CISTERCIAN FATHERS SERIES: NUMBER SEVENTY-SEVEN

Aelred of Rievaulx

The Liturgical Sermons

The Second Clairvaux Collection
Sermons 29–46
Christmas–All Saints

Translated by
Marie Anne Mayeski

Introduction by
Domenico Pezzini

D0141068

α

Cistercian Publications
www.cistercianpublications.org

LITURGICAL PRESS
Collegeville, Minnesota
www.litpress.org

A Cistercian Publications title published by Liturgical Press

Cistercian Publications
Editorial Offices
161 Grosvenor Street
Athens, Ohio 54701
www.cistercianpublications.org

Scripture texts in this work are translated by the translator of the sermons.

1   2   3   4   5   6   7   8   9

Library of Congress Cataloging-in-Publication Data

Names: Aelred, of Rievaulx, Saint, 1110–1167, author.
Title: The liturgical sermons : the second Clairvaux collection : Christmas through all saints / Aelred of Rievaulx ; translated by Marie Anne Mayeski ; introduction by Domenico Pezzini.
Description: Collegeville, Minnesota : Cistercian Publications, 2016. | Series: Cistercian Fathers series ; Number seventy-seven | Includes index.
Identifiers: LCCN 2015048039 (print) | LCCN 2016002173 (ebook) | ISBN 9780879071776 (pbk.) | ISBN 9780879076917 (ebook)
Subjects: LCSH: Church year sermons. | Catholic Church—Sermons. | Sermons, Latin—Translations into English.
Classification: LCC BX1756.A448 L5813 2016 (print) | LCC BX1756.A448 (ebook) | DDC 252/.02—dc23
LC record available at http://lccn.loc.gov/2015048039

CISTERCIAN FATHERS SERIES: NUMBER SEVENTY-SEVEN

Aelred of Rievaulx

The Liturgical Sermons

Contents

INDICES

An Introduction to the Second Clairvaux Collection

Domenico Pezzini

A
n introduction should present the content of a work and at the same time give a foretaste of its beauty so as to attract readers and awake in them the desire to help themselves to a food that is both profitable and tasty. This double quality of a text is precisely what Aelred found in Cicero's *On Friendship* when it fell into his hands. At the time he was a teenager in search of rules to govern his need of love and preserve him from false versions of friendship. He admired that book because, he says, "Immediately it seemed to me both invaluable for the soundness of its views and attractive for the charm of its eloquence."[1] Looking for something that could be a sort of presentation of this book in Aelred's own words, two images came to my mind, so basic and essential that they can be intended as a provision of bread and water.

The Matter of Aelred's Preaching: *The Three Loaves*

The first image has to do with Aelred's conception of the main functions of preaching. He lists three tasks for the preacher: *erudition, correction, and motivation* (S 80.1; CCCM 2B:321).[2] This view goes well beyond the widely diffused idea that reduces preaching either to intellectual catechesis or to moralistic invectives. In the Acts of

---

[1] Aelred of Rievaulx, *Spiritual Friendship* Prol.2, trans. Lawrence C. Braceland, ed. and intro. Marsha L. Dutton, CF 5 (Collegeville, MN: Cistercian Publications, 2010), 53.

[2] Sermons not translated in this volume are cited here and below by sermon number and paragraph number in the editions by Fr. Gaetano Raciti, CCCM 2A–D (Turnhout: Brepols Publishers, 1989–2012).

the Apostles, on the contrary, the preaching of the first missionaries is frequently seen and thought of in terms of exhortation and encouragement, especially when the first announcement, the *kerygma*, had already been preached. On this basis, Aelred translates his well-balanced and integral view into a well-chosen metaphor taken from the gospel: "These, perhaps," he says, "are the *three loaves* sought from a friend, about which our Lord advises us" (Luke 11:5-8). The reference to the parable and the connection with the Advent season, for which Sermon 80 was composed, gives to what seems a mere programmatic list of preaching subjects an emotional context worth noticing. The man of the parable is one who, being in need, goes at night to the house of a friend to ask for some bread. Advent, on the other hand, is a liturgical season figured as "the evening of the world going towards night."[3] Hunger and darkness, in fact, characterize the human compound made of heart and mind, the one inhabited by desire and the other threatened by confusion, both in need of being constantly rectified, enlightened, and motivated. A final typical Aelredian touch closes this paragraph through a prayer addressed to God, "who is my sweetest friend," and to whom the preacher says, "Friend, lend me three loaves, that is the knowledge to instruct, the knowledge to correct, the knowledge to motivate" (S 80.2).

The Manner of Aelred's Preaching: *A Radiant Dew*

The second image occurs in a Christmas sermon (S 93; CCCM 2C:38–42), in which the Word of God made flesh is likened to a "radiant dew" (*ros lucis*: Isa 26:19). Aelred is inviting his hearers to go by imagination to Bethlehem in order to taste and see (*ut gustemus et uideamus*) the Word that has been made (*Verbum hoc quod factum est*). Incidentally, when Aelred mentions using imagination in order to enter entirely into the gospel narratives being meditated on, he is not thinking merely of a sort of an interior reenactment

---

[3] The Advent hymn *Conditor alme siderum* has a stanza beginning *vergente mundi vespere*, "while the world was turning towards its night," stating with these words the situation of humankind when the Son of God came from the Virgin's womb to run his course as the Bridegroom coming to give light and life to the world.

consisting in figuring the scenes but is requiring the involvement of feelings as well. That is why he adds to the biblical *uideamus* his own *gustemus*! Moreover, the two verbs are placed in a sequence that means something, since it seems that taste comes before sight, the eyes of the heart being excited and led by taste!

The double effect of the radiant dew is that it *irrigat et irradiat, fulget et fecundat*: it irrigates and radiates, shines and fertilizes. A light doublet (*irradiat/fulget*) is enclosed within a water doublet (*irrigat/fecundat*), as if the embrace of water or life is necessary for the light or understanding to be efficient and fertile. Aelred's explanation clarifies the message by prospecting four possibilities: two positive, when light and dew work together, and two negative ones, when one exists without the other. In the positive sense, dew waters light (*ros lucis*) when from the truth we perceive a sort of sweetness and the suavity of grace bursts forth, and light shines from dew (*lux roris*) when the suavity experienced in the apprehension of truth makes the soul serene in the light of the same truth.

The opposite result is obtained when dew and light are separated: we have either a knowledge described as "dry and arid" (*sicca et arida*) or a science that is further defined as "dry and blind" (*sicca simul et caeca*) because it lacks all sweetness. The keystone governing this wonderful architectonic passage is the *Verbum quod factum est* of the Vulgate. Unfortunately, modern translations normally prefer to render *Verbum* by "event," thus omitting the link with the verbal metaphor, while the Greek *rhēma*, literally rendered as *verbum* by Jerome, means a "word," which is at the same time an "event," like the Hebrew *dabar*, or, better, a "word that becomes an event" and also an event that is in itself a "word." *Verbum quod factum est* is the angel's announcement materialized in the birth of Jesus, so that this "word" may be "seen and tasted." Here the metaphor of the "radiant dew" takes all its meaning, showing how to combine light and life, which are intrinsically joined to the point that they become two faces of the same coin.[4]

---

[4] For a fuller discussion of this sermon, see Domenico Pezzini, "A Radiant Dew: Aelred of Rievaulx's Art of Preaching," *Cîteaux* 66, nos. 1–2 (2015): 21–68.

Content and Style: How to Approach the Sermons

If one thinks that words are the very matter of preaching, it is easy to understand how Aelred interpreted his ministry of preacher. There must be no divide between words and reality, between words and facts. That is why if the first book from which he draws his sermons is the Bible, the second and no less important is what Saint Bernard calls the book of experience. As in the treatises Aelred cannot conclude the exposition of ideas without substantiating it with the narration of a story, quite often taken from what he presents as his own life, so in his sermons he feels the urge to materialize doctrinal truths and moral principles by a generous use of images and figures, which he usually draws from the words themselves by exploring their iconic content. The various instances of wordplay, rhyme, and assonance and a subtle orchestration of sentences in carefully chosen syntactic structures combine the interplay of sounds and designs, painting and architecture, so that speech becomes material. The least we can say is that Aelred's sermons, like most good medieval literature, need deep attention from the reader, certainly deeper than that we pay to a newspaper article or even to books published in our days.

Basil Pennington's introduction to the First Clairvaux Collection has been structured around some theological and spiritual themes across the sermons: Christ, the Church, Mary, the saints, moral teaching, monastic ascesis, steps on the way to God, community, interiority.[5] This choice has an undoubted interest and needs no justification. It is not, however, the only possible way to organize an introduction. Michael Casey, who also gives "an overview of Aelred's recurrent themes" in his sermons,[6] notes, "The Christology we encounter in Aelred's discourses is conventional and devotional";[7] this statement generally applies to both theological and moral teaching.

---

[5] Introduction to Aelred of Rievaulx, *The Liturgical Sermons*, trans. Theodore Berkeley and M. Basil Pennington, CF 58 (Kalamazoo, MI: Cistercian Publications, 2001), 32–49.

[6] Michael Casey, "An Introduction to Ælred's Chapter Discourses," *Cistercian Studies Quarterly* 45, no. 3 (2010): 279–314, here 302–13. His themes are Christology, anthropology, monastic practices, virtues (humility, chastity, and charity), and vices (curiosity, cupidity, envy).

[7] Casey, "Introduction," 303.

What is original in Aelred's discourses, however, well rooted in a long tradition, are certain preferences and above all the language he uses. Attention to nouns and verbs, adjectives and adverbs, figures and metaphors is essential to take the most profit from reading Aelred's writings. If we limit ourselves to extract raw concepts from Aelred's texts we risk losing much of the radiating charm of his sermons, drying that dew without which knowledge is arid and blind.

That is the reason that I have preferred to adhere to the text of single sermons with the purpose of highlighting the way the argument is developed, in other terms, to mark the "movement" of the discourse. Within this kind of presentation, I have also thought it important to stress some characteristically Aelredian points or accents and occasionally to indicate such linguistic features that may escape the ordinary reader but that are meant to underline Aelred's probable intended emphasis on specific topics, attitudes, or figures.[8]

A Reader's Guide to the Sermons

1. Between Bethlehem and Calvary: Milk and Solid Food

(Sermon 29 *For the Nativity of the Lord*)

It is certainly quite strange to start a collection of sermons with a fragment, but it is not so rare in the transmission of texts in manuscripts. Sermon 29 is the conclusion of a Christmas sermon, whose main body has been lost with a loss of one or more folios,

---

[8] The Second Clairvaux Collection is found in only one manuscript, Troyes, Bibliothèque Municipale, MS 868, dated to the second half of the twelfth century, coming from Clairvaux. Aelred's Sermons are on fols. 51–83ᵛ. The manuscript gathers four different heterogeneous codices. The manuscript containing Aelred's sermons has been bound between a treatise by Odon of Morimond on the symbolism of the number three (fols. 3–50ᵛ) and Gilbert of Hoyland's Homilies 1–3 on the Canticle (fols. 84–90), with another small treatise following. The collection was already damaged when it was copied. Four sermons lack either the beginning (29 and 46) or the end (38 and 42). Identical passages appear in some sermons of the First Clairvaux Collection. A full description appears in the critical edition, *Aelredi Rievallensis Sermones I–XLVI, Collectio Claraevallensis Prima et Secunda*, ed. Gaetano Raciti, CCCM 2A (Turnholt: Brepols, 1989), xiv–xvi. See also Gaetano Raciti, "Deux collections de Saint Aelred—une centaine d'inédits—découvertes dans les fonds de Cluny et de Clairvaux," *Collectanea Cisterciensia* 45 (1983): 165–84.

an accident not rare at the beginning or at the end of a codex.[9] But notwithstanding this drawback, this fragment contains an import- ant message concerning the feeling that is central in any Christmas preaching, in the wake of the angel's message: *Do not be afraid. Lo, I am bringing you good news of a great joy!* (Luke 2:10). Quoting Isaiah 66:10, in which joy is connected with milk sucked from the breasts of God, Aelred centers his reflection on the traditional dis- tinction between milk and solid food. He summarizes what he had said in the lost part of the sermon in a concise statement: "Our Lord Jesus Christ is himself milk for us; he himself is solid food. Solid food because he is God, milk because he is human; bread because he is the Son of God, milk because he is the son of the Virgin" (2).[10] The metaphor clearly suggests that two approaches are possible, one easier than the other, since Jesus' humanity is more at hand, as milk for infants. This is a first stage in the experiential knowledge of Jesus, and characteristically Aelred indulges in this contemplation:

> Brothers, see Jesus in the manger, see him in the lap of his virgin mother, see him sucking at her breasts, crying in the cradle, see him *wrapped in swaddling clothes* [Luke 2:12]; see him also, if I am not mistaken, surrounded by the hay in the stable. This is spiritual milk; these are the banquet foods I promised you for this our feast day. Suck on them sweetly; think on them with tender- ness. Nourish yourselves interiorly with a drink of this milk. But this is for children. (3)

Connecting Bethlehem with Calvary, well within a solid tradi- tion, Aelred then says, "If therefore you are a child, suckle on Jesus in the stable. If you are strong, imitate Jesus on the gibbet of the cross" (4). These are the two extremes of a spiritual program, and Aelred relates them to different stages of the spiritual life, anxious

---

[9] The editor, Fr. Raciti, suggests that probably more than one folio was lost, given the average length of a sermon, together with the reasonable hypothesis that once this text for Christmas was preceded by one or two Advent sermons (CCCM 2A:xiv).

[10] In sections expounding individual sermons, quotations are cited by paragraph num- ber alone, e.g., in this discussion of S 29, this quotation from S 29.2 is cited simply as (2).

to give anybody a chance to imitate Jesus, leaving to everybody to choose what is best for himself or herself.

2. Let Us Go over to Bethlehem and See This Word

(Sermon 30: *For the Nativity of the Lord*)

Another binary pattern appears in Sermon 30, where the start is the impossibility of speaking of such a great event as the incarnation, and on the other hand the necessity to speak to let joy burst out. The dynamic of this sermon is ruled by a refrain running all through it: *let us go over to Bethlehem and see this Word* (Luke 2:15). This sentence echoes another one: *I will go over and see this great vision*, Moses had said (Exod 3:3). With a stroke of genius, playing on the similarity of the texts—a current practice in medieval exegesis—Aelred interweaves Moses' vision of the burning bush with the angelic vision of the shepherds. This connection allows him to draw us into the movement of the shepherds, in the wake of the movement of Moses, both guided by the same need—"go and see"—and accordingly a vision is the central image of this sermon. Against a possible objection about the difference between Moses and the shepherds, Aelred answers, "without a doubt, they spoke of one and the same reality": "*I will go over*, Moses said, *and see this great vision*. What vision? A fire in the bush. And the shepherds said, *Let us go over unto Bethlehem and see*. See what? *The Word that has been made*. . . . The shepherds wished to see the Word, that is, God, in the flesh, and Moses to see the fire in the bush" (5).

The reader must be ready to follow Aelred in a quick series of identifications that flow naturally for him: God in the fire is the Word in the flesh, and the flesh and the bush are one, our human nature. With a detail that becomes crucial for Aelred, a bush has thorns, and this is a reminder of the crown of thorns on the head of Jesus, enough to have Aelred exclaim: "Lord my God, crowned with my thorns!" (6). We may be surprised to find the language of the passion intrude in a Christmas sermon. This connection was indeed quite natural in past ages, when not only treatises and sermons but even such popular poems as the medieval lullabies saw in the cries

of the infant Jesus and in the blood shed at the circumcision pre-
cursory signs announcing the beginnings of his forthcoming passion.

Every word in Aelred's sermon has a sense worth consideration.
Even the clause "go over to Bethlehem" implies "that we go over
all that is visible and changeable, all that varies or may be altered"
(8), so that we might be able to feed on the bread that comes down
from heaven. Where? At Bethlehem, that is, "the house of bread."
There we will see the "vision," both of the Word that has been made
and of the fire seen by Moses. Now "the Lord shows himself to us
in three ways: first, in this world; second, in Judgment; third, in
his Kingdom." But much as was true with Moses, how can we dare
to draw near to God, since the distance between us and him is as
great as that "between light and darkness, death and life, iniquity
and justice, blessedness and misery" (9)?

Here the sermon takes another turn and focuses on our misery,
the very cause of such a distance. The effect is to make us utterly
incapable of reaching God: "There was a twofold misery in us: iniquity and mortality, ignorance and malice, weakness and perversity. In
iniquity, malice, and perversity, there is sin. In mortality, ignorance,
and weakness, there is the penalty for sin. And each of the two, sin
and the punishment of sin, is a misery. Therefore we were made
miserable by both" (10). Incidentally, this is a good example of
Aelred's ability to think, and to write, in binary and ternary structures, of which this paragraph is a perfect combination. The result
is the geometrical clarity of his prose.

Having established the insuperability of the distance separating
us from God, Aelred dramatically asks, "Who will raise us up?" No
one, is the answer, since all of us are overthrown and prostrated in
our misery. But happily, there is "one who stands"; he is the only one
who "can raise up the one who has been overthrown" (10). However,
he cannot do this unless he bends down: "Therefore the one destined
to raise us up was destined to bend himself down, if not entirely
to prostrate himself" (11). This double movement of bending and
raising is structured in four "visions" (*ostensio*), of the manger, the
cross, the Day of Judgment, and the glory of heaven. The first is
about the Son of God's descent into humanity by his incarnation and

death; the second, his sitting as Judge at the right hand of the Father to chastise the wicked and to welcome the blessed. The first vision represents what is normally known as *kenosis*, the self-emptying of God in the person of Jesus (Phil 2:7-8), a gesture so moving that Aelred devotes a long passage (11–13) to describing this event, in which the Lord shows his humility, his smallness, and his poverty. The human response to this manifestation includes four possibilities: the Jews are scandalized, evil Christians are condemned, the beginners in spiritual life are consoled, and the perfect are led to imitation. The first two groups are blocked by their pride and their search for the riches of the world, and thus they cannot understand Jesus' choice of humility and poverty. The beginners are still weak, and they are consoled by seeing that "the misery of our Lord is a share in our misery" (16). The perfect are drawn to his imitation, since they are wise: they have "eyes in [their] head" (Eccl 2:14), and their head is Christ. The conclusion to this section is another example of Aelred's compassionate and balanced attitude:

> Let us console ourselves with the very tiny Jesus because he has been made so small for us. Together with the perfect, let us imitate him as much as we are able, because he has himself tempered his works to the measure of our ability. There is no room for anyone to excuse himself. Let no one consider that I am speaking here of works of divine power, but of those that God did when he assumed our weakness. For our Lord himself does not say, *Learn of me* how to raise the dead or cleanse the lepers, but *Learn of me because I am meek and humble of heart*. (Matt 11:29) (18)

God's showing himself in the Final Judgment and in the Kingdom to come (the two other "visions") takes a much smaller place in the sermon. The Judgment will be the confusion of the proud and the reward for those who have followed the Lord in his humility and meekness. To reach this reward we must now "build Bethlehem in [our] soul," that is, we must practice the virtues shown at the manger, and thus at the end of the road we will "enter into that Kingdom," where Jesus, "sweet and amiable," is waiting for us to welcome us "as his spouse." From vision to vision, Aelred draws the trajectory of our itinerary, until *face to face* (1 Cor 13:10) we see Jesus himself, the Word "that today has been made" (21).

3. The Grace Has Appeared! What Our Response Must Be

(Sermon 31: *For the Epiphany of the Lord*)

Epiphany is a Greek word that means "manifestation" or "revelation" of something hidden and unknown that appears and becomes visible and known. Traditionally, this liturgical feast of Eastern origin, created long before the establishing of Christmas on December 25 in the Western church, focused on three manifestations of Jesus as "the Word become flesh": the revelation to the Magi, the baptism in the River Jordan, and the miracle performed at the wedding at Cana. The dogmatic principle at the base of this celebration was, first, that the birth of Jesus, important as it is, would have meant almost nothing if it had not been known, and, second, what had to be known was the double nature of the person of Jesus: his being man and God at the same time, or what we summarily call the truth of the incarnation. This double nature of Christ was acknowledged by the Magi with their symbolic gifts, proclaimed by God himself in the event of the baptism, and in the miracle of the water turned into wine at Cana, through which "Jesus revealed his glory, and his disciples believed in him" (John 2:11).

Aelred develops the triple dimension of the feast in Sermon 31, which can be easily divided into two parts. The first part describes the three manifestations, which together show how God reveals himself to us; the second analyzes three virtues by which we show ourselves to God in grateful response to his coming down to us and as a way finally to reach him in the heavenly vision. This is a simplified pattern of a rather long sermon, intended to be useful in order not to lose the thread of the argument.

Before offering more detail, let me remind the reader of the meaning of binary and ternary structures in a text. Double sentences, or dyads, are normally used to emphasize a statement by iteration or to create a contrast, functioning thus either as a mirror or as an opposition. In Sermon 31, for example, the three virtues in the second part mirror the three events evoked in the first part. A ternary pattern, technically known as a triad or tricolon, that is, a sequence of three clauses, frequently suggests either a progress (*gradatio*) or a circle and can in this sense be taken as a dynamic structure against the rather fixed and stable double pattern.

Aelred is very fond of ternary patterns, as appears immediately in a sort of background he traces in order to situate God's incarnation in the history of humankind. He views the human condition in three stages: the original beatitude of the creation, the misery of sin after the Fall, and the glorification promised after the redemption realized by Jesus' death and resurrection. God's presence, half hidden in creation, through which his power, his wisdom, and his beauty can be detected, reaches its peak and its heart in the incarnation, by which God enters into our flesh of misery, a supreme sign of his mercy. This descent also signals "a threefold condition of human flesh": what we were "according to creation," what we are "according to condemnation," and what we will be "according to glorification" (5). How to live this dynamic is the subject of the sermon.

The three events celebrated in the feast reveal three aspects of God's presence: "the nations recognized God's grace through a star, the Jews through the sacrament of baptism, the disciples through a miracle" (8). These acknowledgments are reflected in three elements that concretize their reception by the believer—faith, sacraments, and charity—since "without faith, sacraments, or good works, no one can share in the grace of Christ" (8).

It may come as a surprise that Aelred interprets faith in such a pragmatic sense, excluding any intellectual reduction. Probably under the suggestion of the star's leading the Magi along their way through darkness, Aelred joins faith with discernment, the light needed to distinguish a good from a bad behavior. The physicality of the sacrament is the consequence of God's being present in creation, so making creation a revelation of God. So the "Word become flesh" makes Jesus the sacrament of God, as did the rites that were used in the Old Testament, whose carnal meaning is transcended in the sacraments of the New Covenant, of which the baptism is the source.

In the baptism Aelred celebrates Jesus' humility, faith in the Holy Trinity, and the peace signified in the dove of the Holy Spirit. Finally, Cana is the celebration of love, since "water is changed into wine when fear is transformed into love" (16). To see God through faith and to touch God through the sacraments must lead to the very end of the story, charity, through which God's love finds its clearest manifestation. Summing up this first part, devoted to the illustration of what Aelred calls the "mystery," he concludes by saying, "In all these things, *the grace of God our savior has appeared to all people*, illuminating them by faith, sanctifying them by sacraments, setting them on fire with charity" (18).

But here comes the turning point, leading the sermon into its second part: "Granted that this grace appeared to all, not everyone receives it" (18). Mirroring the three revealing events, three virtues respond to God's initiative and receive the grace that has appeared: sobriety, justice, and piety. The spiritual geometry, so characteristic of Aelred, appears in a rule of life governed by these virtues, since we are called to live "soberly in relation to ourselves, justly in relation to our neighbor, and devoutly in relationship to God" (23). The positive practice of the virtues is preceded by a preliminary condition: we will open the door to grace only if we reject impiety and worldly desires—that is, in Aelred's words, "vanity, sensuality, and ambition" (20)—and decisively choose the way of charity. Aelred is more concerned with sobriety, which he interprets mainly as "discretion" as opposed to a sort of "drunkenness, born of indiscreet fervor or a certain obstinacy of mind" (25). Sobriety is a virtue to be practiced in eating and fasting, in talking and in being silent, in keeping vigils and in working. After touching briefly on justice and piety, the sermon concludes by showing in the example given by Jesus as the perfect realization of this virtuous behavior.

4. Waiting for the Coming of the Lord

(Sermon 32: *For the Purification of Saint Mary*)

The Second Clairvaux Collection has three sermons devoted to the feast celebrated on February 2, now known as the Presentation of our Lord to the Temple. In the Eastern tradition it was called *Ypapante*, a Greek word meaning a "meeting," the one between Simeon and the Holy Family.

Sermon 32 takes its theme from an antiphon for the feast, *Adorna thalamum tuum Sion* (*Adorn thy marriage chamber, O Sion*). Simeon and Mary are barely mentioned, while the rich figurative content of the antiphon—with *Sion* meaning "watchtower"—gives Aelred a lot of useful images from which to draw the picture of various degrees of spiritual watchfulness needed to guard and direct human desire to its final destination: the embrace with Jesus in the inner chamber, to enjoy rest and peace with him there.

In a sort of prelude Aelred evokes a Christmas sermon (S 4) in which he spoke of the oil anointing Christ, an oil of which humans were in need, since oil is used "for anointing, because we were sick, for refreshment, because we were famished, for light, because we were blind" (32.1). Then he mentions the miracle at Cana, a gospel passage read on a Sunday after Epiphany, when "you came with Jesus to the wedding" (2) and received *the wine that gladdens the human heart* (Ps 103:15).[11] Then a third food metaphor comes, the "honey of his sweetness," coinciding with a third step, since the right order requires that after the anointing and the drink we pass "from the wedding feast and banquet to the hidden chamber [*ad secreta thalami*]" (2).

Two building metaphors form the basic structure of this sermon. The first, derived from the image of the watchtower, that is, Sion, flows naturally into a recommendation for watchfulness. Using his favorite tricolon, Aelred affirms that "People habitually stand in watchfulness for three reasons: that they may inspect those who

---

[11] Notice the realism of this description: Aelred's listeners—here identified with the disciples—have not merely heard a story but have gone to a wedding. This is indeed the realism of liturgy, which is to be taken as the *repraesentatio* of the mystery it celebrates. The Latin word carries two important intertwined meanings: it figuratively *presents again* the events that constitute the history of salvation, and at the same time it *makes them present* by *re-enacting* them in the lives of the faithful. See Pezzini, "Radiant Dew," 40–41, and Philippe Nouzille, "Temps et liturgie: présence et représentation," *Collectanea Cisterciensia* 73 (2011): 174–86.

are approaching, that they may guard against enemies, and that they may preserve the fruits [of their labors]" (4). Obviously that fiend who is the devil must be rejected, either when he comes by night (that is, in our difficulties) or by day (that is, in our prosperity). Spiritual fruits of virtues must be guarded with care to prevent them from being stolen, and the Lord must be welcomed when he comes. For his advent we must imitate holy Simeon, who "stood in the watchtower, having his eyes on the coming of the one whom he desired, whom he loved" (8), according to the story heard in the gospel of the day.

After this prelude on the watchtower, Aelred uses and allegorically explores another building metaphor, the noun *thalamus*, which the antiphon asks the hearers to "adorn." The noun, here rendered as "your hidden chamber" to indicate intimacy, has a large semantic span, including habitation, house, bedchamber, and metonymically also nuptial bed, in which intimacy and rest are combined.[12] The word frequently appears in Ezekiel 40, where, as Aelred explains, the prophet describes "a certain spiritual edifice" having "an exterior courtyard, an interior courtyard, a vestibule, the domestic rooms, and an interior chamber" (10). This description provides Aelred with a plan in which he identifies five steps of a spiritual journey from the wide exterior to the inmost interior, combining the need for watchfulness with the necessity to adorn the secret chamber where hearers may welcome the coming Lord.

Ancient and medieval authors were particularly fond of allegories, for at least two reasons. The first is dogmatic and consists in the conviction that practically every scriptural word carries a meaning and that the allegory corresponds to the need of reaching a spiritual level of interpretation. The other principle is practical and aesthetic at the same time, by which I mean using figures to enliven and make concrete a speech, an important requirement in an oral culture, in which the message had to be captured in the very instant that it was delivered. To this effect a great contribution came also from the habit of numbering things to develop an argument, starting

---

[12] The NRSV, in Ezekiel 40, translates the word *thalamus* as "recess."

from setting things in dyads and triads so that they could be easily memorized. Figures and images are of the utmost importance for materializing concepts and ideas.

In Aelred's interpretation here, the five parts of the house indicate different faculties, all of which have to be watched so that the soul can be adorned in all its departments to offer a beautiful *thalamus* when the Lord comes. The first stage is memory, seen as the outside courtyard, where everybody and everything is free to enter: "Who can prohibit the good and the bad, the just and the unjust, the clean and the dirty from coming into the memory? All these things rush blindly in" (12).

But a first selection is made in the interior courtyard, which is delight. Many things enter here through those doors, which are the five senses, and entrance is facilitated by focusing attention on the various objects let in by the classic "concupiscence of the eyes, concupiscence of the flesh, and pride of life" (1 John 2:16). Each of these brings with itself a family of vices. In this part of the sermon Aelred is at his best in describing futile imaginations, dangerous sensual behaviors, and striving for honors and the dignities of this world.

But people also feel good desires, which rush in with the bad ones in a mess. It is thus necessary to scrutinize those desires as they enter, as is done in the vestibule, where "the will resides and judges concerning all these things; it deliberates whether it wishes to follow the delight or flee" (18). This statement implies taking into account the distinction between a good and a bad delight, according to whether the object of desire is good or bad. Aelred describes the two final steps with these words:

> The will itself introduces into the domestic quarters that which it chooses. The domestic quarters represent the consent of the will. There the banquet takes place in which people nourish themselves by consenting to their desires, whether for good things or evil. There, within the domestic quarters, the inner chamber is to be found. The inner chamber is affection. When someone acts not from consent alone but with a certain affection, with love and sweetness of mind, [what is accepted with affection] is already in the hidden chamber, as if in a certain interior embrace. . . .

> Blessed is the one who brings [our Lord] through the door into
> the interior courtyard, the one, that is, who gladly thinks on the
> Lord, takes delight in him, and introduces him into the vestibule.
> Blessed are those who deliberate and judge how they may please
> the Lord—by what works, what words, what reflections—and thus
> introduce him into the domestic quarters so that they may consent
> to do, say, and reflect on that which is pleasing in his eyes. (19)

All is said, and the joyous meeting of Simeon with the infant Jesus
becomes possible to everyone.

But Aelred has something more to say specifically on how to
"adorn" the *thalamus*, which he takes as a metaphor for *affectus*,
one of his favorite topics, as appears extensively in his *Mirror of
Charity*. In this sermon, he identifies three parts of affection, which
in the building metaphor of the inner chamber he names "the floor,
the wall, and the ceiling" (21). Our affection leans toward various
objects for three reasons, he says: because they are pleasurable or
useful or simply honest. The "ornament" of these feelings consists
in their purification, unless they go adrift following what might be
called an unconverted concupiscence. Subverting the order, and
somewhat paradoxically, he starts from the ceiling, attaching our
affection for pleasurable things to the consideration of divine charity. If this appears an abstract motivation, hardly effective for the
most terrestrial of feelings, Aelred is explicit in describing what he
intends here: "Brothers, great is the pleasure that comes from seeing our Lord in the womb of his mother, seeing him in the manger,
seeing him today in the arms of Saint Simeon. Great is the pleasure of imagining his words, his miracles, his embrace, and his kiss
in one's heart. This is a great ornament for the ceiling of our inner
chamber" (22).

Imagination, so crucial in Aelred's meditative practice, here
enters again into the discourse. To purify our affection for what
is useful, consideration of the Lord's promises is the adornment
required: "This meditation is like a certain beautiful arch" (23).
Finally, to direct our affection toward what is honest, the floor is our
human condition, and consequently "we ought to consider whose

creature we are and whose image [Rom 9:20]. What can be more virtuous than that the creature love its Creator; the work, its artisan; the servant, its Lord; and the human person, God?" (24). Here is the conclusion of this discussion: "And so if our affection attaches itself to our Redeemer with delight, to the one who has paid off our debt with fervor, to our Creator and Lord with humility, our inner chamber is adorned. This first consideration excludes all sensuality, all greed, and all vanity from our affection" (25).

The final portion of the sermon is a hymn to Mary, who has totally and perfectly realized this ideal in her life: "She is the true Sion, the holy Sion, the decorated Sion, who adorned the inner chamber of her heart with every ornament of virtue. Therefore she received Christ the Lord, not only in her spirit but also in her body, not only in her affection but in her hand, that he might possess her totally, might fill her totally, might totally dwell within her" (28).

5. From Legal Rites to Spiritual Insights

(Sermon 33: *For the Purification of Saint Mary*)

Sermon 33, "For the Purification of Saint Mary," is very long and rather complex. Aelred himself acknowledges that he has spoken for a long time (*diu locuti sumus*: 42), and at the end he deals pretty quickly with the metaphorical meaning of the dove and the turtle, the gifts offered to the temple as a reward for the purification of Mary. The beginning is suggested by the fact that this feast is in continuity with a Jewish rite of purification, a continuity that gives greater relevance to the link between the Old and the New Testaments, involving the need for an allegorical interpretation of ancient rites, according to the often-quoted principle that *All things were contained there figuratively; they were written nevertheless for us* (1 Cor 10:11). In Aelred's words, "The Jewish people had their feasts and sacraments, and we have our own similar feasts and sacraments. But theirs were the shadows and images of the things that were to come. In ours is the truth, that is, that which the previous ones signified" (1). Aelred develops his argument around the signification of the old ritual, intersecting the allegorical interpretation of each word with an itinerary of conversion in which monastic profession, and indeed any Christian vocation, finds its blueprint.

Given the extremely detailed analysis provided by Aelred, it may be useful to divide the text into three parts, to be recalled and kept in focus while reading the sermon: *[1] A woman who, having received seed, bears a male child will be unclean for seven days; [2] on the eighth day, the infant will be circumcised, and she will remain for thirty days in the blood of her purification. [3] She will not touch any seed or enter into the sanctuary until she fulfills the days of her purification* (3; Lev 12:2-4).

1. Aelred actually identifies three elements of the feast being celebrated: "the circumcision of Christ, the purification of his mother, and the offering that was made today. These are great and very profound mysteries [*magna sacramenta*]." Having recognized that "both profound allegories and beautiful moral meanings may be found in that text of Scripture" (5), he says he is going "to say something only about the moral meaning" of the text, although he knows very well that this meaning is based on the allegorical reading.

The first word to be examined is *mulier*, "woman." Here he makes a first bifurcation, since "In Scripture, woman is customarily given sometimes a positive interpretation, sometimes a negative one. When she is interpreted as evil, it is because of her compliance, softness, and weakness; she is interpreted as good because of her fruitfulness or for the affective love that women customarily have toward their children" (6). In the positive sense, "the woman stands for the wisdom of God, that is, for our Lord, Jesus Christ, who sought us, found us, and redeemed us, all with maternal affection" (7). In the negative sense, woman symbolizes a fleshly and vicious life such as was lived before the conversion. But this is not a blocked and hopeless condition, because sick and fragile souls also receive a seed, which is the Holy Spirit, so that they can give birth to some being. This large and open possibility means that from this point on, each of us becomes interested in what Aelred says, although the audience primarily intended is the community of monks.

Another bifurcation now takes place, since "all souls do not bear the same fruit. Some bear females; others males. . . . *Female* signifies a weak and imperfect work; *male*, a strong and perfect one" (9). Aelred applies this double possibility to the man who asked Jesus what to do to possess eternal life (Luke 18:18), explaining that Jesus, seeing the weakness of this "woman," was first content with the birth of a "female" (the observance of the commandments), but when asked for more, he suggested a higher perfection, to leave everything and follow him. The choice to follow Jesus, Aelred notes, "is what it means to bear male offspring" (14). This is the ideal of a monastic vocation, and in this sense both the single soul and, significantly, the whole monastic community is "the woman who, having received the seed, bears male offspring" (12). This view deserves attention, because it hints at the fact that this giving birth to a male, that is, producing a perfect work, is both a personal and a communitarian task, since it is in the community that people both generate and are generated.

The following section concerns the *seven days* during which the woman who has given birth to a male child remains *unclean*. The one who bears female children is in a worse condition, because she is "doubly unclean," meaning that this soul will need not seven but *forty days* for her purification, that is, "both in this life and after this life" (17). The condition of the male-bearer is better. Seven days means "the whole of time" (15), and the consequence is that the work of purifying our uncleanness will last all our life, but when "she goes forth from the body" the soul will be totally clean (16). Before entering in the allegorical interpretation of the seven days, Aelred wisely remarks that "However perfect our works may be within the possibilities of this life, nevertheless it is not possible that our work be without some mixture of impurity, whether of pride or vanity or the appetite for human praise" (19). This statement explains why death may be interpreted as the "circumcision" that took place after the seven days of purification, since it "comes as a kind of sharp little knife and with its bitterness cuts away all that impurity that we have picked up along the way" (19).

Aelred uses the number seven to detail the various steps of this gradual cleaning, a process that shows the same fine psychological introspection he has already admirably displayed in the *Mirror of*

Charity. He produces a concise penitential treatise of the type current in his time, combining the nascent so-called canonical perspective, concerned with the circumstances of sin, with what can be called the medical outlook, which suggested that the penance should correspond to the kind of sin confessed. The itinerary Aelred designs resumes the whole process of monastic life, organized in the following "days," or steps: (1) Conversion, or renunciation of the world, (2) consideration of one's own sins and their circumstances, (3) repentance, (4) confession, (5) compunction, (6) penance through works "appropriate" to the type of sin, including "labors and vigils and fasts," and (7) refreshment of the spirit through "reading, meditation, and prayer" (27).

Surprisingly, when everything seems in order, Aelred reminds us that to avoid the risk of self-glorification and to crown the work of purification, the boy must be circumcised—"that is, let the vice of pride be cut away from all [our] actions," as can be done by means of "that most sharp stone, the humility of Jesus" (28).

2. Two other ritual rules must be analyzed. The first obliges the woman to "remain in the blood of her purification for thirty days," during which time "she will not touch any seed or enter into the sanctuary" (3). Aelred interprets this rule as the necessity for the soul to stay in the remembrance of her sins, since this remembrance "does not defile but entirely cleanses and purifies her" (31). He reads the prohibitions against touching seed and entering the sanctuary as an invitation not to "investigate divinity" (32) or to try to scrutinize profound things. This is advice addressed to the soul who is still a beginner in the spiritual life, who should spend time in considering "her own sins more than the divine purity. However, when she gets to the thirty-third day, she may enter with offerings" (35) into the sanctuary, which is "where secret things are discussed" (34).

3. What offerings? A lamb, or "two turtledoves or two pigeons" (39). This was the offering of the poor, and Jesus took on the condition of a poor person. What does this mean for monks? Here Aelred uses the symbolic reading of the two birds, concentrating in four paragraphs matter that would be enough for an entire sermon. First, he writes, "the dove . . . is without gall, it chooses the best

grain, and it is in flocks, that it, it usually flies in a large group" (43). This behavior, Aelred explains, means to avoid bitterness, follow the examples of the best, and live communally in the company of others. Second, he says, the turtledove "dwells in solitude," "wishes never to have but one mate," and "is a chaste bird" (46). The applications are obvious.

In this long and unusually detailed sermon, it seems that Aelred, as on other occasions (as for example S 74 for the Assumption), is excited by apparently unpromising and poor biblical texts that prompted in him his extraordinary feeling for words and the figures hidden in them. To this feeling we should add his intention to show the spiritual value of apparently carnal prescriptions. Finally, he never forgets the needs of his monastic audience, above all the necessity of being often reminded of their vocation and of the duties it implied. A modern reader can feel frustrated before such abundant food, presented in an apparent jumble of topics, in which it is difficult to find a general and well-organized theme. It is true that, as Michael Casey has said, Aelred's "individual discourses are more significant for certain sections taken as a block than for the whole, since they often combine several seemingly disparate themes."[13] This is also good advice for the reader.

6. How to Wait, Like Holy Simeon, for the Consolation of Israel
(Sermon 34: *For the Purification of Saint Mary*)

After an antiphon from the liturgy of the feast and a legal text from Leviticus concerning the rules for the purification of a woman after the birth of a child, Aelred comments on the gospel passage of the day. Sermon 34, the third for the feast of the Purification of Mary in the Second Clairvaux Collection, focuses on the holy Simeon. He becomes an icon of the man who fervently waits for the meeting with the "consolation" of Israel.

---

[13] Casey, "Introduction," 302.

In this sermon Aelred proposes Simeon as a model, anticipating the idea early on in a sentence that, rather unusually, is a complaint: "The majority of those who begin to serve our Lord either begin tepidly or, if they begin with fervor, remain fervent for a very short time" (2). Thus he implies that habitual monastic practices are being disregarded. Here he speaks in the third person, talking of people who "are tepid and lazy; they are averse to fasts, abhor vigils, and give little weight to manual labor" (2). But shortly afterward the address turns directly toward the actual audience, when Aelred, with a noticeably strong reaction ("For God's sake!" he says), continues with a rhetorical question: "Why do we not meditate on the apostles, martyrs, and other saints who preserved the fervor they felt at the beginning till the last moment before death? But that we may be the more embarrassed, let us think about those who came before the birth of our Lord" (3).

The comparison is obviously unfavorable, and the difference is aggravated by the better behavior of people who had seen and heard nothing of Jesus' life, unlike us, he says: "Daily we see and hear, we discern the cross of Christ; daily we contemplate afresh the passion of Christ, daily the body and blood of Christ is offered before us and for us, daily we hear the gospel of Christ" (4). Implicit here is the fact that the hearers are blind and deaf; the figure of Simeon, taken from the gospel of the day, is meant to awaken them to be ready to welcome Christ in a proper way.

The sermon may be divided into two parts: the first is about Simeon, and the second describes the "consolation" that he was waiting for and that is also offered to us if we behave like him. In fact, using the rhetorical form of iteration called *anadiplosis*, Aelred says, "This man greatly wished . . . to see Christ; and because he greatly wished for it, he greatly desired it; because he greatly desired it, he greatly prayed for it, namely, that he might see Christ, and therefore he received it" (5; Luke 2:28). The repetition of *greatly* connects wish, desire, and prayer to Christ's reception in a sequence of feelings and choices flowing into one another as in a chain of love, of which the adverb sings the intensity, countering the monks' laziness denounced in the introductory paragraphs. Comparing Simeon, whom he calls "truly just," with King Herod, Aelred states that Simeon was "a true king," given that he "ruled himself well because he preserved the members of his body in holiness" (6). Not so, Herod.

But the description of the old man focuses mostly on his being a "man" (*homo*, in the gospel narrative), a noun that Aelred analyzes under the figure of *imago Dei*. This image is in the soul; as for the body, it is what makes us similar to the animals. But our animal part must be ruled by the soul: "The beasts care for nothing else than that which fills their belly, and with a full belly they rest" (9).[14] Our rest must be found elsewhere: Simeon *was a man in Jerusalem* [Luke 2:25]. And if we are like this, brothers, we will certainly dwell in Jerusalem." "Jerusalem . . . means *a vision of peace*" (10). We will have peace and rest when "we expend all our care on our soul[;] then all those battles among our bodily parts will grow quiet, the vices will cease to war against us, and we will dwell in peace on this earth. For we will be upon our earth, that is, upon our flesh, not under it. It will serve us in the doing of good works and not betray us to vice by its vehemence" (11). This is the hierarchical order to be maintained between body and soul if we want to bear and manifest God's image in our life and so to have peace in ourselves.

Besides the composition of body and soul, another thing is required: to be, like Simeon, *iustus et timoratus*, "just and fearful" (Luke 2:25). It is apparently a difficult ideal, since Aelred exclaims, "How few there are, my brothers, who possess these two virtues together" (13). But their joining is necessary for a balanced spiritual life, so that our growth in justice does not eliminate our fear of sinning, a fear that produces watchfulness and discretion. In this earthly journey toward Jerusalem, Aelred reminds us, we are always "beginners," an idea that implies that we must be on our guard "not [to] take pride in our progress." If we remain both just and fearful, "then we will be able safely to wait for the consolation of Israel" (15).

---

[14] See Aelred of Rievaulx, *The Mirror of Charity* 1.21.60–61, trans. Elizabeth Connor, intro. and notes Charles Dumont, CF 17 (Kalamazoo, MI: Cistercian Publications, 1990), 121–22.

In *The Mirror of Charity* Aelred deals at length with different kinds of *visitations* on the part of the Lord: some are meant to awake us when we are lazy, some are meant to console us when we work hard to follow Jesus, some are meant as a reward when we have won our spiritual fight.[15] In this sermon he gives the word *consolation* a large semantic field: "This consolation is the spiritual visitation of Christ, by which he deigns to visit our heart in compunction, in prayer, in the revelations of Scripture or of the sacraments. Perfect consolation is the vision of Christ himself" (19). The ability to see Christ was the response Simeon received from the Holy Spirit, and we too can obtain this vision, Aelred says, provided we "ask for this consolation by habitual good behavior, by worthy dealings with others, by continual prayer" (19).

In any case, this vision is not the fruit of our good actions but a gift of the Holy Spirit. This fact does not encourage us to renounce working: quite the contrary, because Aelred insists that it remains true of Simeon that "at any rate, if he had not prayed or begged with all possible fervor, if he had not devoted himself to good works with perseverance, he would not have received that response" (21). Here he offers another rebuke, perfectly in tune with the third function of a sermon, to animate the community: "If as soon as our head hurts, as soon as we are a little bit weary, we succumb to tepidity, take our rest, and give up the practices by which we ought to make progress, it must be feared that we cannot receive this response spiritually" (22).

Aelred seems anxious to warn his hearers not to sleep in a false sense of security. To this purpose he quotes Saint Paul, who, on the one hand, was certain that nothing could separate him from the love of God (Rom 8:38) but, on the other hand, continued to chastise his body, "lest perhaps," he said, "preaching to others I myself become cast away" (1 Cor 9:27). Aelred comments, "What you must know

---

[15] See *The Mirror of Charity* 2.8.20–64, particularly 2.20, a dense and extremely concise summary of the manner, aims, and effects of these three visitations, a paragraph that concludes with three pictorial metaphors in which the sense of God's action is beautifully concentrated: "The first [visitation] is like a goad correcting someone swerving out of line; the second is like a staff supporting someone weak; the third is like a couch holding up someone at rest" (177).

is that when he says, *I am certain* [Rom 8:38], he is feeling how ardently he burned with the love of Christ, a wondrous affection, which undoubtedly he felt very frequently. And having received that assurance by his affection, he returned to himself and found in his own weakness a reason for fear" (28).

The sermon concludes with the last verses of the gospel of the day. Simeon meets Jesus in the temple in Jerusalem; we will meet him in the temple we have prepared in our heart: "let us turn toward it by pure affections, let us dwell within it by means of good meditations" (30).

There is nothing more to say, since what follows in the gospel passage concerns "the purification of the mother after the birth of a child and the oblation of the child himself" (31), points that require a sermon of their own, as in Sermon 33. But for the time, an important conclusion has been reached: Simeon has indicated a way, and "if you follow this old man's regimen as we have described it, you will enter safely into the temple of your heart; there, without a doubt, Jesus will come" (31). Our part is just to "extend the arms of [our] heart as today holy Simeon opened his bodily arms," and stay with Jesus in "good meditations."

7. About Being Tied by the Cords of Sin and Released by Jesus
(Sermon 35: *For Palm Sunday*)

The reader who approaches Sermon 35, "For Palm Sunday," with the memory full of the well-known images of the triumphal entry of Jesus into Jerusalem will be deeply frustrated. It has been already remarked that Aelred's sermons, although they are attached, and not without reason, to specific festivities, can take their start from almost anything and may choose to develop their theme or themes from almost anywhere. This sermon is a particularly enlightening example of this situation, since what remains of the scenery of Palm Sunday is just the detail of the ass, which moreover comes in only at the very end of the development, leaving the hearer or reader in a state of suspense about when the topic of Palm Sunday will start, and how. The very heart of the sermon is in fact a subtle reflection on Samson's hair explored in its multiple metaphorical meanings. Apart from this curious choice, the reader will undoubtedly admire Aelred's cleverness in the compact way in which he succeeds in structuring his argument.

The sermon starts from a very general principle, the consideration of "the works of our Lord, not those done in the creation of the world, but those that he did for our redemption and that he does daily in restoring us" (1). But even here we may note that the distinction Aelred makes between God's works of creation and his works of redemption and restoration drags the audience's attention from creation and fixes it on God's more personal intervention on behalf of humankind: his redemption and his daily care to heal our wounds and sicknesses.

Aelred first introduces the image of a cord taken from the book of Ecclesiastes, the meaning of which he reveals at the sermon's conclusion. God's action, he says, is characterized by wisdom, strength, and sweetness, and these three attributes form his cord. This image means that they can never be separated: either they operate together and "mutually temper each other" (2) or they become useless and insignificant. Aelred's conciliatory temperament emerges clearly in this remark; his sensitivity to an intrinsic relationship that ties or "federates" things and beings, virtues and vices, persons and societies permeates anything he writes. It has a particular meaning for his doctrine of charity and friendship[16] that is perfectly expressed in the phrase "communitarian personalism," coined by Fr. Charles Dumont to describe Aelred's view of a monastic community.[17] So "wisdom, strength, and sweetness make up *the triple cord that is difficult to break*" (4; Eccl 4:12).

Against this virtuous cord, the devil has his own triple wicked cord, with which he tied our first parents in Eden, a cord made of pleasure, habit, and bitterness: "first he attracted the man, then he tied him up, and finally he knocked him down. He attracted him by

[16] See Aelred of Rievaulx, *Spiritual Friendship* 1.53–58; *The Mirror of Charity* 1.21.59–61.

[17] Charles Dumont, "Le personnalisme communautaire d'Aelred de Rievaulx," *Collectanea Cisterciensia* 39 (1977): 129–48, reprinted in *Une éducation du cœur*, Pain de Cîteaux 10 (Oka, Canada: Abbaye Notre-Dame du Lac, 1996), 309–34.

the cord of carnal appetite; he tied him with the cord of habit; he knocked him down with the cord of bitterness" (5). These are the *funes peccatorum*, the bonds of sin that surround us (Ps 118:61), from which we pray to be delivered, exulting when their chains are broken (see Ps 115:16). The Philistine tried to bind Samson with these cords, just as the devil tried to bind Jesus when he wanted to rouse Jesus' carnal appetite by asking him to transform stones into bread. Samson's force was in his hair, and that of Jesus in the "sword of Sacred Scripture" (6) by which he cut the devil's suggestion. Aelred wishes "to investigate at greater length and with careful distinctions what Samson's hair might be" in order "to learn that we ought not to fear those cords of the spiritual Philistines as long as we preserve that hair" (7).

Hair stands for the thoughts generated by the head. Thoughts may be good or bad: in the first case they should be nurtured, but in the second they must be shaved. This implies a discretional judgment. The most immediately applicable passage in Aelred's allegorical reading of this image is the one in which he gathers the meaning of the "seven hairs" that grew on the head of Samson, here defined as one who is "a man, that is, then he is a Nazirite, that is, *one consecrated to the Lord.*" In this Samson becomes a model offered to all, and here are the "holy, good, and useful thoughts that proceed from his mind, especially those seven hairs by which his strength is preserved" (13). Starting from the fact that hairs are produced from the head "in the front, in the back, on top, and on each side," Aelred invites us to consider things in front of us, behind us, around us, and above us, that is, future things, past things, divine realities, and present reality (14).

More concretely, these fields for meditation available to any person are, for the future, "the fear of punishments . . . the desire for rewards"; for the past, "the remembrance of the evils that he has done . . . the memory of the many benefits that God showed him" (15); and for the present, the consideration of "how small are all of the present realities in comparison with the future and how briefly [they endure]" (16). As for the divine things, only one thing will suffice: God's unity in the Trinity.

These meditations have the effect of making us rest in the bosom of God. But we must never forget that there is another possibility, the one into which Samson fell, resulting in his destruction: the "habit of sleeping in the bosom of the harlot. This harlot is carnal affection" (17). Aelred then describes the temptation we experience when we look for rest where there is only unrest: "[Carnal affection] immediately desires whatever she sees to be beautiful, whatever she thinks pleasurable, whatever tastes flavorful, whatever smells sweet, whatever melodies she hears. At once she surrenders; at once she offers herself, at once she prepares her embrace and her bosom so that she may receive the soul tired out by the labors of this world or temptations. No sooner does the spirit, like a man, betray itself to this harlot than she allows him no rest day or night" (18).[18]

The speed toward the disaster is impressive: three *statim* in the Latin, placed one after the other to mark the rapid descent from desire to surrender, and from surrender to self-offering, rendered here by three instances of *at once*. Also at once, the harlot calls "the barber, that is, the devil," who cuts off the spirit's hair of good thoughts, leaving him bald. "Then he ties him up with the cord of sensuality, he binds him with the cord of depraved custom, he attaches *iniquity to him with the cord of vanity* [Isa 5:18]. Then he takes out his eyes so that he might know neither God nor himself but walk in circles on the mill of the world and be among those of whom it is written, *The impious walk in circles* [Ps 11:9]" (19).

This image of those who "walk in circles," frequently quoted by Aelred[19] and Bernard, alludes to a sterile life seen as a vicious circle, leading nowhere. But there is a rescue, and here, in the final three paragraphs, Aelred arrives at last at the object of Palm Sunday. How? "Perhaps the ass that the Lord had untied and brought to him today was tied by these cords. Yes, indeed, that ass so bound designates human nature that was tied in this way. But the Lord sent his disciples and untied him that they might lead him to Jesus" (21).

---

[18] This is more or less what Aelred says of carnal friendship: see *Spiritual Friendship* 1.39, 1.62–63.

[19] See *The Mirror of Charity* 1.15.47 (CF 17:113), again in connection with the story of Samson.

Aelred concludes by going back to where he had started, the Wisdom of God, identified in the first paragraph as *"reaching strongly from end to end and arranging all things sweetly"* (1; Wis 7:30–8:1). He now comments, "One end was the initial damnation of Adam; the other end, his perfect redemption. From this end to that, the wisdom of God stretches out strongly and disposes all things sweetly" (22). This is indeed the "great work" of the Lord with which Aelred began his reflection, focusing not on the creation but on the redemption and God's daily care in favor of our spiritual health. This is what allows us to join the crowds who, praising God in joy and exultation, follow Jesus not into the earthly Jerusalem "that kills the righteous and the prophets [Matt 23:27], but the heavenly Jerusalem, our mother, that receives all the saints into eternal blessedness" (22).

8. The Four Cardinal Virtues Radiating from the Cosmic Cross (Sermon 36: *For Holy Week*)

There are different ways to meditate on the cross, a subject that oscillates between the realism of a brutal death and the sublime theological significance of the event. Aelred is conscious of the difficulty of maintaining a right balance in the treatment of what is the core of our faith in the redemption, in its double aspect implying both a mystery and an example (see 1 Pet 2:21-25), or, in the words of Pope Leo the Great, its being at the same time *sacramentum et exemplum*. In a sermon for Palm Sunday, Aelred remarks that "nothing was more despicable, nothing more vile, nothing more hateful, nothing more horrible" than that gibbet, but precisely "by means of that gibbet . . . the Lord subjugated emperors, made fools of the wise, instructed the simple and unlearned, glorified the poor" (S 10.27).[20]

According to the great theologian Hans Urs von Balthasar, over the centuries the most difficult point in the theology, spirituality, iconography, and literature of the passion, *the* problem, as he calls it, has been to keep a good balance between reason and feelings,

---

[20] See CCCM 2A:87; Aelred of Rievaulx, *The Liturgical Sermons: The First Clairvaux Collection*, CF 58:179.

speculation and affectivity, mind and heart, "between the personal devotion to the Crucifix and the great patristic vision of the cross as the peak of the whole operation through which God saves us and reveals himself."[21] Aelred's sermon seems to be a congruent response to this need. His exposition offers a well-patterned, almost geometrically organized reflection on the "event," mainly analyzed in its symbolic meaning, from which he derives a list of virtuous behaviors in connection with the manner of the passion and the place where it happened: "The manner of redemption is the passion of Christ; the place, outside the city [Luke 4:29; Heb 13:12-13]. You must know, then, that from this redemption and the manner of accomplishing it, we receive both a way of living and the right location we must choose in order to live in this way" (1).

The first great paradox, and the theological/moral message of the sermon, is that the cross of Christ is a way "both of living and of dying: of dying to the world, of living for God; of dying to vices, and of living in virtues; of dying to the flesh; of living, however, in the Spirit" (2). This "mystery" is illustrated through the well-known paradoxes of the ancient liturgy, especially those linked to the cross as wood (*lignum*), and wood that becomes a boat (*archa mundo naufrago*), needed to cross the sea of this world. The same paradox is seen in the fact that "One who dies on the cross is not on the earth but above the earth; furthermore, the members [of the body] are not cut off but stretched out" (4). This stretching hints at the cosmic meaning of the cross (see Eph 3:18), on which Jesus was placed "as if he embraced heaven and earth," and offers the first pattern of four virtues characterizing the way of living according to the model of the cross.

Aelred introduces these virtues by an invitation not *to fear those who kill the body, because they cannot kill the soul* (Matt 10:28), and it seems that to "carry the cross" ultimately means believing in the saving power of any hardship in life, with the courage needed to accept the cost of the "good works" symbolized in the "four

---

[21] *Mysterium salutis* (Brescia: Queriniana, 1974), 6:202.

dimensions in the cross, namely, length, width, height, and depth" (7). In order, width means charity, which has no boundary, height means hope in the heavenly goods, depth refers to the fear of the now-hidden Judgment of God, and length appropriately serves as a metaphor for perseverance, frequently also mentioned in the Scriptures as patience and constancy.

In correspondence with the way of living, Aelred describes the way of dying, which should better be called a "way of living through death." The "old man," much like the "old life" of sin, must be nailed to the cross until it dies. The nails are the precepts of God, by which what is old in us "cannot move," that is, it cannot have any influence on our behavior. Aelred names only two vices from the classical list, namely, anger and lust, and resumes his teaching in the invitation to refrain from any bad movement: "Just as the crucified cannot move their hands, feet, or other members, so a person who wishes to die in order to live confines and restrains all his members from evil acts through the fear and precepts of God" (14).

A last series of considerations concerns the place where we should live the spirituality of the cross. Two meanings are attached to being "outside the city," where Jesus was crucified. One consists in abandoning in spirit the city of humans, the "evil city that belongs to this world and this present time" (16); the other is the capacity of tolerating the exclusion and insults (Heb 13:13) that this separation implies, since the believer becomes thus an exile (1 Pet 1:1), a foreigner, and a pilgrim.

A final curiosity is derived from the name of the place. *Calvary* means "skull" (John 19:12), but Aelred reads the name in connection with the Latin *calvus*, which means "bald." This interpretation leads him again to the image of hairs, but with another interpretation, as some superfluous part of the body. What follows is an obvious invitation: "Cut back everything superfluous and make a grateful offering of it to the Lord so that you have nothing in this world except what is absolutely necessary. Thus the mount of Calvary may be within you, a true mountain of great excellence and great perfection" (18). The Cistercian ideal was expressed in the motto *nudus nudum Christum sequi*. The cross is the way, and the monks are *professores crucis* Christi, that is, those who profess the cross through their way of living, since to profess means to show in public the reality and the fruit of what the cross means.[22]

9. How to *Walk* in the Spirit

(Sermon 37: *For the Feast of Saint Benedict*)

Aelred wrote sixteen sermons for the feast of Saint Benedict, seeing him as a saint, a founder, and the author of the Rule and taking the opportunity of providing ideals of sanctity to the community born by his initiative of *pater monachorum*. This sermon contains nothing specific about the saint. Rather, its central point is how to celebrate a saint's feast "with fruit," on the traditional principle that the saints get no profit from these festivities—they do not need them—but the profit is ours. In this light, one would naturally think of their power of intercession. Aelred ignores this point, more interested in viewing the saints as models for imitation. The general perspective from which he considers any saint is reflected in the purpose he assigns to the benefits to be derived from the saints' feasts. The principle is that "everyone lives either well or badly, and these celebrations ought to profit both these categories of people" (1).

Aelred goes on to explain what he means by bad or good life, and consequently what profit can be derived from the saints' feasts. First he considers people who behave wrongly: "Those who act badly do so because they are weak and unable to resist their desires, or they are malicious, loving evil and hating good" (2). The profit for the former, he explains, should be a sense of shame, and for the latter fear. Having established this distinction, Aelred concentrates his interest on the weak, so suggesting that theirs is the more normal condition. Since weakness is often taken as an excuse, shame is the

---

[22] See S 10.29, "For Palm Sunday," where in a touching passage addressed to those he calls affectionately "my brothers, my sons," Aelred defines them as people who "not only adore, but also profess, not only profess, but also love the cross of Christ" (*non solum adoratores, sed etiam professores, non solum professores, sed etiam amatores crucis Christi*), ending with the solemn declaration *Ordo noster crux Christi est* (S 10.31; CCCM 2A:87–88; CF 58:180).

practical way of overcoming this instinct of self-justification. No
excuse can be invoked against the fact that Saint Benedict, like any
saint, was a person like each of us:

> What was Saint Benedict? Without a doubt a man like you, like
> him, like me. His flesh is the same as your flesh. You and he are
> both of the same material. Why therefore was he able to do what
> you are not? When but a boy, young and tender, he left the world
> and fled from his parents. You, however, grown-up, wise, and
> prudent, you dream of the world and sigh after your parents. If
> you plead your serious temptations, he, as you know, was tempted
> even more seriously. Nevertheless he resisted in a manly fashion;
> you succumb easily. (3)

This basic remark is the best introduction to a message addressed
to everybody, precisely because sanctity appears to be a normal possibility founded on a famous rhetorical question: *si isti et istae, cur
non ego?* ("If these men and these women were saints, why not I?")
In fact, the consideration of Benedict's sanctity should lead people
to feel ashamed: Aelred repeats the verb *erubescat,* "blush," four
times, addressed to people who are lukewarm, impatient, proud,
and gluttonous. Shame should work as a stimulus to change. Change
starts from the conversion of desire. Desire is shaped by counsels
indicating the direction to take and the works to do in order to go
in that direction. A bad life is directed by the flesh; a good life is
directed by the Spirit. To sum it up, "flesh gives its counsels in order
to draw us to its desires, and the Spirit gives her counsels in order
to draw us to her desires" (7). The choice is absolutely clear. The
clarity of the ideal is integrated with the practicality of the counsels.

Aelred concentrates the desires of the flesh in fornication and
uncleanness. The ways, or the "counsels," leading to the first of
these behaviors are "laziness and talkativeness, . . . familiarity and
conversations with women [remember that he is talking to monks],
. . . [letting] our eyes wander here and there to take in other sights
that we might covet them" (8). The counsels of uncleanness are "to
seek delicate foods so that we may eat to satiation . . . to seek sleep,
indolence, soft blankets, and soft clothing" (8). It seems that the

person is thus agitated between the two extremes of restlessness and satiety, where it would be impossible to find rest and peace and so to be able to move in life with that pace that Aelred describes neither as anxiously running after anything desirable nor as lying inert in self-satisfaction, but as "walking in the Spirit" (13).

Aelred admirably lays out the profile of his ideal of sanctity, which he finds in Saint Benedict, in a series of advisory items: "The Spirit gives counsel that we never be lazy, never wander, never waver, never be profligate in words, but always move toward some good work. She counsels us to be serious, mature, to love silence and quietness. She gives counsel that we spurn familiarity and gossip, which customarily feed unclean desires. She gives counsel that we mortify the members of our body in abstinence, vigils, and manual labor, that we have our heart [fixed] in good meditations, prayers, compunction, and devotion" (10).

Turning back to the desires of the flesh, Aelred identifies two other vices: envy and hate. These are the fruits of a basic self-centeredness, nourished by the decision "to follow [one's] own will, to love familiarity with the high and mighty, and to be called to the council chamber, to the distribution of offices" (11). When these desires are frustrated, envy and hate come to inhabit, trouble, and disquiet the heart. Against this, charity shines as the highest desire of the Spirit, meaning "that we love nothing in this world, that we always seek the good of another rather than our own, that we beware all those entanglements [of councils and offices]" (12). So Aelred points out that the choice Benedict made in his temptation (one of the best-known episodes of his life), a choice through which he conquered "the desire of the flesh through the pain of the flesh" (13), should encourage Aelred's listeners to reject the counsels of the flesh and to follow the counsels of the Spirit.

While a positive shame can stimulate the weak to follow the examples of the saints, Aelred says, the remedy for the wicked is a combination of shame and fear. If one considers what pains a saint such as Benedict had to endure, seeing that "the Lord beats with labors and tribulations the one who has loved and done the good, . . . he will know what the one who loves evil may expect" (14).

Having established this fact, now Aelred provides a summary of the fruits of the celebration of the feasts of the saints:

> If any are tepid, let them begin to feel shame and through shame recover genuine warmth of virtue. If any are evil and cold, let them begin to feel fear and through fear climb out of the coldness of evil to the warmth of charity. Likewise through the feasts of the saints, those who are good and live well can make progress in hope and love. For whoever visualizes himself practicing the exercises the saints performed (and through which they came to holiness) can greatly hope to make progress himself through those exercises and so arrive at holiness. (16)

The finale again brings all our attention to Saint Benedict, celebrated as "such a father, such a guide, and such a teacher" (19). Aelred does not hesitate to qualify the Rule as the materialization of Galatians 5:16: *Walk in the spirit and do not satisfy the desires of the flesh.* This, he says, is what Benedict did and what he taught in the Rule. The refrain of the sermon perfectly applies to Benedict and to his example and teaching. In fact, Aelred asserts that "there is no doubt but that the Holy Spirit has instituted this Rule through Saint Benedict" (18). The paragraph that expands on this statement is worth quoting as an example of Aelred's preaching style, which combines logic, clarity, conciseness, and substance, all ingredients that make the usual tone of oral delivery extremely effective:

> Therefore whoever preserves this Rule of Blessed Benedict, who imitates his life, is certain that he follows the counsel of the Holy Spirit. Whoever follows the counsel of the Holy Spirit in truth is certain that he walks in the Spirit. Whoever walks in the Spirit, however, does not satisfy the desires of the flesh. Cannot the one who walks in the Spirit, who tramples on the desires of the flesh, begin to feel great hope that, because he walks in the Spirit, he may arrive where those who do these things are? Therefore, brothers, walk in the Spirit. (18)

Two instances of "follow the counsel of the Spirit" and five of "walk in the Spirit" hammer the message into the head of the hearers.

Such a fervent iteration sounds more convincing than a subtle argument, especially when it is integrated and substantiated by a shining metaphor, as in this case. Aelred in fact concludes his sermon by describing Benedict as a "burning piece of wood" (Ezek 1:13) and with the invitation to "join ourselves to him," considering "the fervor of his life and the charity of his heart" (21). By this fire, he says, hearers will overcome the fire of concupiscence. Indeed, "no one can be saved except through fire [1 Cor 3:15]. But there is the fire of tribulation and the fire of love" (22). Both are saving fires. Christians should patiently accept the first and burn as much as they can with the fire of charity, because "the fire of tribulation is the beginning; the fire of love, perfection" (23). The saints teach that these are the beginning and the end of the way of the Spirit (Rom 5:3-5), that is, the road map to sanctity, in which any believer is called to walk.

10. The What, How, and Where of Mary's Vocation

(Sermon 38: *For the Annunciation of the Lord*)

The Annunciation is the beginning of human redemption and is at the same time correctly interpreted as the vocation of Mary, or in other words, as the part she had to take, which is also, although in a different order, humans' part in the work for the salvation of humankind. Aelred has devoted no fewer than eleven sermons to this feast, two of which are extant in the Second Clairvaux Collection. The first, Sermon 38, is unfortunately incomplete, but what remains is sufficiently developed and may be taken as a self-contained unit. We can identify in it three parts: the first on the *event*, the second on the *manner*, and the third on *the location* of the event.

1. In full accordance with the theme of Mary's conception of Jesus, the sermon starts by some considerations on the image of the seed. In the monastic community, the seed is largely sown, especially in the liturgical offices and in the reading of the Scriptures. Aelred's point is that "this seed, frequently scattered among you, ought to bear fruit" (1). The memory of the well-known parable suggests a double application. The first concerns Mary's reception of that seed who was Jesus, "for what is today's feast except the seed from which

will spring up the entire fruit of your salvation?" (2). The seed fell
in the earth, where it died, after which Christ brought forth much
fruit (John 12:24-25).

The good ground was prepared by the Law of Moses, since the
commandments were given to "uproot these vices from the earth of
our heart and enable it to receive this grain of wheat, which today
dies in the earth and bears fruit in patience" (3; see John 12:24; 15:2;
Luke 8:8). To bear fruit, this seed that also is to be received must
not fall *on the roadway* (Luke 8:5) but on a ground that is *desert*,
vacant, and *dry* (see Ps 62:3). Allegorically, this means a place where
evil spirits can find no home and no road and where bad desires do
not float. This place, Aelred says, was the heart of Mary.

2. Aelred then devotes a long section to the meaning of *Missus
est angelus Gabriel a Deo*. Why *a Deo*? Aelred asks. Mary did not
need the message, since an interior inspiration could have sufficed,
and it would certainly have been "more excellent than that which
may come through angelic creatures, corporeal signs, or the sound
of external words" (8). But the message was given as a sign of
God's great mercy toward people who would have not been able
to receive and understand the message unless it was announced by
Gabriel, who "was sent by God visibly, and he spoke aloud so that
the mystery could be written about, preached about, and believed"
(9). So the Annunciation, in its very realization, announces God's
amenability and delicate attention to our needs.

As in response to God's initiative of coming down to humankind,
the story also shows that "through the words of the angel to Mary
and the words of Mary to the angel, it would be made manifest
how great was her humility, how undiminished her virginity, how
pure the faith in her heart, and how greatly circumspect she was
in her exchange with others" (10). This is the exact counterpart
of the dialogue between the "bad angel" and Eve, a comparison so
frequently used in the traditional teaching of the church. This section concludes with the analysis of the name of the angel. *Gabriel*
means *strength*, and in this case too he received this name "for us,"
to show even in his name that "through his ministry the incarnation
of the Strength of God was announced" (12).

3. Galilee and Nazareth, Aelred declares, were not chosen by chance. How could he ignore the fact that there is no chance in what God does? One sentence in this sermon has to be considered particularly attentively. The greatness of the event obliges readers to take seriously into account every detail, since "the place, the time, the order, and . . . every syllable of the words, all are full of sacred meaning [*omnia plena sunt sacramentis*]" (13). Thus, guided by his much-quoted *Interpretation of Hebrew Names* by Jerome, he explains first that Galilee means "the migration." What does that mean? "Through the conception and birth of the Lord, the migration of the whole world from the power of the devil and the entry into the kingdom of Christ begins," he writes. Indeed, the conception and birth of the Lord is only the beginning, since "to be sure he was conceived in the flesh only once, but he is conceived spiritually every day" (14).

In the kingdom of Christ, where humankind has migrated, a city must be built: Nazareth, which means "flower." To make the most of this metaphor, Aelred specifies that "there are three aspects to a flower: beauty, fragrance, and the beginning of the fruit" (15). The moral application follows, summarized in a statement: "Beauty pertains to chastity, fragrance to fraternal love, and the hope of fruit to spiritual fervor" (16). Aelred's expounding of charity is worth quoting, since it brings the audience into the life of a monastic community, with its good and bad aspects. Aelred starts with another image: "the human heart is like a vessel filled with honey or poison. As long as the vessel is closed, no one knows what is contained within. If, however, someone takes off the lid, immediately what is hidden within is known by its odor" (17). A silent monk is like a closed vessel, but when he enters into any relation, as when he receives an order or a rebuke, or when he talks with another, then what is hidden emerges. The passage is worth quoting for its vivacity:

> If he is then made angry or gives himself up to slander and murmuring, if also, when he has the opportunity, he gives himself over to buffoonery, laughter, and similar frivolities, he does not offer a good odor to his brothers. He does not have fraternal charity in his vessel but, rather, a weakened will. He has not built Nazareth,

and therefore Christ cannot be conceived in him. In contrast, whoever speaks with gravity, responds with humility, obeys with patience—whoever reveals no bitterness in his voice and shows none in his face—it is as if he gives forth the good odor of good ointment from his full vase. He shows that he has fraternal charity and therefore deserves to be loved by all. (18)

The third aspect of a flower is that it contains the hope of some fruit. This fruit coincides with "spiritual fervor," because "one who is lukewarm, unwilling, and apathetic does not hope for this fruit. If such a person is fervent, then he fervently follows the way of life prescribed for his vocation, he fervently embraces all things; it is in this and because of this that he hopes for great fruit" (19).

Thus, although incomplete, the discourse comes full circle, with a seed at the start and a fruit at the end. How to pass from one to the other is shown in the way Mary received the annunciation, taking the seed not only in her womb but also in her mind and heart at Nazareth, where that seed grew in her and with her as a beautiful, fragrant, and fruitful flower.

11. Mary as a New Eden

(Sermon 39: *For the Annunciation of the Lord*)

To meditate on the annunciation means to consider God's plan to rescue humankind from the consequences of the Fall, which in practical terms signifies contemplation of the beauty of creation materialized in the figure of Eden, the ruinous effects of human sin, and the restoration of the primitive beauty through the incarnation of the Son of God, his life, his death, and his resurrection. Against this theological background, Aelred proposes in Sermon 39 a clear and rather simple plan, easily summarized. The starting point is Eden as a *fertile ground* having a *source* at its center from which *four rivers* flowed to irrigate the whole earth. The allegorical reading gives these figures not another meaning but their full and true meaning. In this light, Mary is the new *garden of delight*, through whom the new Adam enters into the world; her fertility is total, for she is at the same time mother, widow, and virgin;[23] the source is the Holy Spirit, and the four rivers are the four cardinal virtues, practiced to perfection by Mary. The conclusion is for us: if we want to take part, as we ought to, in the work of the redemption, we have to build within ourselves a new Eden, where the new Adam, Christ, can enter and dwell as at home.

Now let us see how Aelred adorns this skeleton, how he succeeds in transforming this plan into a true garden. The first important point is in the very first paragraph, a wonderful overture to set the hearers' feelings in tune with the feast. An old theological tenet affirms that the advantages brought by the redemption were greater than the damages caused by the Fall. Aelred starts by singing a hymn to three "glories" of this day: the immense mercy of God, the excellence of the vocation of humans, called to be one with God, and the abyss of God's plan in making a virgin bear a child. These are undoubtedly truths, but truths that should be emotionally understood and received: "These realities are great, so entirely great that we could in no way perceive them. Nevertheless, we ought certainly to embrace that mercy sweetly, to honor fully with great respect the height that humanity reached, and to contemplate that profound plan with great affection" (1). It is a pity that the English translation cannot render the admirable echoes of the Latin, since *ualde dulciter, cum magno timore, cum magno affectu* are but musical notes that resonate the triple *quantam misericordiam, quantam excellentiam, quantam profunditatem* with which Aelred had described the three reasons that this feast is so joyful.

1. The first tempo of this symphony in praise of Mary as the new Eden is devoted to describing the garden as a fertile ground, since Eden means *voluptas*, that is, "sensual pleasure," turned by Aelred into an "aesthetic pleasure," since he glosses the word as meaning "a beautiful place, full of the most beautiful trees and every physical beauty." The heart of Mary "ought to be called Paradise, a land undoubtedly fertile" (3), since, according to the parable of the sower, she brought forth the fullest fruit (Matt 13:8). Aelred specifies, according to the usual categories of his time, that "thirtyfold

---

[23] See the same principle in S 45 for the Assumption.

fruit pertains to conjugal chastity, . . . sixtyfold fruit belongs to the chastity of widows, . . . hundredfold fruit signifies virginity" (4). What, then, about Mary, who was married, virgin, and widow? For the rest, he compares Mary's virtues to the beautiful trees growing in the garden of Eden, although he mentions only one of these "spiritual trees," patience: "Such a tree is patience: how firmly it stands, how sweet the fruit it bears. So too are piety, humility, and the other virtues" (6).

2. The second tempo is devoted to the image of "the fountain that irrigates that Paradise" (6). Gathering some gospel quotations (John 4:13-14; 7:37-38, 39), Aelred easily indicates in the Holy Spirit the real meaning of this figure, the Spirit who would come upon Mary, as the angel said (Luke 1:35). The conclusion expands the benefit of this water to the whole world, since "this fountain fills the spiritual Paradise with such abundance that it suffices not just for her but for the whole world" (7). The universal work of the Holy Spirit, he says, is realized through the four virtues symbolized by the four rivers of Eden. Prudence, temperance, fortitude, and justice are in fact "the source and beginning of all other virtues but which no one can have at all unless the fountain of the Holy Spirit dwells within him" (9).

The reader will read with great profit what Aelred says of each of these traditional virtues. It would be interesting to understand the reason, if any, that underpins Aelred's sequence. Motivations are found here and there. For example, the primacy of prudence seems to be connected with both wisdom ("No one can arrive at wisdom except through prudence" [10]) and charity ("For without prudence, no one can arrive at charity. Through prudence one knows what one ought to love and what not" [12]). Justice comes at the end, since this virtue apparently incorporates a good number of behaviors, especially with reference to relationships, since it is the virtue "by which one returns to all people what is their due," a principle glossed by Aelred with this advice: "Through this virtue people return fear to their lords, obedience to their superiors, and charity to their brothers. Through this virtue one is unyielding to vices, honest toward other people, humble with companions, and beneficent to those in need" (16). Respect, humility, and mercy are all aspects of justice. All descriptions of the four virtues and their families conclude with a summary that sees them perfectly realized in Mary.

3. The third and final tempo of this "symphony of the redemption" is a sort of solemn triumph celebrating the entry of Jesus, the new Adam, into this newly restored Paradise: "Today, brothers, our Adam [1 Cor 15:45], the Lord Jesus Christ, entered into this spiritual Paradise in order to fight against the *ancient serpent* [Rev 12:7-9; 20:2] that overcame the old Adam. From this comes this festivity, brothers; from this comes the joy. Let us not be afraid. For our *joy ought to be full* [John 16:24]. We need not fear that the serpent will seduce this Adam to evil or entice this woman into sinning" (17).

The concluding exhortation is a prayer and a warning. We pray that, following the example of Mary, we also may become a Paradise for Jesus to enter into. That prayer implies that our heart must become a fertile ground full of the "spiritual trees" of virtues, having at its center the unfailing fountain of the Holy Spirit to water us "with spiritual grace, compunction, devotion, and every spiritual sweetness" and to "wash us from the filth of vices and make us pure and unspotted so that we may be ready for the embrace of our Lord." The warning is not to touch "the tree of the knowledge of good and evil [Gen 2:9]," which is self-will (19). Here Aelred provides a clear echo of the beginning of the Benedictine Rule (Prol.2-3), portraying in this the starting point of a history of salvation meant to repair the history of the Fall. This new history—performed in an exemplary way by the new Adam, who was born and grew in the new Eden, which is Mary—is based on the wish of our Lord that we submit and follow his will, not our own, like him who has come not to do his own will but *the will of him who sent* him (John 6:38).

12. The Bodily Passion of Christ That Transfigures Our Evil Spiritual Passions

(Sermon 40: *For the Day of Easter*)

The opposition flesh and spirit, otherwise called letter and spirit or shadow and reality, marks the Christian reading of the relation existing between the Old and the New Testament, the watershed being Jesus of Nazareth, in whom Christians recognize and confess the incarnation of God, in whom the "old figures" find their materialization and the prophecies come true. This relationship became a hermeneutic criterion already widely used in the New Testament writings and adopted in theological literature of any time. This interpretation is sometimes called allegorical reading, which means a transfer of meaning from the letter of the text to its theological, moral, and mystical/eschatological implications, according to the well-known theory of "the four senses" of Scripture. If the principle is clear, its application is not; the history of theology has known ages in which an excess of allegorization prompted a reaction more attentive to the letter and to the basic historical meaning of the texts than to the three allegorical senses.[24]

All of Aelred's sermons incorporate such allegorical interpretation, according to an often-quoted principle established by Saint Paul: *These things happened to them as figures* (1 Cor 10:11). Aelred himself believes that in Scripture "every syllable of the words, all are full of sacred meaning" (S 38.13). Allegory has a substance that differentiates it from a mere metaphor, and it seems that in Scripture something becomes a figure when read in reference to Christ.[25] So in Sermon 40 when Aelred contrasts the physical passion endured by Jesus with the spiritual passion people suffer when they commit sin, the different elements of the passion narrative as he presents them become figures of the different steps of our falling into sin. The principle is that in spiritual falling people are rescued and saved by Jesus' physical suffering. This comparison creates a sort of imaginative illustration of what Isaiah affirmed: *by his wounds we are healed* (Isa 53:5). The resurrection is meant to encourage people to

---

[24] For a history of the development of the four senses of scriptural interpretation, see Karlfried Froehlich, with Mark S. Burrows, *Sensing the Scriptures: Aminadab's Chariot and the Predicament of Biblical Interpretation* (Grand Rapids, MI, and Cambridge: William B. Eerdmans Publishing Company, 2014).

[25] See Pierre-André Burton, "Un art de lire les Écritures selon Aelred de Rievaulx. Principe herméneutiques: transposition et fragmentation," *Collectanea Cisterciensia* 73 (2011): 244–78; Domenico Pezzini, "Radiant Dew," 34–37.

believe in this possibility. The incipit could not be clearer: "As our Lord Jesus Christ deigned to be born for us, to be tempted for us, to be beaten for us, and to die for us, so also did he deign to rise for us. Yet his temptation, scourging, death, and entombment belong to our redemption; his resurrection strengthens our hope" (1).

The five instances of *for us* are the basis of everything that follows, since this intention establishes the link between his suffering and our sins, from which we had to be redeemed, "for without a doubt . . . , whatever he himself suffered in the body is what we have suffered in the soul" (1).

As Judas betrayed Christ by a *kiss*, so our first parents were betrayed by a deceitful kiss, the promise to become as God, with "sweetness and delight on the outside, but poison lay concealed within" (3). As Jesus was subsequently arrested and bound, so we are bound "by our own inordinate desires" (3; Jas 1:14). Then, "thus bound, humanity was handed over to Caiaphas, that is, to cupidity, whose servants and attendants *veiled his face*" (4; Luke 22:64). Impotence and blindness result from following cupidity. After this, humanity is "handed over to Pilate, that is, to the devil, prince of this world," and mocked by other devils (6). But human perversity seems to have no limits. People can "enjoy it when they do evil," and humanity is "thus crowned with thorns because his glory and honor were in his own iniquities" (7). People finally die and are buried because "when they advance so far in their evil life that they neither recognize nor confess their sin, then they are dead from deep within" (8).

To sum it up, "because we had suffered all of these things in the soul, our Lord Jesus Christ wished to suffer all of them in his body and, through the sufferings of his body, to cure the sufferings of our soul" (9). The parallelism established by comparing the "perverse" spiritual passion of our sinful life with the "good" corporeal passion endured by Jesus aims at our conversion. It is a contrast similar to that celebrated in the *Improperia* of Good Friday and in many medieval passion lyrics, in which God's benefits bestowed on humanity were rewarded by ingratitude on the part of men and women.

One wonders why in a Paschal sermon Aelred has given so much space to a reflection on the passion. But this is only the first part of the discourse. The second and more important step draws human lives into the resurrection of Christ, since "who are those who rise with Christ except those who share in all that Christ has suffered?" (9). Those who have risen with Christ are asked to *seek the things that are above* (Col 3:1). Aelred ignores other people, but speaking to his monks, he says, "I wonder whether the apostle speaks especially to you—to you who have certainly suffered many temptations, as if you were being beaten with Christ; to you who die with Christ through daily labors and tribulations; to you who are, as it were, buried in this cloister and in this silence for Christ. You who suffer all these things, not in your soul against Christ, but in your body for Christ, you have certainly risen with Christ" (10).

Here the elements of the passion narrative are spiritually applied in their good sense to some aspects of the monastic vocation, a way of life that traditionally includes three stages: the beginners, the advanced, and the perfect, all called "to seek the things that are above, all according to their own way" (10). The beginners must first fight against carnal vices, striving toward chastity, which is above, and despising lust, which is below. Aelred is always superb at using images: "Above is moderation, which raises the mind to heavenly things; below is gluttony, which drives the mind toward the belly" (12). The advanced are tempted by pride and vanity in their progress; what they have to seek above is humility, because Aelred flatly affirms that *superbae uirtutes uirtutes non sunt*—"proud virtues are not virtues" (13). The perfect must remember that they are still on the road to sanctity and must thus remain humble and always search for better things.

But this is not enough. Aelred remarks that those who are risen must not only *seek the things that are above* but also *savor the things that are above* (Col 3:2). This statement gives him the opportunity to resume one of his favorite topics, the "very great difference" (16) that exists between seeking the truth and savoring it, between a dry and a "dewy" knowledge. After some examples of this kind of interior schism, Aelred specifies that savoring means that one must "frequently meditate upon and thoroughly consider how great is the excellence of truth, what security there is in purity, what happiness in the service of God" (19).

The apparently abstract excellence must produce and be integrated by security and happiness, without which the spiritual life becomes difficult indeed: "By frequent meditation, acquire not only the knowledge of the truth, as many evil people have done, but also the taste for the truth." This is that savoring called *ruminatio*, nourished by *lectio divina*. The result is a combination of mental and affective attitudes, as shown in the apt conclusion: "If thus we have arisen and raised ourselves above the earth in mind, intention, zeal, and love, then we will truly share in the resurrection of the Lord" (19).

13. Days of Creation, Days of Salvation

(Sermon 41: *For the Day of Easter*)

This is the day that the Lord has made: let us rejoice and be glad in it (Ps 117:24). This antiphon is probably the best-known text of the Easter liturgy. Aelred quotes it ten times in Sermon 41, making it the refrain that chains a compact development around the key word, *day*, and in particular *the day that the Lord has made*. *Day* means time, *time* means history; and when history is viewed as ruled by God, it means creation, fall, redemption, and glorification, that is, what is commonly known as "history of salvation," of which the Bible is the narrative and the code from the very beginning to the eschatological completion.

The sermon is organized along two "ways." One describes in five "days" the main stages of the history of salvation; the other interprets the six "days" of the creation as the means chosen by God to repair the world ruined by the sin of humankind. The center connecting these two ways, which makes a true turning point in the whole history of humankind, is the "eighth day," some timeless point that breaks the recurrent seven-day circle and transfers the world from mutability to the stability of God's eternity, whence the creation has come to where it is destined to return.

Aelred magnificently expresses the greatness and joy of Easter day from the start when he inserts between two quotations of the verse of the day one of his cherished triads: "The one who is tired can rest on this day. The one who is sick can be cured on this day. The one who is dead can arise on this day" (1). Note the progress, or *gradatio*, marked in this tricolon. This day comes as the fifth of a sequence that includes the day of eternity, the day of creation, the day of perdition, the day of restoration, the day of resurrection. It seems that time flows from eternity and into eternity and is characterized by mutability and variety, while eternity has neither beginning nor end, since "the day of eternity is God himself" (2).

In describing the content of each day, Aelred signals the differences according to the presence or absence of various moments of the day. So the day of creation "has a morning and an evening" (3), signs of mutability, but no night, since darkness marks the state of a sinful humankind, and night characterizes the third day, a night in which we all were born, "because we all come forth from the mass of perdition" (4). This day "has a morning and an evening. The morning is the day of a person's birth; the evening, his death" (4). This was the condition of humankind until the fourth day came, the day of restoration: "That is the day on which the Lord was made, *when the word was made flesh and dwelt among us* [John 1:14]. This day had a morning in the Lord's nativity, a noontime in the display of his miracles, an evening in his passion" (5). Evening is a time for weeping, but "this weeping does not remain for long, because immediately *joy breaks out in the morning* [Ps 29:6], when the day of glorification begins because of the sublime resurrection of the Lord" (7). This fifth day, the one we celebrate at Easter, opens the way to what Aelred refers to as our resurrection, when *death will be swallowed up in victory* (1 Cor 15:54).

What follows is the heart of this sermon, a true hymn to the glory of heaven, imbued with those high lyrical tones Aelred can use when he talks of the rest, peace, and inner security that form the recurrent dream for which he strove all his life, in friendship and love, in the fraternal community of the cloister as in his diplomatic efforts to reconcile kings and peoples. Paragraphs 8 and 9 are just matter for

contemplation, lulled by the music of their iterations of four key
words: *perfecta, nulla, nihil, quidquid.* What is good will reach perfection and totality (*quidquid* = everything), what is bad becomes
nothing (*nullus labor, nullus timor*), what is against us is removed
(*nihil contra*). And the extraordinary beauty of this construction is
enhanced by the chiasmus, which puts the negative in the middle as
if to be swallowed by the positive placed at the opposite extremes.

This opposition between the whole and nothing actually reflects
the basic opposition between God and Satan, between absolute
good and absolute evil, and hints at our "mixed" situation, which is
the cause of no little pain. In chapter 15 of her *Revelations* Julian
of Norwich writes admirably about the emotional "mutability" that
is the consequence of this ontological condition. But she assures us
that while it is true that "for the time of this life we have in us a
mervelous medelur [*mixture*] both of wele and of wo [*happiness and
misery*]," because we have in us the risen Christ and the wretchedness of Adam's fall (chap. 52), notwithstanding that, "it is Goddes
wille that we holde us in comfort with alle oure might, for blisse is
lasting without ende, and paine is passing, and shall be brought to
nought to them that shall be saved" (chap. 15).[26]

From this vision of the blessed life in the eternity of God, Aelred
comes back to our earthly condition, which after the resurrection of
Christ has radically changed. Now, since "Christ is our Head, and
we are his Body," the consequence is that two statements overlap:
"Today Christ has risen. This is the beginning of our glory" (10).
And what does it mean? It is the rising of a new day:

> This day had a morning when our Lord rose; it will have a noon-
> time when his glory, splendor, and brightness, which begin today
> in the Head, are transferred to all the members, when *our lowly
> body is configured to the body of his brightness* [Phil 3:21]. . . .
> Then our noontime will be transferred into the noon of that first
> day, the day of eternity, so that it cannot fail or fade into evening,

---

[26] *The Writings of Julian of Norwich*, ed. Nicholas Watson and Jennifer Jenkins (Turnhout: Brepols, 2006), 289, 177.

but remains always in its fervor, in its light, in its brightness, in its sublimity. (11)

It remains to outline the second path of the sermon, that is, to highlight the means established by God to restore a fallen creation. For this path Aelred, considering that the Lord divided his creating work into seven days, while having no need of time, finds that this choice was made "undoubtedly because the manner of creation signified the manner of restoration" (15). This argument may seem gratuitous and mechanical, but there is a difference between a God who destroys to make things anew and a Creator who prefers to restore what has been ruined. Doesn't it suggest the same merciful attitude shown in the servant of the Lord, who *will not break a bruised reed or quench a smoldering wick* (Isa 42:3, as quoted in Matt 12:20)?

The works of the re-creation of a fallen humankind are then compared with the six days of creation. The first day, with the creation of *light*, is the birth of Christ, the true light of the world; the second day sees in the *firmament* the excellence of the sacraments; the third day, when the earth produces green plants and fruits, corresponds to the preaching of Jesus, through which a sterile ground brought forth "the fruit of penitence," seen in the conversion of Zacchaeus (Luke 19:1-10) and of the sinful woman (19; John 12:3); the sun, the moon, and the stars created in the fourth day are the apostles and their followers; the fifth day, when birds and fish were created, suggests "the miracles of our Savior" (21), which can be called birds because they suggest contemplation and fish because they suggest profundity; finally, the sixth day, when humans were created according to the image of God, indicates the passion of the Lord, by which the human image was re-created, or "reformed in that same image" (22).

With this, humankind returns to Paradise (Luke 23:43), resting in the sepulcher on the Sabbath, to rise eternally on the eighth day. Thus Aelred gives the gospel stories as a pattern showing the ways and the manners of human restoration. It was Jesus who effected this reform of the image, but it requires our response during the *interim* of our life, during which we are called to live "*soberly, justly, and devoutly"* (Titus 2:12), as members of the risen Christ, our Head. In this way, the joy at his resurrection today will lead us to enjoy our own resurrection when the day comes (23).

14. Charity as the Fulfillment of God's Work

(Sermon 42: *For the Day of Pentecost*)

This is the third sermon of the Second Clairvaux Collection to have survived in an incomplete form. It is for Pentecost, and its main theme is the "consummation," in the sense of the perfection or completion operated by the Holy Spirit. Christ's descent on the day of Pentecost crowns his work to redeem humankind, and its presence is mostly seen in charity, which is his peculiar gift and the summit of all virtues.

The discourse is preceded by a long confession of ignorance on the part of Aelred, a device common in medieval literature that Aelred frequently uses.[27] He justifies it as something dark used to highlight the splendor and beauty of speeches better than his own, as pure sweet water may grow sweeter in contrast with the confused water that he is going to give them to drink. This familiar theme of sweetness characterizes the day of Pentecost, which guarantees "sweetness, consolation, hope, and security" (3).

A completion supposes earlier stages, and the sequence in this case appears in the verse Aelred quotes at the beginning: *Behold, I will consummate a new covenant with Jacob. . . . I will give my laws into their minds and write them on their hearts* (Heb 8:8-9; Jer 31:31-32, 33). The first covenant is put under the Law given through Moses; the new one is ruled by Grace and Truth, which "are not just given but brought about and fulfilled *through Jesus Christ* [John 1:17]. For the perfection of the law is charity" (6). So Christ is the one who operates the passage from the Old Law to the New, and he does it through the gift of the Spirit. Aelred clearly summarizes this transition in the statement, "Charity is preserved through the pouring forth of the Holy Spirit. The practice of charity fulfills the

---

[27] On Aelred's so-called incompetence, see Casey, "Introduction," 293–98.

new covenant. . . . I will show you life brought to fulfillment in the new covenant; this life was not in the old covenant, and I will bring you to fulfillment in the new covenant" (6).

The rest of the sermon teaches us how to grow to fulfillment, since what was shown in the life of Christ and brought to completion through the descent of the Spirit must become "our own" (10). Following a procedure he adopted in Sermon 27, "For the Feast of All Saints," Aelred intertwines the seven days of creation, the seven gifts of the Holy Ghost, and seven of the eight Beatitudes to build a rule of life in the Spirit modeled on Jesus' life. Again, the moral teaching is absolutely traditional, as was the practice in classic and medieval preaching to organize doctrinal tenets and moral principles in numerical sequences, a good procedure for assisting people to memorize what they received through oral delivery. The number seven was one of the favorite choices: to those already mentioned (creation, the gifts of the Spirit, and the Beatitudes) could be added the seven sacraments, the seven petitions of the Lord's Prayer, and the seven deadly sins. What is original in Aelred's treatment in this sermon is the fact that he introduces a new patterning element, the ages of Jesus, an appropriate addition since the object is to see how Jesus grew to perfection so that we can imitate him.

The incomplete sermon preserves only four parts, attached to four ages: *infantia, pueritia, adolescentia, iuventus,* but the whole plan survives, since Aelred announces it at the start:

> In his infancy he taught humility, and in his childhood, piety; in adolescence, knowledge; in young manhood, strength. In that strength, he fought to the finish, unto death, and by his death he overpowered death. His resurrection followed, in which he revealed the secret of his plan. He ascended into heaven, drawing our understanding toward heavenly things, and today, through the infusion of the Holy Spirit, he gave an understanding of wisdom, the perfection of charity, the fulfillment of the law. (8)

The three stages currently missing from the sermon are the resurrection, the ascension, and the infusion of the Spirit. The connections are ingeniously established, and we may imagine that they were heard with relish and delight, enhanced by a certain surprise at seeing how Aelred had newly organized well-known spiritual themes in webs of figures and principles. One example suffices to show Aelred's procedure:

> In infancy he taught humility, which is born in us through fear of the Lord and confession of sins. If we listen diligently to him crying out, *Do penance, the kingdom of heaven is approaching* [Matt 3:2], [it is] as if we were hearing him say, *Let there be light* [Gen 1:1] at the beginning of our re-creation. First he says, *Let there be light,* so that the morning star may arise in our hearts and there may be a division between the light of our new conversion and the darkness of the iniquity we have committed. *And let there be evening,* out of consideration for our weakness, *and morning* [Gen 1:5] for the beginning of our enlightenment. Thus, out of the spirit of fear of the Lord [Isa 11:3], let there come for us *a first day* [Gen 1:5], like our first blessedness. All this was shown to us by the Lord, first by example in his infancy and afterward by word in his preaching when he said, *Blessed are the poor in spirit*—that is, the humble and God-fearing—*because yours is the kingdom of heaven* [Matt 5:3]. (9)

If the first day means the *timor Domini,* childhood in the second day is connected with *pietas,* that is the cult of God, nourished by the creation of the firmament, that is, Holy Scripture, which has as its fruit the beatitude announced to the meek.

The third day corresponds to Jesus' adolescence, during which he encouraged *scientia,* the gift of knowledge. Aelred takes the opportunity to reaffirm that "it was not necessary for us to know the nature of herbs or the movement of the stars, but rather to know what and where [the Lord] is, his daily failings, how much he advances, how much he regresses" (12). The gathering of the waters (our thoughts) performed in the third day is ordered to the end that "*a dry land appear* [Gen 1:9] in our heart, where we thirst for God and experience a shower of compunction coming from above" (13). Compunction evokes tears; that is why this day is marked by the beatitude that proclaims, *Blessed are they who mourn.*

The fourth day is devoted to Jesus' *iuventus*: "In his young manhood, he showed strength [*fortitudinem*], teaching us so *to hunger and thirst for justice* that we would not fear to suffer either *persecution* [Matt 5:6, 10] or death for justice's sake" (14). As in Sermon 27, Aelred here extends the eighth beatitude to include the other seven, since it recalls how hard it is to live in poverty, meekness, and so on. The metaphorical interpretation of the greater and lesser lights, which helps discernment, is truly illuminating, since it joins in hierarchical position Christ and the church in their complementary function, as both in prosperity and adversity, "The greater light, which presides over the day, is the example of the Savior himself, which prevents us from being exalted in the day of human achievement; the lesser light, which presides over the night, the stars, is the example of the patience of the church, which prevents us from being overthrown by the cruel night of persecution" (14). Strength is then connected with the beatitude addressed to those *who hunger and thirst for justice*.

A further useful element for reflection is the fact that Aelred gives for each day subtle interpretations of evening, morning, and full day, three stages that mark a progress from what may appear as a painful or even negative situation (evening) through a recovering of hope (morning), leading to the experience of the beatitude prefixed to the day. For example, in the fourth day, "although it might be evening, given the consideration of human persecution, let there be morning if we remember divine justice. Thus from the gift of the Spirit of strength let there appear to us the fourth day, namely, the fourth beatitude" (14).

Behind what may appear an abstract and formal organization of standard themes, shrewdly but artificially interlocked, we have in fact a well-structured spiritual treatise, full of subtle psychological insights. A slow and close reading reveals in this apparently unpromising sermon that well-balanced wisdom that is one of the best characteristics of Aelred's pedagogy. Numbers, figures, and their connections seem to be only useless husks, but when seriously and sympathetically analyzed they reveal how useful they are for memorizing a doctrine by fixing it to elegantly structured patterns of thought, to brilliant images and metaphors that will continue to shine in the mind of the hearer or reader. This too is a gift of the Holy Spirit, which Aelred names *imagination*.

15. From the Yoke of Iniquity and Misery to the Sweet Yoke of Charity

(Sermon 43: *For the Nativity of Saint John the Baptist*)

John the Baptist incarnates the ideal of monastic vocation, particularly in what is thought to be the apex of this choice: the solitary life. The feast of John's Nativity was a day on which the abbot was required to preach to his community. The subject chosen by Aelred for this sermon appears highly original and in a sense paradoxical. In fact, while exalting the hermit's ideal as the summit of Christian discipleship and thus a vocation appealing to very few people, Aelred at the same time tends to water down its singularity and to deal with it in a way that allows him to say that the virtues apparently typical of the solitary life are better understood "as a rule for the spiritual solitary, such as we all ought to be" (23).

In this respect, the introductory paragraph has a great relevance. Holiness, Aelred says, is possible for everybody on the principle that in God's house *there are many mansions* (John 14:2). This phrase reflects the fact that "there are differences in life, different ways of living, different degrees of perfection—if I may say this" (1). This restrictive clause applied to perfection, of which there are not different types but different degrees, apparently implies that "differences" do not coincide with "hierarchies." Aelred, in fact, perfectly in tune with the mentality of his time, establishes a sort of "scale of perfection," when he lists in an ascending pattern the different conditions of the married, widows, monks, and solitaries, but he corrects the possible strictly hierarchical interpretation of this list by stating that "in every state in life in the church, people can be saved if they are able to live according to the designation and rule of their state in life" (3). He supports the statement with scriptural examples: Zachary and Elizabeth for married people, Anna the prophet for widows, the primitive church community in Jerusalem for monks, and John the Baptist for solitaries. Each state has its rules of perfection. Predictably, "the total perfection of the monk is in giving up his own will" (5); this is the basic moral principle of the Benedictine Rule.

The path of holiness is modeled on the solitary life, but with the intention of drawing a rule ultimately applicable to everybody, with opportune adaptations. First, to avoid any simplification, Aelred specifies that "some are solitary only in body, others only in spirit, and still others both in body and spirit. . . . These two are solitaries to be praised" (6). The real starting point of the sermon is a passage usually adapted to solitaries, if not reserved for them, in which "Saint Jeremias describes their perfection and the very way of perfection itself when he says, *It is good for a person to carry the yoke from his adolescence; let him sit alone and be silent because he has been raised above himself*" (7; Lam 3:27-28). The transfer of what seemed to be valid for solitaries to an ideal of perfection valid for all is thus assured. The sermon is consequently structured around some points taken one by one from the quotation: the ages of the spiritual life and the various types of yokes describe the human anthropological condition; the program to reach perfection is indicated in *stability, solitude, and silence*; the final objective consists in *rising above oneself*.

Aelred considers only the first three stages of a person's life, those preceding the condition of *vir*, meaning a mature adult man. These are infancy, childhood (*pueritia*), and adolescence: "In infancy, ignorance rules; in childhood, evil desires rule; in adolescence, reason and sense arise against vices" (8). Only when we are conscious of our wounded human condition and start under the guide of reason to enhance virtues and fight against vices, he says, do we really enter into that process aptly called "adolescence," during which—as the verb *adolesco* indicates—we grow toward adulthood.

An important and decisive element of this consciousness as Aelred describes it consists in being aware of and taking into account the fact that in our life we are oppressed by three yokes, but also that paradoxically we can become free only by submitting to two other yokes. The oppressing yokes are the yoke of iniquity, the yoke of misery, and the yoke of infirmity; the virtuous yokes that free us are the yoke of the fear of God and, above all, the yoke of charity. The oppressing yokes are imposed on us by the devil, partly because of our responsibility as a consequence of the Fall; the virtuous yokes are freely chosen and are the paradoxical way by which we are made free.

The yoke of iniquity refers to the bad instincts inhabiting our souls. The yoke of misfortune (*infelicitas*) has to do with the miseries and sufferings of this life. The yoke of weakness (*infirmitas*) combines the preceding two and is defined by Aelred as "the impossibility or the difficulty of doing good" (13). This is the yoke under which we habitually suffer; it partly derives from the "corruption of nature" and partly from "unrelenting habit," in the establishment of which our responsibility is implied (13, 14). Aelred is clear: "People place this yoke upon themselves" (15). As a result he spends extra time examining the ways we create this third yoke, at the same time emphasizing the care we must take to sustain our good will so as to prevent bad actions from becoming bad habits through iteration.

To escape this oppression we must submit ourselves to the yoke of our Lord. This yoke is double, combining fear and love. First, the irrational child (of the second age), considering personal shortcomings, assumes the fear of the Lord and opts for a new way of life, thus entering into the third age: "This fear compels such people to accept the yoke of law and discipline, that is, to be under the power of another and to live under one or another written rule, as we do under the Rule of Saint Benedict or as canons do under the Rule of Saint Augustine. At this point their adolescence begins, because then they begin to resist vices and sins and to be strong against the devil and his persuasions" (19).

In this state, carrying the yoke can be very painful, but if people persevere "they will certainly grow from adolescence into perfect adulthood; thus they will receive the yoke that is sweet and the burden that is light" (20; Matt 11:29-30). A stair, even the *scala paradisi*, has many steps; on a stairway one goes up and down and sometimes, maybe for a long time, one may sit down on a certain step, being incapable of moving or unwilling to do so. Schemes and patterns help discernment; they indicate the potential dynamic of life and are not to be taken as photographs of a regular irresistible ascent.

John the Baptist now comes to the foreground. As Aelred does with Mary, after describing an ideal of sanctity he is eager to affirm that there has been someone who has lived that ideal, who has made the ideal come true: "Blessed John the Baptist, this man of whom we speak today, bore that yoke without a doubt, not just from his adolescence but even from his infancy, because even in the womb of his mother he was full of the Holy Spirit, who is love, charity, and sweetness" (21).

This passage opens the way to the more practical part of the sermon, which offers "a rule for the spiritual solitary, such as we all ought to be" (23). This rule has three parts and an objective, according to the verse of Lamentations quoted as the theme of the sermon: sitting in solitude and being silent in order to elevate ourselves. As Aelred explains: "*sitting* signifies stability, *silence* signifies quiet, and *being raised up* signifies the heights of contemplation" (24). His attention is particularly captured by the instinct to wander (*vagatio*), both in body and in spirit, a bad curiosity that is the worst threat to the quiet and peace of the soul. Paragraphs 25–27 present a series of vivid pictorial scenes of the restless monk, a gallery of the kind of portraits of which Aelred is an indisputable master and for which the accelerated pace of the concise sentences enthralls the reader. The conclusion is a kind and gentle invitation: "Therefore, brothers, let us sit, so that we may persevere in quietness of body and spirit; let us be silent, so that we may remove both from our mouth and our heart all that is meaningless, suspicious, and disparaging; thus we may be able to be raised above ourselves" (28).

The end of this spiritual journey requires that people become capable of rising above themselves. People's homes are where their love is. They may lower themselves beneath themselves, as happens when they direct their love to inferior creatures. Or they may preserve themselves within themselves, as when they direct their love to themselves, but in this case they meet with their own wretchedness. The best approach is to raise their love above themselves, reaching at the same time their fulfillment, precisely as John the Baptist did: "The blessed man whose feast day we celebrate today knew and understood this. He held all earthly things in contempt—all earth's delights, all earth's vanities, all earthly pleasures and honors—and he raised his whole heart above himself to the one who is truly blessed and eternal. Therefore he is eternally blessed with him" (31).

It may be useful to remember that Aelred is not saying that inferior loves, so called according to their object, must be discarded. Everybody knows that such a response is impossible, and Aelred knows very well how to appreciate the beauty of creation and knows that it is necessary to love oneself, in body and soul. The point is not to confuse things, not to love "transitory and perishable things" as if they were eternal. The point is not to confuse what is partial with what is total, that is, not to turn our "whole love" (*totum amorem*) toward ourselves but to reserve "the whole" for God only. God is "above us," and so God becomes the lodestar guiding all our choices as regards what is "beneath us and within us," since the love of God gives a sense of direction to our life and to our loves: we become what we love! *Vagatio*, pretending to go everywhere, leads nowhere; attaching to everything leads to nothing. A concentration of energies, in quiet, in solitude, in silence, in fact reaches the highest target possible, eternal blessedness, as did Saint John: "he raised his whole heart above himself to the one who is truly blessed and eternal. Therefore he is eternally blessed with him" (31).

16. The Joy of the Friend of the Bridegroom

(Sermon 44: *For the Nativity of Saint John the Baptist*)

Church festivities are joyful events, especially those that have their origin in the gospel. It is said of John the Baptist that *many will rejoice in his birth* (Luke 1:14). We are among these many; therefore we must rejoice. Joy is then the subject chosen by Aelred for this second sermon for the Nativity of Saint John. He starts from the apparent paradox of a saint famous for the severity and austerity of his life who was announced as a *joy for many*, who "leapt for joy" (Luke 1:44) when still in the womb of his mother, who in one of his few statements about himself proclaimed that he was *the friend of the bridegroom, who stands and hears him, and rejoices greatly at the bridegroom's voice,* concluding with, *For this reason my joy has been fulfilled* (John 3:29).

Aelred starts with a note of sound realism, saying that in our postlapsarian condition there is no such thing as "perfect joy," because "this body weighs us down, the devil troubles us, temptations attack us; from all this comes sadness." The foundation of our joy is "the hope we have in the Lord, through whom we will be freed from these evils" (3). But even now pain is not necessarily against joy. He quotes the example given by the Lord of the "sadness" preceding childbirth, which is followed by the "joy" of a newborn baby, a metaphor of the "good works" generated by our hard efforts to overcome temptations. He also adds that "we ought to rejoice not only because of the reward given for these tribulations but also because we are worthy to suffer some trouble for our Lord and to pay back something to him for the trouble he himself suffered for us" (5). Therefore we can rejoice in the feasts of the saints "insofar as we take care to imitate their faith, their manner of life, and the suffering they endured for the Lord" (6).

Where did the joy experienced by John come from, Aelred asks. Certainly not from the possession of earthly goods or from the exterior success he enjoyed for a time, when he positively discarded the idea that he was the Messiah. This joy was interior, as he himself affirmed, and came from his being the friend of the bridegroom. We all share in this joy with John, since "Christ is the bridegroom of the soul," any soul (9). So we are interested in knowing what is implied in being Christ's friends. Aelred picks up the two conditions specified by John himself: *amicus stat et audit,* the friend stands and listens.

First, the friend stands: "he is not moved, he does not waver, he does not fall but stands" (11). Aelred uses appropriate iconic verbs to contrast with this standing: the friend does not fall (*non cadit*) from a good life into an evil one, he does not lie down (*non iacet*) under vices and sins, he keeps (*tenet*) the right way, he does not "fly upward" (*non uolat*) (12), carried by the wind of pride. In contrast, "Adam . . . wished to fly and be like God. He did not wish to be a friend but an equal; therefore from being a friend he was made a wretched slave" (12). Incidentally, this portrait of interior stability and good sense of direction is one of the pictorial and concise spiritual programs frequently found in Aelred's discourses.

Second, the friend *listens*. This attitude marks a progress, since stability indicates a personal quality, while listening implies a relational situation proper to friendship. In fact, Aelred expands this second theme more than the first, with seven paragraphs rather than two. Obviously the quality of this listening depends on who it is who speaks to us, or, better, what we consider him to be like. Adam heard the Lord speaking as a judge, David as a king, Moses as a teacher. But, says Aelred, "which is the soul that can say, *I will listen to what you speak within me, Lord God? Within me*, he says. There the friend of the bridegroom stands, there he listens to him and rejoices with great joy at the voice of the bridegroom" (14).

Where does this voice come from? Quoting Ezekiel 1:22-25, Aelred says this voice is to come "sometimes . . . from below the firmament, sometimes from the firmament itself, sometimes from above the firmament" (15). The first voice is that which comes through the mediation of the beauty of created things. The second comes more directly through the wonderful, merciful, and sweet operation of God in our souls. As an example, Aelred mentions that "the soul finds joy within herself when she considers that fishermen become rulers of the whole world, publicans become evangelists, thieves are changed into preachers!" (17). The third voice comes from the revelations offered by God himself beyond any mediation: "If [John] had such joy in him when in the narrow confines of his mother's womb, just imagine what kind of joy he had in his heart when he saw him, when he touched him with his hands, when he saw the Holy Spirit descending like a dove upon him, when he heard the voice of the Father from heaven" (19).

Seeing, touching, hearing: this is certainly an interior joy, but it reaches us through our senses. This joy awakes our joy as far as we imitate John's life. How? By praising him, with praise that is actually our life. To celebrate the saints means not only singing hymns to their glory but rather transferring their life into ours.

A series of final considerations is attached to the figure of John as an angel comes "to prepare the way of the Lord" (Mal 3:1; Matt 11:10; Luke 7:27). A well-known biblical story is introduced at this point: the wrestling between Jacob and the angel at the ford of the Jabbok River (Gen 32:22-30). The story, because of its deep ambiguity, has received multifarious interpretations. Here is how Aelred reads it, focusing his attention on the angel's blessing and its being delayed until dawn: "Jacob stands for the holy fathers who came before the incarnation of the Lord; by tears, prayers, and a good life, they wished to constrain our Lord to take flesh, he who would remove this curse and give a blessing. Because of their great desire, they were almost impatient, but he was waiting for the time he had himself foreseen together with the Father. Perhaps the wrestling match signified that [conflict]" (22).

The apparition of John is the sign that dawn has come, and dawn announces the coming of the full sun, the coming of the bridegroom whose presence will give joy to all his friends. This is how Aelred concludes his sermon, in a way that proves unquestionably that liturgical feasts both represent and make present in us the figures and the events of the history of salvation: "It seems to me that that [same] angel *prepares the way of the Lord* [Matt 3:1; Isa 40:3; Mal 3:1], not only then but even now, because, following his example, you mortify the members of your body and are eager for the renunciations and austerities of this life. Without doubt the way is prepared by which our Lord wills to come to your hearts so that, like true friends of our Lord *the bridegroom*, you may be able to hear his voice within you and rejoice *at his voice* [John 3:29]" (24).

A final word recalls the cost and the seriousness of this joy. Aelred in fact exhorts us to "hold with all fervor to this way that this friend of Jesus has prepared by his example, so that when we have shared in the austerities he himself endured, we may share the interior joy that he experienced" (25).

17. A Song of Praise to Mary, Our Queen of Mercy

(Sermon 45: *For the Assumption of Saint Mary*)

This is the longest sermon of the Second Clairvaux Collection, a fact that is somehow paradoxical, since the matter concerns a mystery that is more a theological tenet than the narration of an event, and as such is devoid in principle of those affective and human elements so characteristic of Aelred's preaching rhetoric. Notwithstanding these objective limitations, the result is indeed excellent. First, the structure is clearly organized in three parts: a theological section explores the reasons for the glorification of Mary, body and soul (1–12), then the excellence of Mary is visualized in a sort of procession in which Mary goes beyond all other creatures, forming the heavenly Jerusalem to take her place at the throne of her Son (13–34), and finally, she is invoked by the earthly Jerusalem, the church in the world, which trusts in her maternal intercession (35–43).

Contrary to what may be expected, the peculiar qualities of Aelred's language shine with a particular intensity in this sermon: the theological theme is treated with the usual affective tones, the arrival and the glorification of Mary in heaven resembles the drama of a medieval mystery play, and the intercessory prayer to the Queen of Heaven is like a lyrical hymn to the kind and protective maternity of the Virgin. Finally, the well-balanced treatment of Mary, seen not in isolation but deeply inserted into the mystical body of the church, is well in tune with the Mariology of Vatican II, when the Catholic Church succeeded in checking and correcting the drive of an unbalanced theological outlook called by some Mariolatry.

The first part of the sermon starts with an invitation to praise "our Lady, Saint Mary," since in doing so we show her the same admiring and loving attitude that was shown to her by God himself. There is nothing formal or merely ritualistic in this attitude: "What will I say"—Aelred exclaims—"of the tender love that he showed to her when he deigned to sit in her lap, to suck her breasts, and, as a boy, to obey her precepts?" (2). This affective tonality imbues all this section. A short passage suffices as proof: "just as she is more excellent, more blessed, and more gentle among all the saints of God, so too she who is to him not only a creature, a handmaid, a friend, and a daughter but also a mother tastes his sweetness more intimately" (4). All these titles describe Mary's relationship with God in familiar terms. As for us, she is our advocate, our hope, and the mediator (*mediatrix*) between her son and us (3).

Aelred provides a reassuring background with the portrait of Mary as an icon of joy. In the Middle Ages and beyond there were prayers to the joys and the sorrows of Mary. Aelred lists some of her great joys, and although he does not ignore how much she had to suffer during the passion, nevertheless he says that she felt a great joy at Jesus' resurrection and one still greater at his ascension: "But today we ought to rejoice with her even more, because today her joy was filled up to the brim" (4). Because of her perfection Mary "was in great woe after the glory of his ascension, when his corporeal presence, in which she had greatly delighted, was taken from her" (6).

But this misery was lightened and enlightened by the hope of a better and stronger reunion with her son; it became practically an energy fostering her desire, which today is realized. Aelred offers one of the best summaries of the meaning of the assumption, not only for Mary, but also for us: "Therefore he provides us with a great cause to jump up with joy. Our queen, our Lady, our mother, our own *flesh and our blood* [Gen 29:14] is raised up above the choir of angels as one ready to pray for us. She is conveyed to the right hand of her son as one ready to protect us. If therefore she is *for us, who can be against us?* [Rom 8:31]" (8).

Aelred's sense of the union between Jesus and Mary verges on identity. Seeing her as one with the mediator, her son, he called her *mediatrix*, daringly using for her what Saint Paul says of Christ. In another sermon for the assumption, where he shows Mary as solemnly advancing toward the throne of God, she is invoked by the heavenly citizens with the prayer addressed to Jesus by the two disciples at Emmaus: *Mane nobiscum Domina!* (S 73.6–7).

In Aelred's time the bodily assumption of Mary was not universally believed. Aelred, together with Isaac of Stella, is among those who, although with some reservations, suggest it as a possibility. Since this is a particularly important theme in the history of theology, here is what Aelred writes on the problem:

Today he receives her in that place and conforms the body of
his most blessed mother to his own body, with its proper glory.
Granted that I may not dare to affirm this—because if someone
would wish to deny and vigorously to refute it we do not have the
sure testimony of the Scriptures to prove it—nevertheless it is
sweet to us to hold this opinion. [We hold therefore] that because
of a very great love for his mother, he who can do all things not
only took her soul to heaven but also raised up her body so that
she might be in his presence with both body and soul and would
already receive the bodily immortality that we all hope for on the
Day of Judgment. It seems altogether credible that the one who
can do all things, he who bore his own holy body above all the
heavens, would also [raise up] the body of his most sweet mother.
Since he received his own body from her, he did not allow her to
be separated from her body for a long time. (9–10)

This is pure theology of love, supported by another argument
more typical of the rational theology according to which, since physical corruption was to be imputed to the Fall, a sinless body "ought
not in any way to be subject to this penalty" (11). But this is not
enough for Aelred, since an uncorrupted body does not automati-
cally imply an assumption to heaven. That's why, summing up his
argument, he affirms that "because it seems to me that the flesh of
the mother may in some way be one flesh with the son, therefore
I believe that where the flesh of the son is, there also the flesh of
the mother may be assumed . . . so that she might live in eternal
blessedness with him, that she might remain with him, reign with
him, rejoice with him, delight in him" (13).

This sense of company, so crucial in the relationships between
Jesus and his mother, becomes the focus of the second part of the
sermon, in which Mary is welcomed by the whole company of the
saints of which Our Lady is the Queen, the title invented for her in
the twelfth century and which gave to the church those admirable
antiphons, perhaps of Cistercian origin, *Salve Regina, Ave regina
caelorum,* and *Regina caeli.* Aelred patterns this second part of the
sermon around the repetition of a verse from the Song of Solomon
taken from the liturgy of the day: *Quae est ista quae progreditur?*

"Who is that who proceeds?" (Song 6:9). The progress is the key image of this part, a word that qualifies Mary as simultaneously the synthesis and the summit of the three classic states of women: motherhood, widowhood, and virginity.

Married women, both "chaste and fruitful" (17), are the first to welcome Mary, who had been bride and mother, as were Sarah, Rebecca, and Rachel, but she could not stop with them because, unlike them, she had also been a virgin. In this subsection Aelred is most interested in Mary's virginal motherhood and the consequent embarrassing pregnancy. He remarks that God did no miracle to preserve her from a possible infamy, implicitly suggesting he preferred to confide in Joseph and Mary's faith in his promises.

To talk of Mary's widowhood may seem strange, but this is the word Aelred uses to indicate the period after the ascension of Jesus, when she was separated from him who was at the same time her son and her bridegroom, because Mary was *mater sponsi et sponsa sponsi*. She is welcomed as a widow by Naomi, her ancestor; Judith, a figure of the church; and Anna, the prophet who had met her in the temple with the infant Jesus. They too desired that she could stop her progress to remain with them, but she had to go on, being also a virgin. Mary is also exemplary in the way she lived her widowhood, in prayer and silence. She was not with the other women at the sepulcher, she did no miracle as Saint Peter did, and she certainly stayed with the apostles, but "in prayer." Why? The answer Aelred finds has simply to do with love: "Each can think what he wishes; I think that the reason is that she so loved her son, our Lord, and so desired him that she could not let herself attend to any outside activity" (23).

The virgins welcome Mary at the end. But this is not the end of her procession. Indeed, only the virgins follow the Lamb *wherever* he goes (Rev 14:4). How? Jesus goes on the way of virtues, and everybody can follow him in one or another virtue, but only virgins imitate his entire way of life and thus follow the Lamb wherever he goes, provided that "beyond the virginity of the flesh, [they] also have other virtues in which they follow him" (28). In this Mary is again an exception, because she "not only followed him but, more than that, in some marvelous way, preceded him by giving birth to him, nourishing him, carrying him in her arms, enfolding him in her lap" (29).

A further step leads Mary to "the highest orders of angels, but the glory of the angels was not sufficient for her" (30). Cherubim and seraphim represent science and love, respectively, but in this too Mary is superior, and so she advances until she reaches the throne of her son.

Incredibly, and paradoxically, this progress of Mary, which by in a sense placing her above all creatures apparently separates her from humankind, has the opposite effect. She becomes on the contrary the center of humanity, giving joy to everybody and hope and confidence to sinners, not only as indeed the Queen of Heaven, but also as Mother of mercy, *Regina mater misericordiae*. Her royalty is her maternity, an unfailing source of mercy. Aelred breaks forth in a beautiful prayer: "O, how blessed are you, most holy Virgin! The heavenly court receives you with great eagerness; the whole church joyfully honors you with many sure signs of great joy. The sinner turns to you with confident eyes in order not to despair; the just one frequently prays to you in order to persevere; the fallen one leans on you in order to rise up; the one rising up seeks your hand in order not to fall short" (33).

Who is this that comes forth like the sun and beautiful as Jerusalem? (Song 6:9). While the first part of the sermon answers the question "Who is this?" and the second describes Mary's "progress" through the heavens (*comes forth* corresponds to the Latin *progreditur*), the third takes its inspiration from the apposition "beautiful as Jerusalem." A predictable and easy interpretation sees Mary as the incarnation of this city. Jerusalem has two parts: one in heaven, one on earth. After seeing the progress of Mary through the heavenly Jerusalem, Aelred turns his eyes to the earthly Jerusalem, the one "constructed of living stones; that part is holy church, and all the saints within are as her stones." Again, he immediately declares Mary's excellence: "She is not compared to any one of the stones in that city but to the city as a whole" (35).

The same idea of Mary as the synthesis or the summary of holiness in all its forms comes again to the foreground, because "she alone has in herself all the virtues that are separate in each separate being" (35). In the believers are many different kinds of beauty; they are like different precious "stones," all of them partially beautiful. Only she can be called *tota pulchra*, wholly beautiful, "not only in her soul but also in her body" (36).

Another part of the liturgical responsory, where beauty is also mentioned, prompts a reflection on the church in connection with Mary: *the daughters of Sion saw her and called her beautiful* (Song 6:8). Sion is another name for Jerusalem, and Sion means "the act of watching" or "the watchtower," an ideal position from which to see something far away: "Such is holy church in this life. It is a watchtower for us to stand in as if at war, fearing always lest our enemies seize us. We must fear, brothers, lest we sleep in this watchtower" (37). To be awake, not to sleep, to keep our eyes on something beautiful, on the "wholly beautiful," to receive comfort and courage in our spiritual struggle: this is our task. Like the heavenly inhabitants, "let us see her excellence, her humility, her charity, her purity. Let us see her, and let us praise her not by the voice alone but also by imitating her. . . . Let us contemplate her glory [in heaven] and not forget her kindness [*pietas*]" (39, 41).

The sermon ends beautifully with the language of doxology and prayer, built on an iteration that is a crescendo of trust and interior consolation:

> May she be our common joy, our common glory, our common hope, our common consolation, our common reconciliation, and our common refuge. If we are sad, let us flee to her, that she herself may gladden us. If we are cast down, let us flee to her, that she may glorify us. If we are in despair, let us flee to her that she may draw us up. If we are troubled, let us flee to her that she may console us. If we suffer persecutions, let us flee to her that she may protect us. If we are out of harmony with her son, let us flee to her that she may reconcile us. May she be our guardian in this life and our protector in death. May she guard us now from sin, and may she then recommend us to her beloved son. Therefore, beloved brothers, let us raise our hearts and the eyes of our heart to this our Lady, our advocate, and our helper. (42–43)

In this admirable passage, in which among other things the ecclesial perspective running throughout the sermon is again worthy of notice, with six instances of *common* in the first sentence, the double aspect of Mary is perfectly summarized in a beautiful parallel: "she is the one who can support us because of her excellence and wills to do so because of her mercy" (43).

18. Blessed Are Those Who Are Pure, Peaceful, and Lovers of Justice

(Sermon 46: *For the Feast of All Saints*)

This last sermon of the Second Clairvaux Collection has lost a great part. If, as we can reasonably suppose, it was originally a commentary on the seven or eight Beatitudes, as is its brother sermon 27, more than a half may have disappeared, since it starts with a comment on the fifth Beatitude, for the pure of heart (*beati mundo corde*), and continues with the sixth, addressed to the peaceful (*beati pacifici*), and the seventh, concerning those who are persecuted for justice's sake (*beati qui persequuntur propter iustitiam*). The running theme seems to be the hardships we have to endure to live a holy life.

This idea can be derived from the image used to describe the incarnation of Christ. He entered into the heavens as if into a tabernacle made of skins when he assumed *the likeness of sinful flesh* (Rom 8:3). In this likeness he appeared black to the Jews, and this blackness means both the weakness and the sinfulness of the flesh, the sorrows Jesus had to endure to redeem the flesh from sin. This is the only biblical image allegorically interpreted that appears in this fragment, but apparently it gives the basic meaning to all the argument. Indeed, "blackness" in its double sense must be cleansed and eliminated if we want to join the company of the saints in heaven: "if we wish to have this beauty within us, it is necessary for us to cleanse our hearts and be peacemakers" (2).

It may be that Aelred had also joined the four previous Beatitudes in pairs. The double pattern characterizing the blackness is immediately evident, since, Aelred says, "purity of heart is twofold.

For first the heart ought to be cleansed from greed, afterward from weakness" (2). Cupidity is like a beam in the eye of the heart that prevents us from seeing God, and to take it away is to purify our heart. To do this we enter a struggle, in which we can only be either conquerors or conquered, cleansed or more soiled. There is no other way to realize "perfect peace" in our heart, "peace between the self and the neighbor, between the flesh and the spirit, between the spirit and God" (4).

A condition of perfect peace, rest, and inner security will be reached only in the future life, and Aelred wisely observes that although we cannot *have this peace* as perfectly as we would like in this life, nevertheless we ought to *make peace* in this life. The intrinsic impossibility of perfection in this life is not enough reason to renounce striving toward it. Moreover, this struggle against our weaknesses and vices makes us more similar to the Son of God, "who is truly the peacemaker, who destroyed the devil, who reconciled human nature to God" (5). The saints did so not without hard efforts both to conquer and to preserve this peace "not only among the successes of this world, but more fervently still in the midst of its persecutions" (6), as the following Beatitude indicates in its address to *those who suffer persecution for justice's sake* (Matt 5:10).

This statement has a more general meaning, referring not only to external persecutions but also to internal temptations and difficulties. Aelred formulates the basic principle in clear words: "Let each one judge as he will; it does not seem to me that a person can simultaneously have delight of the mind and care for the belly [*delectationem mentis et curam ventris*], nor have eternal rest there if he does not experience hardship here" (10). The opposition between mind and belly is made stronger by being expressed in a rhyme.

Aelred contrasts the strength the saints showed in their troubles with the weakness of those "who cannot suffer one stern sermon for Christ," the one "who abandons the state of life in which he first began to serve Christ," those who "when they cannot have all their own will, when they happen to hear one harsh word, immediately threaten to depart" (7). To keep faithful to our purposes and promises there is no better way than to fix our eyes on the blessed vision of God and his saints, which is "perfect happiness," a vision which is given only to those who are pure of heart. This keeping our eyes on God creates a virtuous circle, from vision to behavior and from behavior to vision.

Vision means also knowledge, and Aelred defines this knowledge of God as "the summit of perfect blessedness" (11). To describe this vision Aelred has recourse to his most intense affective vocabulary, as if to stress the materiality of something that is difficult to perceive when we suffer for any reason. *Vision* turns into hearing, embrace, taste. In it are "such satisfaction . . . such fullness," "such jubilation, such praise, and such glory that there is nothing better to desire" (14). Again, "in that vision, true peace is to be found; there true happiness, there tranquility, there perpetual steadiness, there true rest, a dwelling place, true delectation, the end and consummation of all good things. If such a homeland pleases us, brothers, then the road to it—be it as hard as we have said above—also pleases us, and we do not turn away from it" (14).

The teaching is always the same. It is true that *"without Christ we can do nothing"* (17), but it is also true that our strength is based on our desire, which must be directed to meet with Christ's indications. To excite, to enhance, and to preserve our desires, an encouraging vision is needed, and what is better than the vision of Jesus among the "company of the saints" (10), who, having run along Christ's hard way, have reached their full happiness? So, "let us ask our Lord that through all the merits of his saints he will hold us to this road and by his compassion lead us to that dwelling place on high, and that he will crown us with eternal joy with them" (17).

Acknowledgments

I must acknowledge the assistance and support of several people. First of all, Mark A. Scott, OCSO, who is presently the abbot of New Melleray Abbey in Peosta, Iowa, as executive editor of Cistercian Publications gave me the task of translating these sermons and encouraged and corrected my work throughout the initial stages. Br. Lawrence Jenny, OCSO, a monk of Genesee Abbey, and Emily K. Stuckey created the scriptural and topical indices; their work is gratefully acknowledged. Marsha Dutton, the current editor of Cistercian Publications, took over the editorial task and has provided her expert editorial advice in bringing this work to completion. It has been a kind of flowering of our friendship of many years.

Abbreviations

Ant	Antiphon
CCCM	Corpus Christianorum, Continuatio Mediaevalis
CCSL	Corpus Christianorum, Series Latina
CSEL	Corpus scriptorum ecclesiasticorum latinorum
Hesbert	René-Jean Hesbert. *Antiphonale Missarum Sextuplex.* Brussels and Paris: Vromant et Cie, 1935.
PL	Patrologia Latina
Resp	Responsory
S, SS	Sermo, Sermones
SBOp	Sancti Bernardi Opera
SCh	Sources Chrétiennes

Works of Aelred

Anima	De anima
Ann dom	Sermo in annuntiatione Domini
Ass	Sermo in assumptionae Sanctae Mariae
Ben	Sermo in festivitate Sancti Benedicti; De Sancto Benedicti
Epi	Sermo in epiphania Domini
Gen Angl	Genealogia regum Anglorum
Heb	Sermo in hebdomada sancta
Iesu	De Iesu puero duodenni
Inst incl	De institutione inclusarum
JB	Sermo in nativitate Sancti Joannis Baptistae
Nat	Sermo in nativitate Domini
Oner	Sermo de oneribus
Orat past	Oratio pastoralis
OS	Sermo in festivitate Omnium Sanctorum

Pasc	Sermo in die Pascae; in sancto Paschae
Pent	Sermo in die Pentecostes
Pur	Sermo in purificatione Sanctae Mariae
Ram	Sermo in ramis palmarum
Spec car	Speculum caritatis
Spir amic	De spiritali amicitia
Vita E	Vita Sancti Eduardi confessoris

Works of Other Writers

Ambrose

| De para | De Paradiso |

Augustine

Civ Dei	De civitate Dei
Enchir	Enchiridion
En in Ps	Enarrationes in Psalmos

Bede

| Hom | Homiliarum |
| In Lc | In Lucae Evangelium expositio |

Benedict

| RB | Regula sancti Benedicti, Regula Monachorum |

Bernard

| Miss | Homilia super missus est in laudibus Virginis Matris |
| SC | Sermones super Cantica Canticorum |

Cicero

| De fini bon et mal | De finibus bonorum et malorum |

Gregory the Great

Di	Dialogues
Hiez	Homiliae in EzOechielem
Mo	Moralia in Job

Horace

| Ars Poet | Ars poetica |

Jerome
Adv Jov   Adversus Iovinianum
Ep   Epistulae
Nom   Interpretatio Hebraicorum nominum

Origen
In Ex   In Exodum
Super Lc   Super Luca

Ovid
Meta   Metamorphoses

Pseudo-Bede
In Lv   In Leviticum

Sermon 29

For the Nativity of the Lord[1]

1. **I**t is certainly not in the beginning, brothers, that the prophet promised this perfect joy to us. For this is the *solid food** of which we read a little while ago. 2. Take note therefore from where it is that we first rejoice: *Rejoice, he says, with joy, all you who were in mourning, that you may be quenched with milk and be filled from the breasts of his consolation.** We have said what this milk is; we have said in what manner our mother the heavenly Jerusalem has served this milk to us. But let us say this more openly and more briefly. Our Lord Jesus Christ is himself milk for us; he himself is solid food. Solid food because he is God, milk because he is human; bread because he is the Son of God, milk because he is the son of the Virgin. This is the milk, then, that Jerusalem serves to us, when the company of the angels announces his nativity according to the flesh.*

3. Brothers, see Jesus in the manger, see him in the lap of his virgin mother, see him sucking at her breasts, crying in the cradle, see him *wrapped in swaddling clothes;** see him also, if I am not mistaken, surrounded by the hay in the stable. This is spiritual milk; these are the banquet foods I promised you for this our feast day. Suck on them sweetly; think on them with tenderness. Nourish yourselves interiorly with a drink of this milk. But this is for children.

*Heb 5:14

*Isa 66:10

*Luke 2:9-14

*Luke 2:12

[1] This is a partial sermon found in two manuscripts; in CCCM 2A Gaetano Raciti identifies it as coming from Clairvaux.

1

What may we do for the youth, what for the elders? The youth are strong; elders have lost the heat of the flesh.

4. If therefore you are a child, suckle on Jesus in the stable.* If you are strong, imitate Jesus on the gibbet of the cross. If you have grown cold toward every carnal action and thought, say with the apostle, *And if I knew Christ according to the flesh, I do not know him so any longer.** And this what the prophet promised, saying, *And when you have turned away from milk, feast by entering into glory,** that is, into Jerusalem itself. For what does it mean to feast by entering into glory except already to taste that glory [that the soul] will have in her going in, when it is said to her, *Enter into the glory of your Lord?** To which end may our Lord Jesus Christ deign to lead us; to him be honor and glory forever and ever. Amen.

*Aelred, Spec car 1.1.1 (CCCM 1:13)

*2 Cor 5:16

*Isa 66:10 LXX; Aelred, Spec car 2.12.30 (CCCM 1:79)

*Matt 25:21

Sermon 30

For the Nativity of the Lord

1. Today affection and ignorance are at war in our heart. Affection drives me to speak, but ignorance bids me keep <silent>.[1]* Perhaps some among you wonder at this conflict, because you think that we are both expert and well-spoken. You ought to reflect that Moses was *skilled with all the wisdom* and knowledge *of Egypt.*† Nevertheless, when he heard that Word of which we must speak, he said, *I have never been eloquent, neither in the past, nor recently, nor now that you have spoken to your servant; but I am slow of speech and tongue.**

*Aelred, S 71.1 (CCCM 2B:220), Spir amic 1.30 (CCCM 1:294)

†Acts 7:22; Isa 33:6

2. Who can contemplate Eternity being born, Power itself failing, Bread going hungry, the Spring itself growing thirsty, without becoming speechless? But who can contemplate the beginning of our salvation, the day of human healing, without bursting forth *in a voice of exultation and praise, the sound of one keeping festival?** God has been made a man; who knows how to speak about that? Our Jesus, our Savior, our joy, comes among us; who can keep silent? And if we can neither keep silent nor speak, what can we do except rejoice? Therefore, *let us rejoice in God, our salvation.** If the angels *see God's face*† in

*Exod 4:10; Origen, In Ex 3.1 (SCh 321:88)

*Ps 41:5

*Ps 94:1; Augustine, In Ps 102.8 (CCSL 40:1458), En in Ps 32, En 2, S 1.8 (CCSL 38:254)

†Matt 18:20

---

[1] Angle brackets indicate words absent from manuscripts but supplied in the critical edition.

*Exod 33:23 jubilation, we ought at least to see God's *back** not without jubilation.[2]

3. I will say more about this. It seems to me that we have, in some ways, a greater reason to cry out with joy than the angels have. They certainly see God, contemplating his wisdom, wondering at his power, enjoying his sweetness, but they see all this in a nature other than their own. *On no occasion did he take the angels to himself.* Because *he* truly *took the seed of* *Heb 2:16 *Abraham to himself,** we see our God, our Savior, our joy, in our very own nature. Therefore, brothers, in order that we may see that which is our joy, that which is our consolation and our glory, *let us go over* *Luke 2:15 *to Bethlehem and see this Word.**

4. Once Saint Moses said almost those words: *I* *Exod 3:3 *will go over,* he said, *and see this great vision.** He wanted to go over and see *a great vision.* He saw a certain bush, and in that bush was fire, and neverthe- *Exod 3:2 less the bush was not burned up.* What, then, was the point of the fire? It was clearly for illumination and not for consumption. This was the great vision of which he said, *I will go over and see this great vision.* It was as if he had read those words that the shepherds said in the gospel: *Let us go over to Bethle-hem,* etc. Without a doubt, brothers, Moses did read those words, but in the book of divine predestination, where God has already done what is to come. There-fore he said, *I will go over and see this great vision.*

---

[2] In Latin and some modern languages, the personal pronoun takes its gender from the noun it modifies and therefore means either *his* or *her* according to context and thereby makes no limitation on the gender of the possessor. This is not true in English, where the gender of the possessive pronoun modifies and limits the gender of the person who possesses. No acceptable alternative to using masculine pronouns referring to God in this grammatical construction presently exists except to repeat the name of God. The translator has chosen to use the latter method rarely and selectively.

5. It seems that there must be some difference between those words of Moses and the words that the shepherds said today, but without a doubt, they spoke of one and the same reality. *I will go over*, Moses said, *and see this great vision*. What vision? A fire in the bush. And the shepherds said, *Let us go over to Bethlehem and see*. See what? *The Word that has been made*. What was it made? Listen to the gospel: *The Word was made flesh.** What did they want to see? The Word in the flesh. What is the Word? Listen to the gospel: *In the beginning was the Word, and the Word was God.** And what is God? Listen to the apostle: *Our God is a consuming fire.** The shepherds wished to see the Word, that is, God, in the flesh, and Moses to see the fire in the bush.

*John 1:14

*John 1:1
*Heb 12:29;
Deut 4:24

6. Will I now dare to say that that flesh in which was the Word that is God, God who is the consuming fire—dare I say that that flesh was the bush? Without a doubt, it is the bush, a bush that had thorns that were not his own but our thorns. Because *it was our infirmities that he bore, our sufferings that he endured; he was wounded for our offenses and worn out for our sins.** Let us remember his passion, let us see in what manner *Pilate* crowned him with thorns and *said, Behold the man.** True man, true flesh, true bush, carrying our thorns. But why on the head? O Lord my God, it is not enough that you may be seen to bear my thorns unless you also bear them on your head! Lord my God, crowned with my thorns!

*Isa 53:4-5

*John 19:5

7. Take note of the three things the Lord wore in his passion: a shining white tunic, a red tunic, and a crown of thorns. The red tunic signifies the blood of martyrs; the shining white tunic, the purity of virgins; the crown of thorns, the compunction and penitence of sinners. He wears the conversion of sinners as a crown. The crown signifies victory. In [converting]

sinners our Lord conquers more than the devil. The Jews saw the flesh of our Lord as a bush, they saw thorns, but they did not see the fire as Saint Moses saw it: *I will go over*, he said, *and see this great vision*.

8. Let us also go over into Bethlehem and see this great vision, this Word that has been made. It is necessary that we go over all that is visible and changeable, all that varies or may be altered, in order that we may withdraw our heart from all vanities and mere sensual pleasures, from everything that feeds on evil delights. Only thus can we take real delight in *the bread that* *comes down from heaven and gives life to the world;**[*]** only thus can our mind become the house of bread, that is, Bethlehem.**[*]** There we will be able to see this Word that has been made; there the fire that Moses desired to see will be shown to us.

*[*]John 6:13

*[*]Jerome, Ep 108.10 (CCSL 55:316)

9. The Lord shows himself to us in three ways: first, in this world; second, in Judgment; third, in his Kingdom. In this world, he is small and humble; in Judgment, great and awesome; in the Kingdom, sweet and lovable. We have been small, and we remained for a long time in corruption, mortality, and iniquity. We lay a long time *in the deep slime* from which the prophet cried out to the Lord, *Save me, O God, because the waters have entered into my very soul.**[*]** How will we be able to rise up, how raise our eyes out of the darkness of that mire to gaze on that brightness, that majesty that is God? How great is the distance between light and darkness, death and life, iniquity and justice, blessedness and misery? Let us not doubt that the distance between God and us is just as great. How can we ever be able to draw near to him?

*[*]Ps 68:2-3

10. Take note, brothers. There was a twofold misery in us: iniquity and mortality, ignorance and malice, weakness and perversity. In iniquity, malice, and perversity, there is sin. In mortality, ignorance, and weakness,

there is the penalty for sin. And each of the two, sin and the punishment of sin, is a misery. Therefore we were made miserable by both. Who will raise us up? No person can, because every person has been overthrown. The one thrown down cannot raise up the fallen; neither can a dead person bring the dead back to life. The blind cannot give light to those in darkness, nor can the unclean person make another clean. But what about the one who stands? How can he raise up the one who has been overthrown unless he bends down?

11. Therefore the one destined to raise us up was destined to bend himself down, if not entirely to prostrate himself. The Lord our God has done this. He has bent way down, all the way to us. Where were we? I have just told you. We were in sin and under the penalty of sin. If he descended all the way down to the sin in which we were mired, he did not bend over but prostrated himself. Completely prostrate himself, however, he could not raise up those prostrate. But though he bent himself down, he did not lose all his strength. He bent down to one and raised us up from the other. He bent down even to our mortality, even to our corruption, even to our weakness.

12. This is the first showing by which he shows himself to us, that is, in our corruption, in our mortality, in our weakness. Let us see this first. We can all see him in this condition. No one has an excuse. In this state, he is small, obscure, and weak; here he is a pauper, and such is his situation that there is nothing in him from which we ought to hide ourselves. *Let us go over*, therefore, *to Bethlehem* today, and *let us see.* There he is so small that he lies down *in the manger.** *Luke 2:7

He is so poor that *he has nowhere to lay his head;** *Matt 8:20
he is so weak that he feeds on mother's milk; he is so obscure that he is *wrapped in swaddling clothes.** *Luke 2:12
To this has our God come down.

13. This is God's inclination, by which he bends down and raises us up,[3] not only from the sin in which we were mired but also from the penalty of sin, to which he himself descended. There, in the vision of his humility, is the beginning of our salvation. Wherefore let us first see our Lord in this humility, in this smallness, in this poverty. And who does not see him in all these conditions? Already it is known through the whole world in what manner God was made a man, an insignificant and poor man.* But not all see him with the same eyes.

*Ps 75:2;
Mal 1:11

14. Some see this reality and are confounded[4] by it; some are condemned, others are consoled, and still others are led to imitation. The Jews see this and are confounded. For they are scandalized when they hear that God considered it proper to enter into the womb of the virgin, that he suffered confinement there for so many months. They are scandalized that God wished to be an infant, that he was able to be hated, mocked, spat upon, and boxed on the ear when he was crucified with robbers. They are proud, and therefore they are ashamed to believe such vile and despicable things about their God.

15. Evil Christians see this to their condemnation. For they are condemned by many aspects of it. They

---

[3] The word *inclinatio*, which Aelred uses here as both noun and verb (translated as *inclination* and *bends down*) means both the human inclination or bias toward an object and the physical act of bending down or toward. Translation cannot capture the force of Aelred's repetition, which suggests that God's bias on our behalf bends God down in the self-abasement of the incarnation. God's action becomes the perfect expression of God's inner intention.

[4] The Latin word *confundere* carries a range of meanings: "to embarrass," "to confuse," and "to defeat or frustrate one's purpose." I have chosen to use the cognate *confound* consistently. Sometimes Aelred combines it with another word for *to embarrass* and clearly means to suggest that he feels defeated in his attempt to lead the monks to holiness.

see great humility in God while they are proud, and great patience in God while they are impatient. They see the great poverty of God while they acquire as much of the riches of the world as possible through pillage, discord, murders, perjuries, and every other evil. They see the lowliness of God while they strive toward the honors of the world through cupidity and ambition. Woe to such Christians! Infinitely better for them not to see Christ than to see and despise him!

16. Next, the beginners [in the spiritual life] see him to their consolation. All of you have experienced this. For what consolation do you have in the miseries of this miserable life, in this poverty, in this lowliness, in these labors and sorrows? Your only consolation is that the misery of our Lord is a share in our misery, his hunger a share in our hunger, his sadness a share in our sadness, his lowliness a share in ours. Better that you possess that in your heart than in my words. But just as those who are not yet perfect see him to be consoled, so the perfect see him so that they may imitate him. Therefore they see him and contemplate his works; they hear his words and draw on them again and again so that they may imitate him.

17. For they are wise who behave in this way, and therefore *their eyes are in their head*, as Scripture says: *The wise one has eyes in his head, but the fool walks in darkness.** Whoever does not know how to keep the works of our Lord always before the eyes and to order life, actions, and words according to the rule is *a fool. He walks in darkness and does not know where he wanders*, because he does not *follow* the light.* The one who is wise, however, always has his eyes *in his head*, that is, in Christ. Therefore, that one goes on the way in the light and knows where he ought to put the foot of his works, because he follows the light of truth. Therefore, brothers, *let us* ·

*Eccl 2:14

*Eccl 2:14;
John 8:12;
12:35; Greg-
ory the Great,
Hiez 1, Hom
2.19 (CCSL
142:29–30)

go over unto Bethlehem, and see this Word that has been made.

18. Let us see him, let us contemplate him, let us not be scandalized like the Jews because of his littleness. Nor let us be condemned along with evil Christians who hold him in contempt. Rather, let us console ourselves with the very tiny Jesus because he has been made so small for us. Together with the perfect, let us imitate him as much as we are able, because he has himself tempered his works to the measure of our ability. There is no room for anyone to excuse himself. Let no one consider that I am speaking here of works of divine power, but of those that God did when he assumed our weakness. For our Lord himself does not say, "Learn of me how to raise the dead or cleanse the lepers," but *Learn of me because I am meek and humble of heart.**

*Matt 11:29;
Augustine, S
69.2
(PL 38:441)

19. Let us who are lowly see him lowly in this world; then we will be secure when we see him in Judgment. For he will show himself in Judgment to both the good and the evil, but not as he shows himself today, small, poor, and of little importance. For today he shows himself wrapped *in swaddling clothes** as if concealed and secret; then, however, *God will come to us openly and not be silent.** On that day the angels will not need to descend as they have done or to say where he can be found, because as *the flash of lightning goes out from the east and appears in the west, so shall the coming of the Son of Man be. Before him there will be a devouring fire; around him, a raging storm.**

*Luke 2:12

*Ps 49:3

*Ps 50:3

20. What will the arrogance of the world do then, my brothers? What? What will it do? Where will those ostentatious displays be, where the arrogance of the worldly, where the beautiful clothes, the fast horses? <Where> will their excess of food be, where their

glorious display and the savage strength of their castles? Truly *the fire will go before him* and *will burn up
his enemies.** How they will tremble then, how they   *Ps 96:3
will shake with fear! How they will desire to hide
themselves and not be able! Then surely *instead of
perfume there will be a stench; instead of the girdle, a
rope. In place of the elaborate hairdo, they will be bald;
in place of the rich gown, a sackcloth skirt.** Whether   *Isa 3:24
they will it or not, they will see Jesus, but in a way
that causes terror, and in terror they will hear him
saying, *Depart from me, you evildoers, into the eternal
fire, which the devil and his angels have prepared.**   *Matt 25:41

21. But you, who now build Bethlehem in your
soul, who have passed over the pleasures of the world,
its secular riches and deceitful honors, you who now
see this very small, humble Jesus, you who are yourselves now small and humble, you will then see his
sweet face, you will hear his most tender voice: *Come
you blessed of my Father, receive the kingdom prepared
for you from the beginning of the world.** Then you   *Matt 25:34
will enter into that Kingdom, and you will see Jesus
sweet and amiable. For then you will be as his spouse,
prepared and ornamented, worthy of his embrace,
because she is without stain or wrinkle. Then she
will taste the great abundance of his *sweetness,* already poured out on the one who loves perfectly, that
sweetness still hidden in this life for those who fear.*   *Ps 30:20;
1 Pet 2:3;
Aelred, Spec car
1.1.2 (CCCM
1:14)

22. O my brothers, what will that glory be, what
that peace, that blessedness, that security, that joy,
that sweetness, which *the eye has not seen nor the ear
heard nor the human heart conceived.** There will be   *1 Cor 2:9
the true Bethlehem, *the* true *house of bread,** which   *Jerome, Ep
108.10 (CSEL
55:316)
will satisfy our *desire for the good,* when *our youth
will be renewed like that of the eagle.*† Let us go over   †Ps 102:5
to this Bethlehem, and there let us see this Word that
today has been made. Let us go over, let us go over

through hope and desire, through love and affection. *Let us see* now *indistinctly as in a mirror* in order that when we will have passed over that which is imperfect, *then* we will be able to see Jesus himself *face to face,** our Lord who with the Father and the Holy Spirit lives and reigns forever and ever. Amen.

*1 Cor
13:10, 12

Sermon 31

For the Epiphany of the Lord

1. **W**hen I contemplate the works the Lord made when he created the world, I reflect on the beauty of the sun and the moon, *the disposition of the stars,** *Wis 7:29 the depth and the width of the sea, the fruitfulness of the earth. All such things delight me, and I say along with the prophet, *How magnificent are your works, O Lord. You have made all things in wisdom.** *Ps 103:24; Aelred, S 35.1 (CCCM 2B:287)* But that meditation and contemplation do not ravish my whole soul, because in all these I do not see my Lord with respect to the whole. I can see something of God's power in these things, something of God's wisdom, something of God's beauty, but still I do not see that which has a greater savor, that which delights more.

2. When, however, I turn my eyes to the work of his mercy and contemplate that ineffable grace he provides for the wretched, those for whom he wished to become miserable himself, that contemplation indeed draws me in, to the very marrow and guts of my soul. I begin to say with the prophet, *What return shall I make to the Lord for all of his mercies to me?** *Ps 115:12 This memory, brothers, ought to be sweet to you always, but today especially, when this very *grace of <God> our savior has appeared.** *Titus 2:11 As the apostle says, *grace has appeared,* etc. Up until today, brothers, the grace of God was as if hidden, but today it has appeared. The apostle does not say, "today begins the grace of God," but rather, "it has appeared."

3. This grace was hidden in the deeds of the patriarchs, in the words of the prophets, in the ritual sacrifices and the observances of the Jews. This grace was concealed in the lamb of Abel, the thigh of Abraham, the stone of Jacob, the tunic of Joseph, the bush of Moses, the rod of Aaron. For the lamb that [Abel] *offered* is the one that John pointed out today at the River Jordan, saying, *Behold the Lamb of God who* *takes away the sin of the world.** It is also God himself foreshadowed in Abraham's thigh when he spoke to his servant saying, *Put your hand under my thigh and* *swear to me by the God of the heavens.** From this thigh came the flesh of holy Mary, from whose flesh the God of heaven was born.

*John 1:29

*Gen 24:23

4. He is the stone that, according to the prophet Daniel, was *hewn from the mountain without hands,** the same that Jacob anointed, signifying him of whom the prophet said, *God, your God, has anointed you* *with the oil of gladness above your fellows.** He is the fire in the bramble-bush that Saint Moses saw.** This reality is twofold: the fire and the bramble-bush. Our *God*, as the apostle says, *is a consuming fire.** And *the* *earth, cursed by the doings of Adam*, brings forth *thorn* *bushes and prickly plants** like the bramble-bush. This earth is human flesh; whoever works therein finds only thorns, that is to say, painful thoughts and the stings of bad passions. As the apostle says, *Whoever* *sows in the flesh reaps the corruption of the flesh.**

*Dan 2:45;
Gen 28:18

*Ps 44:8
*Exod 3:2

*Heb 12:29;
Deut 4:24

*Gen 3:17-18

*Gal 6:8

5. Today true fire shone in true flesh, when the Son of God appeared in our mortal substance. Although there was no sin in that flesh, there was nevertheless the *likeness of sinful flesh*. As the apostle says, *He sent his son in the likeness of sinful flesh.** You can distinguish a threefold condition of human flesh: according to creation, according to condemnation, according to glorification. In Paradise, human flesh was

*Rom 8:3

in the condition of creation, that is, the state in which it was created. In this misery, the flesh is condemned for its corruption, that is, the state in which it has been condemned for sin. In the Day of Judgment, the flesh will be glorified when our Lord *will reshape our lowly body, fashioning it to his glorified body.**   *Phil 3:21

6. In Paradise, the flesh could be called happy and justified; in this life, the flesh of sin and misery; in that [final] blessedness, the flesh of happiness and glory. In Paradise, human flesh enjoyed great happiness because it suffered no misfortune and great justice because it experienced no sin. In this life, it both suffers misery and is born and nurtured in sin. In the Day of Judgment our flesh will be happy and glorious, when *the just shall shine like the sun in the kingdom of their father.** Our Lord has flesh from the   *Matt 13:43 flesh of Adam. Because he comes and restores the flesh of Adam to its pristine condition, he has in his flesh something of that state in which Adam was in Paradise and something of that state in which he was in exile. He had both the justice of the one condition and the misery of the other.

7. Therefore he does not come in sinful flesh, but *in the likeness of sinful flesh.* This is grace, and a great grace indeed. A great grace because the one who had no stain of sin in him willed to suffer the punishment of sin. Hidden up to now, this grace has appeared today. This grace came into the world before these days, but today was the first time it was made known to the world. *The grace of God our savior has appeared,* as Scripture says, *to all people.** Before this,   *Titus 2:11 God *was known among the Jews, God's name was great in Israel.** But *today, from the rising of the sun unto its setting, God has a great name among the nations.*†

   *Ps 75:2;
   Aelred, S
   68.7 (CCCM
   2B:193)
   †Ps 106:3;
   Mal 1:11; Ps
   75:2; Aelred,
   Iesu 2.18
   (CCCM 1:265)

8. For today, the nations recognized God's grace through a star, the Jews through the sacrament of

baptism, the disciples through a miracle. The first recognition comes from an inspiration of faith, the second from the reception of the sacraments, the third from the infusion of divine charity. For at first we are enlightened by faith, then we are sanctified through the sacraments, and thus we are made firm in good works through charity. See, brothers, how the grace of Christ appears in these three, without any doubt, because without them, that is, without faith, sacraments, or good works, no one can share in the grace of Christ.

9. The star signifies faith. For the star shines in the night, not in the day, because the rising brilliance of the sun conceals its brightness. You know that it is [now] the night, the night in which *all the beasts of the forest** prowl about. In truth, brothers, we often experience that it is night. *We walk in darkness,** and often we do not know what we ought to do, whether we must speak or keep silence; often we do not know what to pray for.* Often while we are doing one good thing, we are prevented by our ignorance from another. Someone wishes to fast because of hearing that fasting is a good work, but because of walking in darkness, such a one sometimes exceeds the limit and suffers the loss of other good works.

10. This kind of thing customarily happens in regard to vigils and labors. Someone loves silence because of hearing that silence is good. But because it is night, this person often does not know the path and wanders off it. Because of the importance attributed to silence, this person does not wish to rebuke a brother, and silence causes perdition for the one and for the other. Another wishes to rebuke his brother, but because of not knowing the brother's weakness, he acts according to his own zeal and accuses the other with excessive severity. The brother

*Ps 103:20

*1 John 1:6;
Ps 81:5

*Rom 8:26

collapses into a worse state because of the rebuke. As the apostle says, *We do not know how to pray as we ought*. Therefore Saint Job says, *I am anxious about all my works.** *Job 9:28

11. Therefore, my brothers, as long as this night remains, *let us walk in faith*, as the apostle says, *and not by sight.** For faith is that star that leads us in this *2 Cor 5:7 night, but afterward the day will come, and the true sun will rise, which *will illuminate the things hidden in darkness and will reveal the thoughts of the heart.** *1 Cor 4:5 Then the brightness of that star will undoubtedly be hidden, because there will be no faith, but sight. But whoever has faith in Christ must receive the sacraments of the holy gospel.

12. Up to [the birth of Christ], the sacraments of the Old Testament flourished, because *the law and the Prophets were in force until John.** Our Lord was cir- *Matt 11:13 cumcised on the eighth day, he was presented in the temple on the fortieth day, his mother was purified, a sacrifice was offered for him, and once each year he went up to the temple. All of these actions and events pertain to the Old Testament. Today the Lord instituted the sacraments of the New Testament, without which no one can be saved, and his astonishing grace appeared at his baptism. 13. What a grace is this, that the Son of God stripped himself and mingled with sinners, that he who committed no sin might receive baptism with those who received baptism to do penance for their own sins. What a grace it is that he who created all things, he who rules all things, he who fills up all things and sustains all things yielded himself into the hands of his servant. And why would he do this? In order that he might sanctify the waters of baptism, that he might institute the sacrament of the perfect gospel, that he might give an example of humility.

*Titus 2:11

*Mark 16:16

14. This grace *has appeared to all people** because *the one who believes and is baptized will be saved.** In the baptism of our Lord the rule of correct faith is shown to us, by which we believe in the Father, the Son, and the Holy Spirit. For the Holy Spirit appeared in the likeness of a dove and remained over him, and the voice of the Father was heard: *This is*

*Matt 3:17

my beloved Son, in whom I am well pleased.* Thus the whole Trinity is revealed: the Father in the voice, the Son in the man, the Holy Spirit in the dove. 15. Rightly did the Father reveal himself in the voice,

*Ps 32:9

because God *spoke and all things were made.** The Son too is rightly revealed in the man, *who was made*

*Rom 1:3

from the seed of David according to the flesh.* Similarly the Holy Spirit is revealed in the dove, *through*

*Rom 5:5

whom charity is poured forth *into our hearts** so that, like the dove, we may be free from the poison of bitterness and have peace with all. That is what the kiss of the dove signifies: that we offend no one but rather love everyone. *For love is patient, is kind; charity does*

*1 Cor 13:4

not envy nor act falsely, etc.*

16. The Holy Spirit is the one who makes the groan of the dove in us, as the apostle says: *For the Holy Spirit himself intercedes for us with unerring*

*Rom 8:26, 34

*John 2:9

groans.* The Spirit changes the water into wine for us;* in this the grace of God appears in a most astonishing way for our salvation. Water is changed into wine when fear is transformed into love. O, what a grace! See, brothers, and pay attention to that same grace in yourselves. What do you do? What do you suffer? And in what manner do you act, how do you suffer? Labors, vigils, silence, cheap clothing, rough food—are these not your afflictions of soul and body? 17. You have suffered these things, but you do not suffer alone. Many poor people who hasten from door to door suffer these things. What is the difference between you and them? A great one certainly. For they suffer unwillingly, they seek as much support for their body as possible, often importunately, often inconveniently. Often they steal; often they lie. Why? Because they do not drink the wine of Jesus. You do drink that wine; therefore you bear all these things with exultation, and you rejoice to sing with the prophet, *I will run along the ways of your commandments, when you give me a docile heart.**   *Ps 118:32

18. In all these things, *the grace of God our savior has appeared to all people,* illuminating them by faith, sanctifying them by sacraments, setting them on fire with charity. Granted that this grace appeared to all, not everyone receives it. *There is no one who escapes the heat,* because *the voice of those who have preached this grace goes forth to the whole world* and *their words to the ends of the earth.** As Scripture says, *this grace teaches*   *Ps 18:7, 5
*us to reject godless ways and worldly desires that we might live soberly, justly, and devoutly in this world.**   *Titus 2:12
Surely it teaches us to reject godless ways through the illumination of faith, to reject worldly desires through the sanctifying power of the sacraments, that we might live soberly, justly, and devoutly, set afire by charity.

19. To be sure, this is the rule that the grace of God teaches: that we first turn away from evil, rejecting ungodliness and worldly desires, and then that we do good, living soberly, justly, and devoutly.**   *Ps 36:27
cording to this rule, we should first reject ungodliness. Ungodliness, properly so called, is unfaithfulness, and the unfaithful are properly called the ungodly. This is the foundation of every good: that we first cast away unfaithfulness and have a sincere faith in God, because *without faith it is impossible to please God.**   *Heb 11:6
But because many pollute their faith by unclean works, we ought to reject not only ungodliness but also worldly desires.

20. My most beloved brothers, please take note that we may also have those worldly desires. Worldly desires are threefold: vanity, sensuality, and ambition. Thus worldly desires are the desire for meaningless [things], for sensual pleasures, and for honors. These are the three things that worldly people desire. They desire meaningless trappings, such as the beauty of their garments, the speed of their horses, the flight of their birds of prey, the keen senses of their dogs, the spectacle of their games. These are all vain things, void of permanence and truth. They desire also sensual pleasures, such as delicacies at the table, different kinds of drinks, satisfaction of their appetites, and such like. They desire also the honors of this world, such as a kingdom, a retinue, episcopal status, and such like.

21. My most beloved brothers, please take note that we may also have those worldly desires in small and insignificant things that others have in great things. For we desire meaningless trappings if we take pains with our cheap clothes, anxious that they may appear now too large or too narrow, now too short, now too long. If we attend to these details, if we busy ourselves concerning them, we have not fully let go of worldly desires. Similarly, if we wander willingly here and there, if we listen willingly to *empty words** and respond in kind, if we listen willingly to rumors and repeat them, we are certainly not free from worldly vanity.

*RB 4.53

22. Because if we mutter about our food or sleep, if we occasionally judge or disparage someone in our heart concerning such matters, we have not yet fully conquered the sensuality of the world. We may still have an appetite for honors, insignificant and meaningless as they may be. If anyone desires to be prior or abbot or cellarer or anything of this sort, if he

chooses to do as much as he can to achieve them, envies those who have them, and disparages them as much as possible, he has undoubtedly dirtied himself by worldly desires.

23. But *the grace of God our savior has appeared to all, teaching us to renounce ungodliness and worldly desires that we may live soberly, justly, and devoutly in this world.** Soberly, Scripture says, and justly and devoutly: soberly in relation to ourselves, justly in relation to our neighbor, and devoutly in relationship to God. Brothers, sobriety is a great virtue. Sobriety is the opposite of drunkenness. There is drunkenness of body and drunkenness of spirit. Drunkenness of body is when someone abandons reason or thoroughly disturbs his own good sense because of excessive drink. However, spiritual drunkenness is sometimes good, sometimes bad. 24. It is bad when through some intemperance or passionate desire a person is not able to serve the ends of justice. It is good when through revelation or contemplation or an excess of human love someone goes beyond sense and reason, drunk from *the abundance of the house* of God and *from the torrent of its pleasures** that he has drunk. Describing this drunkenness, the apostle says, for *if we are out of our minds, it is for God, if we are sober, it is for you.** A certain prophet, reproaching someone who had not attained this drunkenness, says, *you have drunk, and you are not made drunk.**

25. Saint Moses defines bad drunkenness, that which is produced by bad wine, in this way: *from the vine in the vineyard of Sodom and from that of Gomorrah.** The vineyard of Sodom is the love of the world from which the wine of lust and avarice gushes forth; this wine customarily inebriates people and turns them from all sense and reason. By this drunkenness they are put to sleep, and to them the

*Titus 2:11-12

*Ps 35:9

*2 Cor 5:13

*Hag 1:6

*Deut 32:32

*Joel 1:6
prophet says, *wake up, you drunks, and cry.** There
is also another drunkenness, born of indiscreet fervor
or a certain obstinacy of mind. Rather, the fervor
and obstinacy are themselves a kind of drunkenness,
which makes one exceed the bounds of discretion and
one's own possibilities.

26. For all of these reasons it is necessary that
we live soberly. This is the virtue that preserves us
unhurt from every sort of bad drunkenness so that we
act without excess but with all moderation and discretion.* If you are excessively silent, you are judged to
*RB 64.12;
31.12; 70.5
be drunk. If extremely loquacious, you are judged no
less drunk. If you fast over much, you are made drunk
by excessive fervor or a certain obstinacy of mind. If
you indulge in banquets and sensual foods, the wine
of earthly sensuality has snatched sense and reason
from you. If your vigils and works are above the limit,
you have lost good sense. If you are tepid and lazy,
you have fallen asleep in a pernicious drunkenness.

27. All these sorts of evil and damnable drunkenness are to be avoided, in order that we might live
soberly. But just as sobriety serves us, so does justice
serve our neighbors. For justice is that virtue by which
we pay back to someone what is his own.* Among our
*Aelred, SS
39.16, 55.25
(CCCM
2A:316, 2B:88),
De oner 31.8
(CCCM
2D:282), Spec
car 1.32.91,
1.33.96, 3.31.75
(CCCM 1:53,
56, 141); Ci-
cero, De fini bon
et mal 5.23.65
†Aelred, Spec
car 1.33.96
(CCCM 1:56)
neighbors, there are those who are above us, those
who are equal to us, and those who are below us. If
therefore we wish to live justly, it is necessary that
we offer an abject humility and obedience to those
above us, a chaste affection and mutual respect to our
equals, and a devout compassion and providential care
for those inferior to us.†

28. In all these things, the grace of God our Savior
has appeared, by which he teaches true faith against
impiety and a renunciation of the world against
worldly desires. For in the gospel itself, Christ says
of faith, *This is the work of God: that you believe in*

the one whom the Father has sent.* And he also says,   *John 6:29
If you would be perfect, etc.* Grace itself teaches us   *Matt 19:21
to live soberly, saying, *see that your hearts are not
weighed down with carousing and drunkenness, etc.**   *Luke 21:34
The same passage teaches us to live justly when it
says, *render unto Caesar that which is Caesar's and
to God what is God's.** But if we do all such things   *Matt 22:21
for the riches or honors of this world, we are surely
totally lost, and our Lord says of us, *Amen I say to
you, they have received their reward.**   *Matt 6:2, 5

29. Therefore the grace of God teaches us to live
not only soberly and justly but also devoutly, that
we may do all such things with a simple spirit and
an upright intention.* Our Lord also revealed these   *Titus 2:12;
commandments to us not only in words but also in   Aelred, Spec car
deeds. For he showed sobriety when he fasted for   3.31.75 (CCCM
forty days and forty nights.* He showed justice when   1:141)
he paid the debt of obedience to the Father and trib-   *Matt 4:2
ute to Caesar.* Likewise, when he spent the night   *Matt 22:21
in prayer and when he preached and *cured the sick*
during the day,* he undoubtedly demonstrated justice   *Luke 6:12,
without fail, exhibiting prayer to God and care for   4, 40
the neighbor.

30. Therefore, if we have become skilled in these
things, we will await *a blessed hope,** securely and   *Titus 2:13
without a doubt—a blessed hope that hopes for life
eternal, the joy of Paradise, the presence of Jesus
Christ. This is a blessed, reasonable hope. For this
hope is not confounded,* this hope does not perish.   *Rom 5:5
But *the hope of the impious will perish.** This is not   *Prov 10:28
to be wondered at, for they hope for worldly riches,
secular honors, the delights of the flesh, and empty
vanities: and *the world and its cravings are passing
away.** Therefore the hope of the ungodly will perish.   *1 John 2:17
But yours, brothers, your hope is certainly blessed,
because it is grounded in and hopes for those things

that cannot die. *For heaven and earth will pass away, says the Lord, but the word of the Lord remains forever.** This is the word of promise that cannot perish, *because whatever God has promised, God is also powerful to do.**

*Matt 24:35;
1 Pet 1:25;
Isa 40:8
*Rom 4:22

31. Therefore, brothers, we await a blessed hope that is not poor, nor perishable, nor transitory but remains forever like God. We await also *the coming of God in great glory.** Brothers, today our God appeared small and humble, but on that day he will appear great and awesome. Today his grace appeared, but on that day his glory will appear. Whosoever in any way receives him in his smallness will surely and certainly see his greatness, and whoever is not ungrateful for his grace, however he may now express it, will then undoubtedly participate in his glory.

*Titus 2:13

32. But because we have dragged out this sermon at length, let us ask for the grace of which we have spoken so that true faith may pour down into our hearts like the light of the star. Let us pray that we may preserve in their fullness the sacraments of Christ that we receive. Let us pray that our fear may be converted into true love, as the water was changed into wine. Let us pray that, confirmed in good works, we may await the blessed hope and the coming in great glory of God, our Savior, Jesus Christ,* to whom be honor and glory with the Father and the Holy Spirit, world without end, through forever. Amen.

*Rom 16:27

Sermon 32

For the Purification of Saint Mary

1. **A**dorn thy marriage chamber, O Sion.* Before this day, we spoke to your char-ity on the day of our restoration, that day of exultation and joy, when *the light shone in the darkness*,* health in our sickness, life in death. As much as we could, we then served you the spiritual oil that our doctor, Jesus Christ, brought to us. We were in need of that oil for anointing, for refreshment, for light: for anointing, because we were sick; for refreshment, because we were famished; for light, because we were blind.* You have exulted greatly in this anointing, and it delighted you to cry out, *Your name pours out like oil.**

2. Then you came with Jesus to the wedding, and *new wine, the wine that gladdens the human heart** was set before you. And from that moment on, you have continued to exult and rejoice that you were able to glory and say, *The king brought me into his wine cellar.** Notice the beautiful order. First our Lord nourishes us with the oil of his mercy, then he makes us drunk on the wine of his exultation, and today he feeds us with the honey of his sweetness. Therefore, brothers, however good it may be, however joyful, to linger at these nuptials and over this wine,* of which we have recently spoken, nevertheless it is right that we follow the proper order.* The right order is that we come from the wedding feast and banquet to the hidden chamber.

3. Therefore adorn thy hidden chamber, Sion. O Sion, O Sion, adorn thy hidden chamber. The spiritual

*Ant and Resp for the Purifi-cation (Hesbert 3:1293, 4:6051)

*Ps 3:4; Aelred, S 4.1 (CCCM 2A:37)

*Bernard, SC 15.3.5 (SBOp 1:85)
*Song 1:2; 2:4

*Ps 103:15

*Song 2:4

*Ps 132:1; Matt 17:4

*Aelred, S 50.38 (CCCM 2B:39)

25

bridegroom wishes to come there this very day, that
bridegroom who is so beautiful, pure, and holy that
he cannot bear any disgrace, any stain, or any filthiness in that chamber he wishes to enter. Therefore,
Sion, adorn thy inner chamber. To whom do I speak?
To Sion. Sion may be interpreted as the watchtower
or the act of being watchful. What soul ought to be
called the watchtower? In what soul does the rational
mind always stand as if in watchfulness?*

*Aelred, S
45.37 (CCCM
2A:363);
Jerome, Nom 39
(CCSL 72:108);
Augustine, En in
Ps 50:22 (CCSL
38:615)

4. People habitually stand in watchfulness for
three reasons: that they may inspect those who are
approaching, that they may guard against enemies,
and that they may preserve the fruits. And we have
enemies, those whom it is necessary to guard against;
we also have fruits that it behooves us diligently to
preserve. Something is coming toward us—and it usually comes to us often—to which we must always pay
close attention. For these three reasons, we must always be vigilant, standing always as if in a watchtower
so that we may say with the prophet, *I stand upon my*
*watchtower every day.**

*Isa 21:8 Vulg;
Hab 2:1

5. You know well who our enemy is. Certainly,
our *enemy* is the *devil, who goes around like a roaring*
*lion, seeking whom he may devour.** Plainly the one
who wishes to anticipate and guard against his assault
must not sleep but always stand as if in a watchtower.
We have no security by day or by night. Sometimes
he comes in the day; at other times he comes in the
night. In the night, he inflames us to impatience,
grumbling, or hatred because of the adversities and
tribulations of this life. In the day, he draws us by the
joy and good fortune of this life toward sensuality or
vanity. Therefore let our mind always stand as in a
watchtower to guard against this enemy.

*1 Pet 5:8

6. We also have the fruits, such as *charity, chas-*
*tity, joy, peace, patience,** and others of this kind.

*Gal 5:22-23

These are certainly good and useful fruits, but there are many thieves who endeavor to steal them from us. Envy waits in ambush that it may take charity away from us. Fornication wishes to corrupt chastity, sadness to corrupt spiritual joy, and discord peace. Brothers, it is not to be wondered that we love such fruits. Blessed is the one who loves them and guards them well. His soul rightly deserves to be called Sion, that is, a watchtower.

7. Again, you know for whose coming you ought always to have your eyes open. The Lord himself reveals it in the gospel: *Be watchful*, he says, *for you know not in which hour your Lord will be about to come.** Therefore, brothers, may your soul be as a watchtower in which the mind always stands alert and anxious to watch and not sleep. May our soul always have before its eyes that day when *the Lord, our God, will come openly and not be silent*, when *the fire will flare up before his face and a raging storm around him.**

*Matt 24:42

*Ps 49:3

8. Beloved brothers, consider holy Simeon, whose story is read in today's gospel; with what solicitude he stood in the watchtower, having his eyes on the coming of the one whom he desired, whom he loved. Surely, brothers, the one who was then about to come was the humble, gentle Lord, who came to save the world, not to judge it.* The one who is about to come now will come in a terrifying, glorious way, with power and terror, that he may judge the world and render to *each according to his works.** Therefore we must work at our *salvation with fear and trembling,** with great care and solicitude, and always anticipate his coming,* so that our soul may be Sion, as the Lord says to us, *Adorn your hidden chamber, Sion.*

*John 3:17; 12:47

*Matt 16:27
*Phil 2:12; Eph 6:5

*RB 4.47

9. Surely, brothers, it is no small thing that your soul can hear this voice. It is a great thing to prepare

for our Lord a hospitable place where he may refresh
himself, as Martha did.* It is also great to prepare for
him a large dining-room, arranged in such a way that
he may eat the Passover with his disciples.* But it is
much greater to prepare for him a hidden chamber in
which he may rest. Therefore he says to Sion alone,
Adorn your hidden chamber. We wish to consider
what sort of hidden chamber this is.

10. We read in Ezekiel about a certain spiritual
edifice, founded on some mountain, that the prophet
saw in the spirit. There he describes an exterior courtyard, an interior courtyard, a vestibule, the domestic
rooms, and an interior chamber. He speaks there also
of the number and dimensions of these rooms, their
width, length, and height.* But this is not *the time
to speak** of all these things. One thing only I say:
we ought to seek this edifice in our soul. The external courtyard, the interior courtyard, the vestibule,
the domestic rooms, and the interior chamber are all
there within our soul. Blessed is the one who builds
and ornaments this edifice in the soul in such a way
that our Lord wills to dwell there.

11. Already we may see the differences between
these rooms. You know that the exterior courtyard
lies open to all, and scarcely anyone is forbidden entry.
In the interior courtyard, men are customarily ad-
mitted all together, but it is guarded with moderate
diligence so that those who are obviously enemies
do not come in. The vestibule is like a portico where
judges customarily position themselves; they listen
to many and judge among them, deciding who are
to be denied entrance to the household quarters. At
that point, those whom they highly esteem and judge
worthy of table fellowship with the family patriarch
enter into the domestic quarters.*

*Luke 10:38

*Luke 22:11-12

*Ezek 40
*Eccl 3:7

*Aelred, Iesu
3.29 (CCCM
1:275)

12. Let us understand this edifice to be entirely within our soul. As it seems to me, our memory is like the external courtyard; let all of us consider very carefully how this applies to ourselves. The memory is an open courtyard. Who is prohibited entry there? Do not the good and the bad, friends and enemies without difference or discretion, enter there? The memory is a courtyard, and the courtyard is outside. Who can prohibit the good and the bad, the just and the unjust, the clean and the dirty from coming into the memory? All these things rush blindly in. What, then, are we going to do? Let us guard the door of the interior courtyard so that they do not enter there.

13. The interior courtyard is delight. Something enters there as if through a door, because of our zeal for meditating on it. Consider how it happens: sometimes, whether we are sitting or standing, we direct our thoughts toward ourselves; we record the things we have heard or seen, or rather everything that we have experienced through our bodily senses, namely, through sight, hearing, taste, smell, or touch. These are like five doors through which everything we have spoken of above enters into the memory as into an external courtyard. Do not good and bad things alike enter through these doors?

14. *Concupiscence of the eyes** enters in that way, with as it were a large family. It leads with it the beautiful and the vain; it places before your eyes costly garments, cities, castles, public gathering places, market days, fables and old songs, debates and hunts. For all these things pertain to curiosity, which is the meaning of *concupiscence of the eyes*. These things come into the memory; they come up to the interior doorway, that is, the zeal for reflection. For they wish that we reflect at length on all these things, that through such

*1 John 2:16

reflection they may be able to come into the interior courtyard of delight.

15. In a similar way *concupiscence of the flesh* with its family enters the exterior courtyard, whence it strives to press forward into the interior courtyard with its family: banquets, drinking sessions, impurities, fornication, sensuality, and many sorts of unclean and impure things.* Pride of life also strives to enter the interior courtyard in turn with honors, preferential treatment, and the dignities of this world. But is it only those evil things that enter the courtyard of memory? Does not charity also enter from the other side, and with it joy, peace, and sweetness?*

*Rom 13:13; Col 3:5

*Gal 5:22

16. Contempt for the world enters too, bringing with it spiritual freedom and joyfulness of spirit. Similarly patience brings along a disregard for injuries and the endurance of tribulations. What about chastity? Does it not enter with its flowers and pleasant odors, spreading out all its perfumes of marvelous sweetness, *with the aromas of myrrh and frankincense and with the perfume of every exotic dust?** Among these many things that we turn over in our mind, it is up to us which ones we introduce into the interior courtyard by opening the door.

*Song 3:6

17. Think about this carefully. For if, when all these things come into our memory and run around in a disorderly manner, we choose something to consider carefully and linger over it, we are opening the outer door of the house. For such consideration is the outer door through which something enters into delight. We have all experienced what I am saying. If some carnal pleasure comes to us in memory and we then begin to reflect on it intently, at once we feel a certain delight. Thus the enemy enters into the interior courtyard. But who can protect the courtyard so that no enemy enters? We must protect the vestibule.

18. The vestibule is deliberation. For first we remember something, and then we reflect on it; from that point on we feel delight about this matter, and then we deliberate on whether or not we will satisfy that delight. There, in the act of deliberation as if in a vestibule, the will resides and judges concerning all these things; it deliberates whether it wishes to follow the delight or flee. The will itself introduces into the domestic quarters that which it chooses. The domestic quarters represent the consent of the will. There the banquet takes place in which people nourish themselves by consenting to their desires, whether for good things or evil. There, within the domestic quarters, the inner chamber is to be found. The inner chamber is affection.

19. When someone acts not from consent alone but with a certain affection, with love and sweetness of mind, [what is accepted with affection] is already in the hidden chamber, as if in a certain interior embrace. Blessed is the one who excludes and rejects all vain and sensual fantasies that may come into the memory and who there receives our Lord Jesus Christ. Blessed is the one who brings him through the door into the interior courtyard, the one, that is, who gladly thinks on the Lord, takes delight in him, and introduces him into the vestibule. Blessed are those who deliberate and judge how they may please the Lord—by what works, what words, what reflections—and thus introduce him into the domestic quarters so that they may consent to do, say, and reflect on that which is pleasing in his eyes.

20. If people do all of this cheerfully, even if at first with some difficulty and labor, they introduce the spouse, that is, our Lord Jesus, into the domestic quarters, but not yet into the inner chamber. To such souls the Holy Spirit says, *Adorn your inner*

chamber, O Sion, and receive Christ the King. It is as if the Spirit is saying, "you have the Lord Jesus in your domestic quarters, where you experience how good he is, how meek and humble of heart."* You have labored by day in imitation of his humility; now adorn your inner chamber so that you may rest in his embrace. There you may be at leisure to see *how sweet he is;** there you may experience that he is sweet, and you may feel that his *Spirit* is *sweet above honey and his inheritance above honey and the honeycomb.** Therefore, adorn your inner chamber, O Sion.

21. Let us see in what manner we ought to adorn this inner chamber. The inner chamber is, as I have said, affection, and it has three parts: the floor, the wall, and the ceiling. See how this is to be understood. Sometimes our affection leans toward pleasurable things, things that give delight, and sometimes toward useful things, that is, toward something that may be useful to us, although it may not give delight. Sometimes it leans toward virtuous things when, to be sure, the affection anticipates neither delight nor profit but is drawn because the thing is virtuous and becoming. We ought to adorn each of these three categories of affections as if they were the three parts of our inner chamber.

There are three considerations that, if they are rooted and strengthened in our heart, will, without a doubt, adorn the chamber. 22. Insofar as our affection leans toward pleasurable things, we ought to adorn it by the consideration of divine charity. We must consider the love by which God *did not spare his own Son, but handed him over for all of us,** and the love by which the same Son, *because of the greatness of love by which he loved us, handed himself over to death** and *was counted among the wicked.*† Brothers, great is the pleasure that comes from seeing our Lord

*Matt 11:29

*Pss 33:9; 45:11; 1 Pet 2:3

*Sir 24:27

*Rom 8:32

*Eph 2:4
†Isa 53:12;
Aelred, S
67.4 (CCCM
2B:182)

in the womb of his mother, seeing him in the manger, seeing him today in the arms of Saint Simeon. Great is the pleasure of imagining his words, his miracles, his embrace, and his kiss in one's heart. This is a great ornament for the ceiling of our inner chamber.

23. Next, insofar as our affection leans toward useful things, it must be ornamented by a consideration of the divine promise. For what did God promise to us? How much glory, how much happiness, what riches, what honors? What, then, may be more useful to us than to desire all that God promised, seek after it, and finally possess it? This meditation is like a certain beautiful arch.

24. Next, insofar as our affection is drawn to virtuous things, it must be ornamented by a consideration of the human condition. We ought to consider whose creature we are and whose image.* What can be more virtuous than that the creature love its Creator; the work, its artisan; the servant, its Lord; and the human person, God? This meditation is surely a beautiful ornament.

*Isa 29:16; Rom 9:20

25. And so if our affection attaches itself to our Redeemer with delight, to the one who has paid off our debt with fervor, to our Creator and Lord with humility, our inner chamber is adorned. This first consideration excludes all sensuality, all greed, and all vanity from our affection. Therefore, adorn your chamber, O Sion, and *receive Christ the King** with all your affection, all your love, all your delight, and every sweetness.

*Ant and Resp for the Feast of the Purification (Hesbert 3:1293, 4:6051)

26. The text says "Christ the King." To the king belongs power, to the Christ, anointing. Power makes him awe-inspiring; anointing makes him lovable. Jesus is in truth my awe-inspiring, lovable Lord. It is necessary, brothers, that we not separate these two, but that in our soul the meditation on his power always

be linked to the meditation on his sweetness. The first leads to awe, the other to love. Therefore, receive the king that you may fear him; receive the Christ that you may love him.

27. What joy it is, brothers, when our Lord has entered into the inner chamber, crossing over into our affection so that our total affection possesses him. Whether this be because of the superior manner in which he has loved us or because he created us or because he has promised such and so many good things, how gentle his embrace and how ardent his kisses will then be. There is no impurity in his love, nothing soiled, nothing vicious; he himself was *conceived by a virgin and by a virgin given birth.** For the Lord Jesus has been conceived without concupiscence, without any fleshly pleasure, without any iniquity. Therefore his love is entirely holy, entirely pure, entirely virtuous. Therefore, my brothers, let us discern between good and evil love.

*Ant and Resp for the Feast of the Purification (Hesbert 3:1293, 4:6051)

28. Wherever love is chaste and holy, not seeking earthly goods but heavenly ones, there love is good. There love belongs to the Son of the Virgin, to the one who was a virgin when she conceived him and bore him, the one who remained a virgin after his birth. She is the true Sion, the holy Sion, the decorated Sion, who adorned the inner chamber of her heart with every ornament of virtue. Therefore she received Christ the Lord, not only in her spirit but also in her body, not only in her affection but in her hand, that he might possess her totally, might fill her totally, might totally dwell within her. Through her merits and prayers, may we also deserve today to purge our heart and our soul so that, purged from vices and ornamented with virtues, we may be spiritually worthy to receive Christ the King, our Lord, who with the Father and the Holy Spirit lives and reigns, God without end. Amen.

Sermon 33

For the Purification of Saint Mary

1. < **T**he woman who has borne a male child, having received seed, will be unclean for seven days, etc. >* As you know *Lev 12:2 and have already heard, before the coming of our Lord there was a certain people who believed in him, that is, the Jews; after his coming, another people believed, namely, the Christians. The Jewish people had their feasts and sacraments, and we have our own similar feasts and sacraments. But theirs were the shadows and images of the things that were to come. In ours is the truth, that is, that which the previous ones signified. Therefore the apostle says, *All things were contained there figuratively; they were written nevertheless for us.** There they were prophesied; *1 Cor 10:11; 9:10; Rom 4:24; Aelred, SS 54.4, 76.7 (CCCM 2B:67, 287) here they are fulfilled.

2. But you ought to know that even now we have certain feasts born in some way from the customs observed by our ancient fathers. Better we say, though, that their feasts were celebrated figuratively, that is, as a foreshadowing of the future when we would have them in truth. For example, it was because Christ would be our Passover in the future that they in their Passover sacrificed a lamb. 3. You ought, therefore, to know that the feast that we celebrate today, namely, the Purification of Saint Mary, pertains in some way to the custom that they had. For such was the precept in the law of Moses: *A woman who, having received seed, bears a male child will be unclean for seven days; on the eighth day, the infant will be circumcised, and*

35

she will remain for thirty days in the blood of her pu-rification. She will not touch any seed or enter into the
*Lev 12:2-4 *sanctuary until she fulfills the days of her purification.** Because Blessed Mary fulfilled this law, we celebrate this feast today in her memory.

4. First you ought to consider the wonderful humility of our Lady and to imitate it, as much as you are able. Although she was unstained, nevertheless she wished to be seen as stained by all. Although she contracted not the slightest stain from the sweet infant that she bore but was rather purified by him from all sin, nevertheless she willed to purify herself by sacrifices. Don't think that she did this because of the strict requirement of the Law. For she did not
*Lev 12:2 bear a son through *receiving seed,** not she to whom the angel Gabriel said, *The Holy Spirit will come upon you and the power of the most High will overshadow*
*Luke 1:35 *you.** Therefore, brothers, she did this entirely because of her humility and our necessity.

5. It is for a great purpose that all these things were done, namely, the circumcision of Christ, the purification of his mother, and the offering that was made today. These are great and very profound mysteries,[1] but there is no time to speak of all of them properly. We wish to say something for your edification, only about that precept of the law. Granted that both profound allegories and beautiful moral meanings may be found in that text of Scripture, nevertheless, we think to say something only about the moral meaning

---

[1] The word that Aelred uses, *sacramentum*, is multi-layered. It is the word that the Vulgate uses for the Greek *mysterion*, a reality that bears the presence of God. It becomes the name of those liturgical rites that are considered especially and specifically sanctifying. It was also used to designate the higher or spiritual meaning of the text of Sacred Scripture. Here, and elsewhere in Aelred, the resonances of all three meanings are present.

because of the shortness of the time. For the one who
speaks ought not to reflect so much on what he feels
in himself as on what others may feel in themselves.
For people listen willingly when what they hear from
another they also find in themselves.

6. Let us see who that woman is who, having
received the seed, bears a male child. For spiritual
conception and birth is quite like bodily conception
and birth. Spiritual conception is that of which Isaiah
says, *O Lord, by your Spirit we have conceived and we
have borne the spirit of salvation.** Similarly we ought   *Isa 26:18
to understand this woman spiritually. In Scripture,
woman is customarily given sometimes a positive interpretation, sometimes a negative one. When she is
interpreted as evil, it is because of her compliance,
softness, and weakness; she is interpreted as good
because of her fruitfulness or for the affective love
that women customarily have toward their children.

7. She is given a good interpretation in the gospel,
as when the Lord says, *The kingdom of heaven is like
the leaven that a woman hides in the three measures
of meal.** Similarly, *What woman having ten drach-*   *Matt 13:33
mas, etc.* In these places the woman stands for the   *Luke 15:8
wisdom of God, that is, for our Lord, Jesus Christ,
who sought us, found us, and redeemed us, all with
maternal affection, *because of his great charity.**   *Eph 2:4

8. Woman receives an evil signification in Isaiah,
where it is said of the Jews, *And the women will domi-
nate them.** For here *the women* signify those who   *Isa 3:12
were delicate and compliant and had nothing virile
in themselves. Thus when you were in the world,
when you were tasting nothing except the flesh, when
you loved the compliance of the flesh, its softness
and vices, then your soul was a woman and a vicious
woman at that, a sinner, an adulterer who had an
adulterous demon for a husband.**   *Luke 7:37;
                                           Mark 8:38

9. But often our Lord Jesus Christ also joins himself even to such a soul and places there his seed. The seed of our Lord, who is a true man, a true man *potent in work and in word**—his seed is the Holy Spirit. From that seed, souls are conceived: *O Lord, from your Spirit we conceive and we have given birth.** But not all souls bear the same fruit. Some bear females; others males. See how they differ, those who bear male offspring from those who bear females. *Female* signifies a weak and imperfect work; *male*, a strong and perfect one. 10. Our Lord approaches someone who has fallen into adultery, fornication, uncleanness, and similar criminal vices, someone who takes delight in them. If our Lord puts his seed in that person—who then begins to fear on account of his sin—he may begin to reflect and resolve to correct himself, in order that he might lay hold of a better life. His soul is then like a woman, who receives the seed.

11. But if he begins to devote himself to a somewhat fragile and imperfect life, if he for example takes a wife and leads with her a chaste life, to be sure he bears not male but female offspring. Again, if he has devoted himself to a lukewarm life in which he lives according to his own will and has similar delights, he receives a certain seed and gives birth but bears female offspring. 12. What soul is it that receives seed and bears male offspring?[2] I do not have to search

*Luke 24:19

*Isa 26:18

---

[2] Aelred has already indicated that gender here is entirely a matter of allegory. Nonetheless, from this point on, the use of the feminine noun *alma*, "soul," for all persons and especially the monks Abbot Aelred addresses requires pronoun usage that can be confusing in English. In Latin, the subject is usually contained in the verb form and no pronoun is required. But English does require one, and the use of *she* to replace *soul* means that the feminine pronoun often indicates the monk. As translator, I use *she* when Aelred is writing about the woman in the biblical text and *he* when Aelred is extending

long. If I well consider this whole community, you are all the woman who, having received the seed, bears male offspring. And see how the Lord himself distinguishes those two births in this place.

13. A certain woman, that is, a certain soul, who had received the seed and wished to give birth, said to the Lord, O *Lord, what must I do to possess eternal life?** That soul certainly received seed and therefore wished to give birth, that is, to do some work through which she might be saved. And the Lord said, *Do not commit murder, do not steal, do not commit adultery, and other similar commandments.** The Lord saw the weakness of this woman; he did not wish to tell her at once that she should bear male offspring, but at least female. Because she was not able to grasp the perfection of the gospel, he wished that at least she should fulfill the law. 14. She answered, *These things I have done since my youth. What still is lacking to me?** She bore female offspring and thought that that was sufficient. But the Lord showed that she had still not advanced far enough. For he said, *There remains one thing lacking to you.** You have borne female offspring. *If you would be perfect*, it is necessary for you to have male offspring. *If you would be perfect, go, sell all that you have and give to the poor and come, follow me.** That is what it means to bear male offspring.

15. Already you see, and I think that you exult because when you received the seed of the Holy Spirit you did not bear female but male offspring. But let us see what the Scripture says about this woman who bears a male child. She must be considered unclean

*Luke 18:18

*Luke 8:20

*Mark 10:20;
Matt 19:20

*Luke 18:22

*Matt 19:21;
Luke 18:22

---

the allegory to situations that are specifically about the experience of the monks. When the pronoun replaces *alma* and refers to the souls of human persons more generally, I try to follow Aelred's consistent allegory and use female pronouns.

for seven days. Therefore, brothers, when a certain soul gives birth to a perfect work, that is, when she leaves the world, let her not take pride nor glory in her purity; then she fulfills the seven days. Seven days signifies the whole of time, because all of this time runs in increments of seven days.

16. Therefore, however long she lives in this life, however long she bears this fragile flesh, however long she walks amid the snares of the devil, however long she sees another law in her members, *fighting against the law of his mind,** however long she beats her breast and says, *Forgive us our sins,** however many male offspring she bears, however many perfect works she does, her soul is not perfectly clean. For who will glory in having a chaste heart?* Nevertheless, let her be joyous and happy, because, provided that she bears masculine offspring, provided that she lives a perfect life, when these seven days have run their course, that is, when she goes forth from the body, she will be clean.*

17. But not so the one who bears female offspring. For that one will be doubly unclean. The soul that is all tangled up in the cares of the world, whose plans* are about a wife,† children, and frequently worldly profits, even though she does not commit horrible, damnable sins, must nevertheless necessarily be purged after this life. The wood, hay, or straw that she had built up on the foundation of Christ must be burned. She will be saved, but only as if by fire.* Therefore, the soul that bears female offspring will be unclean for forty days, that is, both in this life and after this life.

18. However unclean she may be through these seven days, that is, in this life, the soul that bears masculine offspring will nevertheless be clean after this life, when she will have been freed from *the body*

*Rom 7:23

*Matt 6:12

*Prov 20:9

*Ps-Bede, In Lev 12 (PL 91:346 AB)

*2 Tim 2:4; Luke 21:34 †1 Cor 7:33-34

*1 Cor 3:12, 14-15

*of this death,** which merely weighs us down and
stains us. Nevertheless she does not enter into the
sanctuary* immediately after the seven days. We can
understand this sanctuary as that perfect blessedness
that we will receive on the Day of Judgment. Even if
holy and perfect souls enter immediately into heaven
after this life, nevertheless this is not yet the fullness
of the blessedness when they recover their bodies on
the Day of Judgment.

19. Then after those seven days, that is, after this
life, the woman who has borne a male offspring is
made clean and the infant is circumcised. However
perfect our works may be within the possibilities of
this life, nevertheless it is not possible that our work
be without some mixture of impurity, whether of
pride or vanity or the appetite for human praise. At
the very least, less discreet dealings with others creep
into our works. Therefore this child that is our work
cannot be so circumcised in this life that all filth is
done away with. As a certain saint says, "Our evil
deeds are entirely evil but our good deeds are not entirely good."* This will be so throughout these seven
days. Then death comes as a kind of sharp little knife
and with its bitterness cuts away all that impurity that
we have picked up along the way.*

20. Let us look at another interpretation of these
seven days and the others that follow, brothers, so
that the whole [range of meanings] may be referred
to this present time. It seems to me that it is lawful
to set out different foods according to the different
infirmities,* so that if by chance one kind of food
does not please someone, then another may. Let us
speak therefore about whether *this* meaning pleases,
and let each receive the one that pleases him more.
Therefore, brothers, the woman—that is, the soul—
that bears male offspring—that is, that follows the

*Rom 7:24

*Lev 12:4

*citation
unidentified

*Ps-Bede, In Lev
12 (PL 91:346B)

*RB 39.1-2

perfect gospel—is not perfectly clean immediately
after she leaves this world, but only after she passes
through the seven days.

21. The first day is the moment of renunciation.
On that day, the infant is born, that is, it is the opportunity for perfection about which the Lord teaches,
saying, *If you would be perfect, go, sell all that you*

*Matt 19:21;
Luke 18:22

*have and give to the poor and come, follow me.** Up to
this point the soul is unclean because of sins. Therefore she must begin to reflect and call to mind what
she has done, how much she has sinned, how much
she has offended her Creator. She did this in childhood and that in youth, [something] in this place
and [something other] in that, in this particular time
and in that particular time. She ought to consider all
these things because of the differences among sins.

22. For it is one thing to sin in childhood, another
in youth, and still another in old age. Similarly, it
is worse to sin in church than in some other building, and the one who sins on holy feast days does so
more gravely. Again, the manner of sinning must be
considered; one way of sinning is more shameful and
more serious than another. Likewise in regard to those
persons against or with whom one has sinned, for it
is more grievous to sin with one person than with
another. The soul begins to have such a meditation
after its conversion, and the consideration of sin itself
is like the second day.

23. The second day is entirely daylight. For the
sun begins to shine brightly on the one who knows
her own sins and begins to consider them attentively.
In calling them to mind, she begins worthily to do
penance for sins. For when a person truly sees her
sins, then she says, "O, how could I have done this?
How could I have thus offended my Creator? How
could I have sunk to such shameful and horrendous

sins?" This penance is as the third day. But the soul is still unclean until she begins to move toward oral confession. 24. Then she comes to the superior and confesses her sins, and that confession is as the fourth day. But because she is confounded[3] in confession and blushes from shame, there usually follows a certain groaning and compunction. Then she begins to groan and weep that she has committed such foul and shameful things. And this groaning, or perhaps the compunction, is as the fifth day. Already this woman is perceived to be clean.

25. Certainly she is clean, in a measure, but in a measure unclean. She is clean because she has confessed her sins and cried for them. But that is not sufficient for conscience, which until now has submitted to the stains of sin. Confession does not suffice until she does penance, that is, until she does such works as are appropriate for penance. In no way can conscience have peace unless the flesh, which took delight in base and filthy things, has been afflicted by contrary actions. 26. Insofar as she has sinned through gluttony and drunkenness, she wants to be tormented through hunger and thirst. Insofar as rich and luxurious foods have compelled her flesh toward wantonness, she wants to nourish chastity with meager, tasteless food. Insofar as she took pride in expensive dress, she wants to be humbled by mean, rough garments. Insofar as she fostered idle and sordid thoughts through laziness and sleep, she wants to banish such useless, foolish thoughts by vigils and manual labor. Therefore penitent action is the sixth day.

27. But even as she represses sordid and useless thoughts through bodily labors, it is necessary that she nourish good and pure thoughts through spiritual

---

[3] See S 30n3.

exercises. For just as the flesh is disciplined through labors and vigils and fasts, so the spirit is refreshed through reading, meditation, and prayer. Spiritual exercise is therefore like the seventh day. If someone among you wishes to reflect upon himself, he will see indeed that even if the woman bears a masculine offspring, she will be unclean for seven days until the boy is circumcised on the eighth day.*

*Lev 12:2-3

28. Therefore, she will not be cleansed by all these actions unless the boy is circumcised. For those who hold to this way and hasten well through all these days will undoubtedly be tempted by pride and vanity; the more they progress in these things, that much the more they are certainly tempted to exalt themselves. Let such search for a stone, or rather let them receive that most sharp stone, the humility of Jesus, and let that child—their spiritual progress—be circumcised, that is, let the vice of pride be cut away from all their actions. Henceforth, the woman will not be unclean.

*Lev 12:4

29. Nevertheless *she will remain in the blood of her purification for thirty days.** O, great mystery! What is the blood of purification? As I believe, some souls remain in the blood of their contamination, others in *the blood of their purification*. To remain is to rest, as one does after some labor. Such remaining [argues for] a certain security. The blood is sin, brothers,

*Ps 50:16

about which David says, *Free me from bloody ones.**
30. At some time or other you have seen or heard about a person—indeed you have been such yourselves, who took delight in your sins and remembered them with a certain pleasure. Many take delight in their vices to the point that they linger [in them], and the more shameful they are, the more glorious they seem to themselves. These are the ones who remain in the blood of their contamination. Of such

it is written, *They rejoice with evildoers and exult in evil things.** Those who *sit in the seats of the wicked*† and teach others to imitate their wickedness and base behavior remain as if secure in the blood of their contamination.

*Prov 2:14
†Ps 1:1

31. There are others who, even though they too have confessed and been converted to God, nevertheless [experience] fear and sorrow and have their sins before their eyes. They say with the prophet, *I know my iniquity, and my sin is always before me.** Before God, they review *all their years, troubled in spirit.** They are like the woman who remains—that is, she perseveres—in the blood of her purification. The remembrance of her sins does not defile but entirely cleanses and purifies her. Secure, she is able to say to God, *You have fully washed me from my iniquity and cleansed me from my sin, but [only] if she truthfully says what follows: Because I know my iniquity.**

*Ps 50:4-5
*Isa 38:15

*Ps 50:4-5

32. Therefore this woman, who *has borne a male offspring* and is cleansed in the manner we have described above, *remains in the blood of her purification. She does not touch any seed, or enter into the sanctuary.** What is this all about? Just as *no one is good but God alone,** because in comparison with God no one is good, no one is holy except God alone, because in comparison with God, no one is holy. For however long she is in the blood of her purification, that is, for however long she must remember her sins, this woman is prohibited from touching grain. This means that she is prohibited from thrusting herself forward to know and investigate divinity. For this is the touch of the body; it is both rational and intellectual.

*Lev 12:2-4
*Luke 18:19

33. There are others who, as soon as they have left the world, begin to wish to scrutinize profound things; they want to understand something of the sacrament of the body and blood of the Lord, or of

baptism, or, as I have said above, of divinity, as if by reason. To do so is to wish to touch every grain, that is, to investigate all the more profound mysteries. The woman* is restrained from such audacity, especially in her first conversion, when she must remain in the blood of her purification, that is, when she properly has compunction for her sins and is purged by this purification.

*i.e., of whom we are speaking

34. *Let her not enter into the sanctuary.** The sanctuary is where secret things are discussed. That is why the prophet says, *Until I enter into the sanctuary of God and understand the new things about them.** Indeed, wishing to know why the same things happen to both good and evil people alike in this life, he says, *This is hard work for me until I enter into the sanctuary of God,* etc.* One who pours out her soul above herself enters into the sanctuary of God and passes *into the place of the wonderful tabernacle up to the very house of God.** By a certain power of contemplation she is carried away to the throne of God,* where she sees the invisible and hears the ineffable.

*Lev 12:4

*Ps 72:17

*Ps 72:16-17

*Ps 41:5

*2 Cor 12:4; 5:10

35. At any rate, she is not capable of this, this woman who newly gave birth, that is, the soul converted to God only a little while before. Such a soul must still consider her own sins more than the divine purity. However, when she gets to the thirty-third day, she may enter with offerings. It seems to me that in this number we can understand both the perfection of work and the perfection of faith. Thirty is a multiple of the number ten, which signifies the perfection of works because of the commandments, and the number three, which signifies the perfection of faith because of the holy Trinity, to which our entire faith returns.*

*Ps-Bede, In Lev 12 (PL 91:346C)

36. Therefore this soul, recently converted, first hastens to do good works and to believe firmly, to

pluck all heretical suspicions from her heart. Otherwise she will not be able to touch holy things, that is,
to touch them by reason or intellect, because unless
she believes, she does not understand;[4]* nor will she
be able to enter the sanctuary, because faith and work
constitute the road to the sanctuary. Now let us hear
with what kind of offerings she ought to enter: *Let
her bring a spotless lamb for a holocaust or a pigeon
or turtledove for sin.* *

37. Who is this lamb? It is not our task to explain
to you why the law required the immolation of the
lamb. To be sure, it signified the future immolation
of that devout, meek, and innocent lamb* to whom
you daily cry out, *Lamb of God, who take away the
sins of the world,* have mercy on us.† Therefore, let
the one who wishes to enter into the sanctuary of
God and touch holy things offer this Lamb. But how
do we offer this Lamb? This is the Lamb whom *God
has made wisdom and justice and sanctification and
redemption for us.* * Therefore the one who can offer
wisdom, justice, sanctification, and redemption to
God, the one who without doubt offers this Lamb,
is the one who imitates the Lamb.

38. Such a one can enter into the sanctuary, probe
the secrets, and touch holy things with the touch of
the mind. But you say to me, "I see that someone can
be just, wise, and sanctified before God and can thus
offer to God wisdom, justice, and sanctification, but I
do not see in what way he can offer redemption." So
listen to John the apostle: *Just as Christ has laid down
his life for us, so we ought to lay down our lives for the
brothers.* * If therefore you can die for your brother, if,
by your word and teaching, you can also rescue *those*

*Isa 7:9

*Lev 12:6

*Aelred, S 3.39
(CCCM 2A:36),
Gen Angl (PL
195:716B)
†John 1:29

*1 Cor 1:30

*1 John 3:16

---

[4] This clause echoes Anselm of Canterbury's dictum, *credo ut
intelligere.*

*Prov 24:11

*being led to death,** that is, bring back to true life those who are dead in spirit, you have offered redemption.

39. But who among us, brothers, can meet the requirements for offering this Lamb? Let us not grow sad. For the divine word consoles our poverty. Read the Law: *If one cannot afford a lamb, let her offer two turtledoves or two pigeons, one as a holocaust and the

*Lev 12:8

*other for a sin-offering.** This is the offering that was offered for our Lord in the temple today. But why was a lamb not offered? Perhaps it was not necessary to search for a lamb because the true Lamb was already being offered to the Father, the Lamb that was the type? There is another very beautiful reason that the holy fathers discuss, namely, that because he was made a poor man for us, he preferred to choose the

*2 Cor 8:9;
Bede, In Lc
1.2 (CCCL
120:63), Hom
1.18 (CCCL
122:129)

offering of the poor.*

40. I am still amazed by one thing in the words of the gospel. Already in the law it was said that an offering ought to be made for the woman herself so that she could be fully cleansed. Nevertheless the gospel says, *They gave according to the custom of the

*Luke 2:24; Ant
and Resp for the
Feast of the Pu-
rification (Hes-
bert 3:4104;
4:7307, 7406)

*law for him a pair of turtledoves or two pigeons.** What then? Do we say that the evangelist is lying? Absolutely not. Perhaps he wishes to reveal to us by these words that the most Blessed Mary does not stand in need of purification. But what then? Does her son need it? He certainly does need it, but only if you understand in what way he needs it.

41. If seated now in heaven he needs bread, drink, garments, and hospitality, do you wonder that established on earth he needs an offering? In what manner does he need bread and similar things? If you need them and you are his members, then he truly needs them. He says just this in Judgment: *When you have done it to one of these, the least of mine, you have done

*Matt 25:40

*it to me.** Because his members as a whole needed

this offering, he needed it, and because he has been made that offering for us, it has certainly been made for him. His mother did not need it, because she was purified. He needed it because not all of his members were yet purified.

42. So, brothers, if any soul—perhaps we are that soul—that *has borne male offspring* and fulfilled *the days of purification* as we have described above is so poor that she cannot offer that Lamb—as already interpreted—*let her offer two turtledoves or two pigeons, one as holocaust and the other as a sin offering.* *In these two kinds of birds, a great mystery is entrusted to us. But because we have already spoken for a long time, we cannot fully investigate these birds. Nevertheless we will briefly explain that the pigeon shows us how we ought to behave openly with our brothers, the turtledove how we ought to behave in secret before God. For the pigeon lives in society, the turtledove in the desert.*

*Lev 12:8

43. Because it would take a long time to say all that may be said about these birds, let us see three things about the nature of the dove. It is without gall, it chooses the best grain, and it is in flocks, that is, it usually flies in a large group.* We ought to preserve these three things, spiritually understood, among our brothers. For all who live in community ought to be without gall, that is, to be on guard lest any bitterness show in their words, deeds, exclamations, or responses. Whatever they do ought rather to have a taste of charity or indicate some interior sweetness.

*Bede, In Lc
1.2 (CCCL
120:64), Hom
1.18 (CCCL
122:130)

*Aelred, S
67.23 (CCCM
2B:187)

44. They ought also to choose the best grain. There are some who when they see that another has grown lax through negligence or childishness wish to imitate him. When corrected for their negligence, they immediately say, "Does not so-and-so do the same?" These are not the doves of God; they do not

offer a dove and therefore cannot enter into the sanctuary. Those who imitate the dove choose the better
grain, that is, they imitate with great zeal those in
the community who behave better, more maturely.

45. They ought also to fly in a flock, that is, they
ought to live communally, in the company of others.*
Those who love always to be singular, never seek to be
with others, and try always to act according to their
own will do not fly in a flock. But the one who always
holds fast to the company of others and tries as much
as he can to follow the orderly arrangements of the
community, he flies in a flock. These three qualities
render us *without reproach before others*.*

46. Let us see three qualities in the turtledove
that render us *without reproach before* God. That the
dove dwells in solitude signifies a total contempt for
the glories of the world, the same as we ought to have
in the depths of our heart where God alone sees. That
the dove wishes never to have but one mate signifies
the pure love that we ought to have for our spouse,
the Lord Jesus Christ. As a consequence, we must
never associate with an adulterous devil through any
vice. That the dove is thus a chaste bird signifies that
we ought to avoid all allurements of the flesh and the
hidden filthiness that God alone can see.*

47. If therefore we offer these birds in such a way
and, like them, give forth a sigh as our song, we will
without doubt enter into the sanctuary and begin to
touch sacred things with a certain sweetness of mind.
Those things, to be sure, are preserved for us in the
future through our Lord Jesus Christ, to whom be
honor and glory forever. Amen.

*Bede, In Lc
1.2 (CCSL
120:64), Hom
1.18 (CCSL
122:130); Au-
gustine, S 64.4
(PL 38:426)

*1 Thess 2:10;
3:13; Rom 12:17

*Jerome, Adu
Jov 1.30 (PL
23:252B);
Bede, Hom
1.18 (CCSL
122:130);
Gregory the
Great, Mo
32.3, 4 (CCSL
143B:1629)

Sermon 34

For the Purification of Saint Mary

1. When I reflect on the holy fathers who went before us and think about their life, the love they bore for God, and their fervor in good works, I am greatly embarrassed that we are just now so wretched.* I am plainly confounded,[1] seeing among us such tepidity and idleness that it seems to me we fulfill what the Lord said in the gospel: *Because iquity abounds, the charity of many grows cold.** 2. Truly, brothers, the charity of many does grow cold in this time. The majority of those who begin to serve our Lord either begin tepidly or, if they begin with fervor, remain fervent for a very short time. We see many who go back to the vices they had abandoned or, as if strengthened by the grace of God, progress to the point where they seem to be somewhat peaceful about their sins of the flesh—sins that I and even worldly people consider the most disgusting sins possible, worthy of damnation. They become sure of themselves, as if it were no longer necessary for them to labor very much in good exercises as they did at first. And thus they are tepid and lazy; they are averse to fasts, abhor vigils, and give little weight to manual labor.

3. Therefore, and for the most part by the just judgment of God, they continue until they begin to

*Bernard, SC 2.1 (SBOp 1:8); Matt 5:12; Eccl 1:10
*Matt 24:12

---

[1] The Latin is *confundar*. Here it is given its stronger meaning, indicating a condition beyond embarrassment. See S 30n3.

be buffeted by the very sins that they thought they had previously conquered. What seemed at first to be easy for them is made wholly difficult. And rightly! For greatly are those deceived who consider that they need not carry on their physical exercises, however long they live in this mortal body. For God's sake! Why do we not meditate on the apostles, martyrs, and other saints who preserved the fervor they felt at the beginning till the last moment before death? But that we may be the more embarrassed, let us think about those who came before the birth of our Lord.

4. They had never seen him in the flesh, never heard his sweet voice in the gospel, never seen his passion, and nevertheless they loved him so fervently that they were able to do almost nothing else than meditate on him. Wretched as we are, have we gained any ground on them, we who have seen what they had not seen and have heard what they had not heard?* Certainly we have. Daily we see and hear, we discern the cross of Christ; daily we contemplate afresh the passion of Christ, daily the body and blood of Christ is offered before us and for us, daily we hear the gospel of Christ.*

5. But if we do not intend [to hear it] for our edification, let us hear to our shame what the gospel today narrates for us of a certain holy man who saw nothing of all this yet nevertheless fervently loved it all. *There was a man in Jerusalem whose name was Simeon,* it says.* He was one of those about whom the Lord said to his disciples, *Many kings and just men wished to see what you see;* but he was not among those about whom Jesus added, *but they did not see.* For, to be sure, this man greatly wished to see, that is, to see Christ, and because he greatly wished for it, he greatly desired it; because he greatly desired it, he greatly prayed for it, namely, that he might see Christ, and therefore he received it.*

*Luke 10:24

*Aelred, S
26.3 (CCCM
2A:210)

*Luke 2:25

*Luke 10:24;
Matt 13:17

*Luke 2:28

6. Truly just was he, this holy Simeon, truly a king. At that time, proud Herod resided in his palace while this old man lamented, perhaps in some corner of the temple. Nevertheless, Herod was a most worthless servant while the latter was without a doubt a true king. The former because of his pride and greed was not able to rule himself; he did not know how. The latter ruled himself well because he preserved the members of his body in holiness. Therefore the former was the servant of his vices; the latter, the king of all his bodily members.* 7. For this reason was it said so beautifully of him in the gospel, *There was a man in Jerusalem.*† Clearly, he ought justly to be called a man. For he was living the way it is proper for a man to live, a man created *in the image of God.** For those who do not want to preserve human dignity may be compared to the *senseless beasts*† and behave like them.‡ Perhaps that is why he was living in Jerusalem, so that he might keep vigil there and pray there and await that day with tears there, there in the temple of God. *And that man was just and fearful.*#

8. O beloved brothers, if only we might wish to imitate this old man! Oh, if only we knew how to be men ourselves and understood that we are created *in the image and likeness of God!** What belongs to this dignity, brothers of mine? To be sure, we humans are made of two natures. We have a body; we have a soul. In the nature of our body we are like beasts, for the image and likeness of God is not in our body. Rather, it is in our soul that we are made to the image and likeness of God. Let each one see if he lives according to what makes for the image and likeness of God or according to what makes for the likeness of a beast. Let each see, I say, whether he cares more for that which sustains the body or for that which should sustain the soul.

*Aelred, SS 1.16, 28.10–12 (CCCM 2A:6, 231–32)
†Luke 2:25
*Gen 1:27; Aelred, S 41.22 (CCCM 2A:329)
†Ps 48:13, 21
‡Aelred, S 49.3 (CCCM 2B:22–23), Anima 2:20, Spec car 1:2.6 (CCCM 1:713, 15)
#Luke 2:25

*Gen 1:26; 5:1

9. For the beasts care for nothing else than that which fills their belly, and with a full belly they rest. They seek for nothing except that which belongs to the body. [Imagine] the one who lives thus, therefore, who thinks of nothing else but his belly all day long or of how he can be at leisure, of how he can be sated or at rest. What was said of Saint Simeon cannot be said of him, at any rate, namely, that he was a man. No, he is rather a cow or a pig like those the prophet called out to: *Hear me*, he said, *you fat cows.** Of course, by these words he does not call irrational cows to listen to him, but those who, with the morals of cows, think of nothing other than their stomachs. He does not wish to call them beef or bulls, but cows. By living a soft life, they have lost whatever is virile in their humanity and are justly called by a feminine, not a masculine, name.

10. In truth one who considers his dignity already cultivates, nourishes, and feeds that part of himself that is in God's image with good thoughts. If such a one does not hesitate to discipline that part of himself that is in the likeness of the beasts by hunger, thirst, vigils, and manual labors, [knowing] their usefulness, he ought to be called a man. Such was Saint Simeon, about whom the evangelist said, *There was a man in Jerusalem.** And if we are like this, brothers, we will certainly dwell in Jerusalem. The name Jerusalem, as you know, means *a vision of peace.** If we are [like Simeon], we shall see peace, and we shall dwell in this vision of peace.

11. For if we disdain carnal pleasures and reject completely the bestial side of our nature, if, as people ought, we expend all our care on our soul, then all those battles among our bodily parts will grow quiet, the vices will cease to war against us, and we will dwell in peace on this earth. For we will be upon

*Amos 4:1

*Luke 2:25

*Jerome, Nom 50 (CCSL 72:121)

our earth, that is, upon our flesh, not under it. It will serve us in the doing of good works and not betray us to vice by its vehemence. 12. O brothers, if we have ever experienced labors and sorrows, temptations and spiritual warfare*—or if we do so now—let us desire the victory so that, having conquered the worst passions that disturb us, we can dwell in peace upon the earth. Let this peace be seen in us so that it may also be said of us that we live in Jerusalem, that is, in the vision of peace.

*Aelred,
Inst incl 30
(CCCM 1:664)

13. *And that man*, it says, *is just and fearful.** How few there are, my brothers, who possess these two virtues together. Lukewarm and wretched, if we think that we have made even some spiritual progress or other, we begin to feel a certain security, and with security comes pride, as I said a little while ago. It is as if we were already beyond fear, and, unless the Lord looks upon us and permits us to be buffeted by vice and tempted, we soon come to the point where we make light of spiritual practices and abandon them. 14. Blessed is that holy Simeon, who was both just and fearful. Blessed are all those who imitate him, who likewise learn to be just in such a way that they never cease to fear. For Scripture says, *Blessed is the man who is always on guard.** Brothers, while we are in this mortal body we are able to sin, and, while we are able, we must always be fearful lest we do sin.

*Luke 2:25

*Prov 28:14

15. Therefore if we are men, if we have begun to dwell in Jerusalem, that is, in that peace of which we have just spoken, understand what I have said: if we have begun. For who feels this peace perfectly within? We ought nevertheless to make progress in this peace and lessen the internal warfare as much as we can. If therefore, as I have said, we live as men, not as cattle, if we begin to dwell already in this vision of peace, if we do not take pride in our progress but are both

just and fearful—as is said of this holy man—then we will be able safely to wait for the consolation of Israel, like the one of whom the evangelist says, *And he was*
Luke 2:25   *waiting for the consolation of Israel.**

16. My brothers, you know well just what that consolation is that holy Simeon was waiting for. It is, brothers, what the Lord had promised through the
Ezek 34:11   prophet: *I will look for my sheep and I will visit them.**
He was waiting for this because he was one of those sheep that belonged to the true Israel. I say that he was waiting for the one who first sent the prophets and patriarchs to come himself to visit and console his sheep. He was waiting for this, he desired this, he begged for this with many tears and prayers. 17. But what, then, are we saying, my brothers? Because he came only once in the flesh, because he has already
Aelred, SS 9.1,   retreated from us in the flesh,* is there nothing to
13.25 (CCCM   meditate upon, nothing to wait for? On the contrary,
2A:70, 110),   brothers: if we imitate this old man, to some degree
Anima 3.5   we too will wait for the consolation of Israel. For we
(CCCM 1:733)   greatly need the one who consoled Israel with his bodily presence to console our Israel spiritually. The
Jerome, Nom   word *Israel* means *the man seeing God.** We seek
13 (CCSL   Israel in our soul, and we both desire and wait for
72:75)   his consolation.

18. You ought to know, beloved brothers, that our soul has a certain faculty through which it can see corporeal things and distinguish among them. The Lord also gave it a certain faculty through which it can judge between good and evil. It has a still higher faculty, capable of seeing God himself. This faculty or natural power of our soul, namely, the intellect, we can call Israel. For the intellect is like the person meant to rule his sensual and carnal appetites. The intellect can be called Israel, that is, the one seeing God, because it was created precisely to see God.

19. This consolation is the spiritual visitation of Christ, by which he deigns to visit our heart in compunction, in prayer, in the revelations of Scripture or of the sacraments.[2] Perfect consolation is the vision of Christ himself. Let us desire this consolation, beloved brothers. Let us ask for this consolation by habitual good behavior, by worthy dealings with others, by continual prayer. But if we experience this desire within us and make progress in it, we must not become proud or attribute such progress to our own merits. For when the evangelist commends Saint Simeon to us by saying that he had all these good qualities, he carefully adds, *And the Holy Spirit was with him.**

*Luke 2:25

20. My brothers, from that Spirit came the desire, the justice, and the fear that [Simeon] had. From that same Spirit comes whatever good we will or desire. Therefore, brothers, let us preserve his presence in our heart and not flee from it by our bad behavior. Let us desire the consolation of Israel so ardently, so fervently, with such perseverance, that we may experience what the evangelist asserts about Saint Simeon: *And he received as a response from the Holy Spirit that he would not see death until he had seen the Christ of the Lord.**

*Luke 2:26

21. My brothers, Simeon received this response from the Holy Spirit whether through a vision, an interior inspiration, or a voice spoken to him: that he would not die in the flesh until he had seen the physical presence of our Lord. Blessed is the one who received this response, blessed the one who deserved to see that sweet vision, blessed the one who prayed

---

[2] Aelred's word is *sacramentorum*. In the context, it seems to mean something other than scriptural interpretations already mentioned. Therefore I have translated it as *sacraments*. See S 33n1 above.

and wept with such perseverance that he deserved
to receive that response. At any rate, if he had not
prayed or begged with all possible fervor, if he had not
devoted himself to good works with perseverance, he
would not have received that response.

22. Brothers, let us also beg and pray and devote
ourselves to good works. For what do we think, beloved brothers? If as soon as our head hurts, as soon
as we are a little bit weary, we succumb to tepidity,
take our rest, and give up the practices by which we
ought to make progress, it must be feared that we
cannot receive this response spiritually. May you not
be burdened by what I tell you, brothers. *For woe*
is me if I do not tell you!*   23. The more I love you,
the more do I desire your perfection and the more
do I fear your defection. For I have not said this as
if I would discredit you in any way. Surely, brothers,
I discredit none of you. Whoever says to me, "I am
weak"—I believe you. But, my brothers, I warn not
only you but myself lest we believe in ourselves too
quickly. Know this, most beloved ones, this flesh is
a deceiver and, unless we take precautions, we fall.

24. I believe that you wish to hear what that spiritual response is that we ought to desire and wait for.
But I fear that I cannot explain to you in any way
what I understand on that point. Nevertheless I will
express it as best I can so that you may at least form
an idea about that which you have perhaps experienced yourselves. For these things that I am about
to put into words for you must not be said to carnal people who have not experienced anything like
them. For they are not able to receive them. For *the*
man who lives in his animal nature does not perceive
*what belongs to the Spirit of God.** But you who are
spiritual, listen to what I tell you if I am able to put
it into words in some way.

*1 Cor 9:16

*1 Cor 2:14

25. If someone among you has been accustomed to frequent prayer, has drunk deeply of frequent meditation, has frequently been visited by compunction, has been moved sometimes either in prayer or meditation so that he can feel in his heart what the apostle says—*The Spirit gives testimony to our spirit that we are children of God**—that one has received a *response from the Holy Spirit that he will not have seen death until he has seen Christ the Lord.** Have you understood this? Yes, certainly, if you have experienced it. And you have understood!*

*Rom 8:16

*Luke 2:26

*Aelred, Oner 21.26 (CCCM 2D:192)

26. But here I will speak more openly about this. Whoever has occasionally burned in this way with the love of God, with some sweet feeling for Jesus Christ, may in his excess of love be seized by such a great sense of security that he seems sure and certain that he will not be damned but saved, and without any ambiguity. Such a one has received the response from the Holy Spirit that he will not see death until he has seen the Christ, that is, that he will not incur the death of his soul until he has seen Christ. Not that he will die after that, but that until he has seen Christ he can fear death. For when he sees Christ, then he will certainly live better.

27. This is the same manner of speaking used when it is said of Christ, *It is proper for him to reign until he puts all his enemies under his feet.** Not because he will not reign thereafter, but because in the interim his enemies will doubt his reign. I say this not because we ought to wait for assurance of our salvation in this life but because the mind can sometimes be so affected by a love and desire for Christ that it feels that it already enjoys such assurance in that hour. For when someone returns from that moment of deep love, he quickly discovers within what he ought to fear for himself. And in order that

*1 Cor 15:25

we may prove what we are saying, let us see both convictions in Paul.

28. For he says, *For I am certain that neither death nor life nor any other creature can separate us from the love of God.** He says otherwise as well: *I chastise my body and bring it under subjection, lest perhaps preaching to others I myself become cast away.** And in another place, he says, *If in some way I may be present at the resurrection of the dead.** If he is certain of his salvation, how can he fear? What you must know is that when he says, *I am certain,** he is feeling how ardently he burned with the love of Christ, a wondrous affection, which undoubtedly he felt very frequently. And having received that assurance by his affection, he returned to himself and found in his own weakness a reason for fear.

29. *Brothers*, whoever has experienced this affection, *let him rejoice* humbly *in the Lord,** and strive that you may be able to experience the same. But what I wish to impress upon you is that you will not be able to come to this point by idleness or pride, but by labors, vigils, fasts, tears, and contrition of heart. Whoever receives this spiritual response, however, can rightly be called Simeon, that is, the one who listens to tears.* For you see that the interpretation of his name teaches us how we ought to arrive at his virtue.

30. But let us see what the evangelist says next concerning this saint: *And he came into the temple in the Spirit.** He was obviously taught by the Holy Spirit, brothers, when he came at that moment into the temple in Jerusalem, where Holy Mary with her most sweet son was about to come. If we wish Christ to come into us, we must prepare a temple for him in our heart, for to such a temple does he willingly come. But in order that we may be led by the Holy

*Rom 8:38

*1 Cor 9:27

*Phil 3:11

*Rom 8:38

*Phil 3:1

*Jerome, Nom 10:65 (CCSL 72:30, 141:25)

*Luke 2:27

Spirit to enter this temple, let us turn toward it by pure affections, let us dwell within it by means of good meditations.

31. *And when his parents led the child Jesus in so that they might fulfill what the Law prescribed.** We do not now wish to speak about this prescription of the Law concerning the purification of the mother after the birth of a child and the oblation of the child himself, because the hour is short and the service longer than usual. For there are many things to be said about these points, and they require their own sermon. However, you know, brothers, that if you follow this old man's regimen as we have described it, you will enter safely into the temple of your heart; there, without a doubt, Jesus will come.

*Luke 2:27

32. But because I hope that you will hold to this way that you have already practiced, of preparing a temple in your heart, I hope that today he will enter into you. Therefore open yourselves up wide and extend the arms of your heart as today holy Simeon opened his bodily arms. May you be worthy to have your spiritual arms filled with Jesus Christ, our Lord, who with the Father and the Holy Spirit lives and reigns forever and ever. Amen.

Sermon 35

For Palm Sunday

1. When I consider the works of our Lord, not those done in the creation of the world, but those that he did for our redemption and that he does daily in restoring us, it seems to me that I ought to exult and cry out in the voice of the prophet, *How magnificent are your works, O Lord! You have done all things in Wisdom.** Our Lord is Wisdom, and therefore he makes all things wisely. He himself is Strength, and therefore he does all things strongly. He himself is Sweetness, and therefore he does all things sweetly. For *Wisdom conquers wickedness, reaching strongly from end to end and arranging all things sweetly.**

*Ps 103:24;
Aelred, S
31.1 (CCCM
2A:250)

*Wis 7:30–8:1

2. This wickedness is from the devil, principle of all the evil that we commit, the cause of all the evil that we suffer because, as Scripture says, *through the envy of the devil death has entered into the world.** Our Lord Jesus Christ conquers the wickedness of the devil wisely, strongly, sweetly. Wisely, for he must hide the mysteries; strongly, for he must restrain his tyrannies; sweetly, for he must put lowly realities before the mind. And see how these three work together and how wisdom, strength, and sweetness mutually temper each other. 3. Without strength, wisdom is weak. Strength without wisdom is blind. Wisdom enables us to know what must be done, but without strength we cannot do it. Again, with strength we can do what must be done, but without wisdom we cannot know how it must be done. Again,

*Wis 2:24

62

wisdom without sweetness is cunning, and sweetness without wisdom is stupid. Similarly, strength without sweetness is rash, and sweetness without strength is lax. Through these two, wisdom and strength, we do our work, but if we do it without sweetness, surely we are discouraged in that work.

4. But our Lord, just as he does all things in wisdom and disposes all things in strength, so in himself he rests sweetly.* Wisdom, strength, and sweetness make up *the triple cord that is difficult to break*,† the cord with which our Lord Jesus *tied that strong man with a strong hand** and tore to pieces *the equipment in which he trusted*.* That cord of our Lord is the opposite of the triple cord with which the wickedness of the devil tied up our first parent. And therefore it was necessary that Wisdom conquer wickedness and that one cord tear apart the other.

5. Consider the three cords by which the devil conquered the first parent. Notice: first he attracted the man, then he tied him up, and finally he knocked him down. He attracted him by the cord of carnal appetite; he tied him with the cord of habit; he knocked him down with the cord of bitterness. Don't you recognize these cords? Are they not the ones you lament every day, for which every day you cry, *The bonds of sins have surrounded me*?* Have you not often felt how these chains are broken? Have you not then exulted and said, *You have broken my chains*?*

6. These are the cords with which the Philistines wished to bind Samson. But as long as he preserved his hair unharmed, he easily broke them. Afterward, however, when the harlot cut his hair, he was tied up immediately by these cords.* The great Philistine wished to tie our Samson by these same cords: *If you are the Son of God, speak and these stones will become bread*.* He wanted to attract him by the cord of carnal

*Aelred, S 61.5 (CCCM 2B:140)
†Eccl 4:12
*Matt 12:29

*Luke 11:22; Jerome, Nom 68 (CCSL 72L:145)

*Ps 118:61

*Ps 115:16

*Judg 16:4-21

*Matt 4:3

appetite, but the true Samson broke that cord and ran him through with the sword of Sacred Scripture: *It is written, not by bread alone does one live, but by every word of God.** He did not give his hair over to a harlot, as did the other Samson.

*Matt 4:3;
Aelred, S
61.9 (CCCM
2B:141)

7. We wish to investigate at greater length and with careful distinctions what Samson's hair might be. We ought to do this willingly, since we may hope for a useful result: namely, to learn that we ought not fear those cords of the spiritual Philistines as long as we preserve that hair. Hair is produced by the head and can be cut without pain; nevertheless it adorns the head and protects it from heat and cold.* Understand: just as our exterior man has diverse members—feet, hands, stomach, head—so too the interior man has its members. But the exterior man is our body, and therefore its members are corporeal. Our interior man however is spiritual, and therefore its members are spiritual.

*Aelred, S 3.20
(CCCM 2A:31)

8. These members of the perfect soul are described in the Canticle of Canticles. There it is also said of the head and the hair: *Your head is like Mt. Carmel, the hair of your head like the purple garment of a king, secured by pins. You have wounded my heart, my sister spouse, by one hair on your neck.** The head of the soul is the mind, which is the seat of reason. From it, the vital force proceeds through all the members of the soul. From this head, hair is produced, and sometimes it is appropriate to shave it if we wish to cross over to the embrace of Booz, like Rahab the harlot.* At other times, hair grows that we ought to sustain and preserve and burn up as a sacrifice to the Lord.*

*Song 7:5; 4:9

*Josh 6:25

*Num 6:18

9. If the soul that does not yet belong to the people of Israel wishes to cross over to the embrace of the true Israelite, he ought certainly to shave his hair.* Similarly, the one who is leprous cannot be

*Deut 21:10-12

made clean unless he shaves his head.* But he who   *Judg 13:5
is the true *Nazirite of the Lord* ought to sustain his
hair, and *holy will he be who lets his hair grow.** Such   *Num 6:5
was Samson before he grew accustomed to resting in
the bosom of the harlot.* Consider carefully these   *Judg 16:19
differences. The law prescribed that if any woman
had been captured in battle by an Israelite man, she
had to cut her hair and cut off her fingernails if she
wished to change sides and marry him.* Now see why.   *Deut 21:10-12

10. As we have said, the head of the soul is the
mind, which is the seat of reason. From it are produced thoughts, as if they were the hair of the head.
See how appropriate this comparison is. Consider the
number of the individual hairs, how they grow and
are cut without our feeling it. Who can count all of
his thoughts? Who can feel them as they come and
go? But as many individual hairs as the head produces,
just as many are the thoughts produced by the heart,
of which there are some that ought to be sustained
and some that ought to be cut off. And hear how the
Lord himself described these hairs: *Evil thoughts proceed from the heart*, he said, *adulteries, fornications,
murders and blasphemies.** Who does not see that   *Matt 15:19;
Mark 7:21-22
such hairs must be cut off?

11. Sometimes he goes to war, *the true Israelite in
whom there is no guile,** *who has* certainly *committed   *John 1:47
no sin, in whose mouth there is found no guile.** *From   *1 Pet 2:22
his mouth*, rather, *comes forth a long sword, sharp on
both sides*, as described in the Apocalypse.* That is   *Rev 2:12
the sword of which the apostle says, *The word of God
is living and effective, able to penetrate better than any
two-edged sword.** With this sword, he attacks his   *Heb 4:12
enemy, pierces him through, wounds and kills him.
He attacks by preaching, he pierces him through by
accusing him, he wounds him by pouring out his love,
he kills him by destroying whatever evil lives on.

*Ps 33:9;
1 Pet 2:3

12. It is from among such people that he takes a wife, a tender and delicate soul. He wishes that she go over into the embrace of charity, to the sweetness of a delightful intimacy; he wants her to be his spouse and *taste how sweet the Lord is*.* But without a doubt she is not worthy to be married to such a true Israelite unless she rejects those hairs that she nourished among the enemies of the Lord—that is, the thoughts with which she delighted herself among unclean men and spirits—and rids herself of useless works. Likewise that soul that is leprous, stinking, and filthy with the bloody waste of willfulness cannot be fully cleansed from this passion unless she first cuts off those filthy thoughts that set her on fire and shook her deeply by their filth.

*Judg 13:5;
16:17; 13:4
†Deut 32:32

*Hos 1:2

13. But the one who is *the Nazirite of the Lord*, first of all, is not a woman but a man; then he is a *Nazirite*, that is, *one consecrated to the Lord*, who not only does not eat anything *unclean* but does not even touch it.* He drinks no *wine from the vine of the Sodomites*; neither does he eat *grapes of gall*† or a cluster of grapes of bitterness. This one *meditates on the law of the Lord day and night*, his *thoughts* on *judgments*.* He sustains his hair and saves it, namely, those holy, good, and useful thoughts that proceed from his mind, especially those seven hairs by which his strength is preserved.

14. Hairs are produced from our head in the front, in the back, on top, and on each side. Consider how this may be. Some things are in front of us, some behind us, some things around us, some above us. Before us are future things, after us, the past. Above us are divine realities, around us, the present reality. From these things certain thoughts are produced in the heart of him who is the true Nazirite, that is, the one flowering forth in virtues.* There are especially

*Jerome, Nom
62 (CCSL
72:137)

seven thoughts that preserve him in spiritual strength
so that the wicked Philistines, that is, unclean spirits,
may not harm him or bind him with those cords of
which we spoke a little while ago.

15. From the future, this Nazirite always has in
his heart two kinds of thoughts: one kind is derived
from the fear of punishments, the other from the
desire for rewards. Again, about the past, there are
two kinds: one from the remembrance of the evils
that he has done, the other from the memory of the
many benefits that God showed him. From the first
is born a certain shame, arousing in him hatred of
self; from the other a certain piety stimulating him
to an affection for the Lord God. Perhaps this is what
the spouse in the Canticle speaks about: *You have
wounded my heart, my sister spouse,* etc.* *Song 4:9

16. Again, about the present realities, there arise
two kinds: how small are all of the present realities
in comparison with the future and how briefly [they
endure].* Again, of divine realities only one thing *Aelred, Oner
can be considered. For whatever we consider about 21.26 (CCCM
God ought to conclude with his unity. Otherwise, we 2D:195)
are in error. If we consider wisdom, power, strength,
providence, goodness, or other like qualities, all these
things are one in God. For *the Father* and the Son *and
the Holy Spirit are one.** *1 John 5:7;
John 10:30;
17. These are the seven hairs that it behooves our 17:21-22
Nazirite to preserve diligently; then undoubtedly he
will be protected from the bonds of sins. For who could
ensnare with any cord of sin the one who always keeps
in his memory eternal punishments, eternal rewards,
his own evils and the benefits of God, the vileness of
temporal things, the brevity of mortal life, and above
all the undivided unity of the Trinity? Let him take
such care that he forms no habit of sleeping in the
bosom of the harlot. This harlot is carnal affection.

*Ezek 16:25;
Jerome, In
Ez 4:16 (CCSL
75:181)
*Aelred, Spir
amic 1.39
(CCCM 1:295)

18. The true harlot is the one who spreads her legs apart[1] for all those going by.* She at once desires whatever she sees to be beautiful, whatever she thinks pleasurable, whatever tastes flavorful, whatever smells sweet, whatever melodies she hears.* At once she surrenders; at once she offers herself, at once she prepares her embrace and her bosom so that she may receive the soul tired out by the labors of this world or temptations. No sooner does the spirit, like a man, betray itself to this harlot than she allows him no rest day or night.

19. Woe to the miserable person who lays his head in her bosom that he might sleep there! Immediately she brings the barber, that is, the devil, who first cuts off his hair, that is, he robs him of all his good thoughts and leaves him bald. Then he ties him up with the cord of sensuality, he binds him with the cord of depraved custom, he attaches *iniquity to him with the cord of vanity.** Then he takes out his eyes that he may know neither God nor himself but walk in circles on the mill of the world and be among those of whom it is written, *The impious walk in circles.**

*Isa 5:18;
Aelred, S
62.7 (CCCM
2B:147)
*Ps 11:9

20. In this way did the malice of the devil conquer the human person. First he attracted him with the cord of sensuality: *Taste*, he said, *and you will be like God.** Afterward he tied him with the cord of evil habits. Then he scourged him with the cord of damnation. But the Lord freed him from evil sensuality by the wisdom of his doctrine, he untied him from evil habits by the taste of his sweetness, he redeemed him from eternal damnation by the strength of his passion.

*Gen 3:5

21. Perhaps the ass that the Lord had untied and brought to him today was tied by these cords. Yes, indeed, that ass so bound designates human nature

---

[1] The Latin reads *she spreads her feet apart.*

that was tied in this way. But the Lord sent his disciples and untied him that they might lead him to Jesus. For this purpose the patriarchs were sent, for this the prophets, and for this afterward the apostles were sent, that this ass might be untied and led to our Lord and thus fully freed. For he could not be fully freed before the one came who conquered the malice of the devil, the one who *reached from end to end strongly and arranged all things sweetly.** *Wis 7:30–8:1

22. One end was the initial damnation of Adam; the other end, his perfect redemption. From this end to that, the wisdom of God stretches out strongly and disposes all things sweetly. Through this whole time the wisdom of God punished human beings for transgression; nevertheless, with wondrous benevolence God arranged what was fitting for salvation. The law and the sacrifices were given to that end, and for that reason there were also the prophets, miracles, divine oracles, and symbolic actions.

23. But, beloved brothers, because Christ, the author of sweetness himself, has come and already untied the ass—that is, human nature—from the bonds of the devil and sits upon him, let us follow our Lord with praise, exultation, flowers of virtue, and palms of victory. Let us say to him, *Blessed is he who comes in the name of the Lord, hosanna in the highest!** Let *Mark 11:10
us not cease to follow in his footsteps until he brings us into Jerusalem, not the earthly city that kills the righteous and the prophets,* but the heavenly Jeru- *Matt 23:27
salem, our mother, that receives all the saints into eternal blessedness. May our Lord himself lead us there, Jesus Christ, who with the Father and the Holy Spirit lives and reigns, God, forever and ever. Amen.

Sermon 36

For Holy Week

1. **O**ur Lord Jesus Christ worked for our salvation not in one way only but in many. Because his mercy provided for our redemption, he accomplished it in such a way that he might be an example for us. Behold, my brothers, how at this time you call to mind our redemption; therefore pay diligent attention not only to the redemption itself but also to both the manner by which redemption was accomplished and the place in which it was done. The manner of redemption is the passion of Christ; the place, outside the city.* You must know, then, that from this redemption and the manner of accomplishing it, we receive both a way of living and the right location that we must choose in order to live in this way.

2. Let us accept now the way of living that comes from this cross of Jesus. Do I say a way of living or of dying? Certainly both of living and of dying: of dying to the world, of living for God; of dying to vices, and of living in virtues; of dying to the flesh, of living, however, in the Spirit. Therefore in the cross of Christ there is death, and in the cross of Christ there is life. There, the death of death and the life of life. There, the death of sins and the life of virtues. There, the death of the flesh and the life of the spirit. Why, however, did God choose this kind of death? Because

of both the divine mystery[1] itself and the example [to be given]. Then, too, because our illness was such that the remedy should fit it in this way.

3. It was certainly fitting that we who had fallen through the wood would rise up through the wood. Fitting that he who conquered through the wood would himself be conquered through it. Fitting that we who chose the fruit of death from the wood would be given the fruit of life from the wood. And because we fell from the stability of this most beautiful earth into the *great and spacious sea,** it is fitting that wood be prepared for us by which we would cross over that sea. For no one can cross the sea without wood, nor this world without the cross.*

4. Let us now say something of the hidden meaning* of the cross. One who dies on the cross is not on the earth but above the earth; furthermore, the members [of the body] are not cut off but stretched out. They are so stretched out in width and in length that the crucified is extended in four directions, so that he seems to enfold the four parts of the world and to take possession of heaven and earth at the same time. When the cross is erect, the head is toward heaven, the feet are stretched toward earth, and the outstretched arms are positioned between heaven and earth. If the crucified is laid on the earth, one part [of his body] is toward the east, another toward the west, the third toward the south, the fourth toward the north.

*Ps 103:25

*Aelred, S 22.2, 3 (CCCM 2A:176)
**mysterium*

---

[1] The Latin *mysterium* defies precise English translation. It suggests the presence of the divine reality in sacred actions and is connected to the development of the word *sacramentum*. It also contains the idea that the external words and works of the Lord always have a deeper, divine significance. Because it continues to be used with its medieval implications in theological circles today, I have used the English cognate here but have attempted to nuance it appropriately.

5. Therefore do you see how Christ chose this kind of death as full of some divine meaning or other? The apostle explains it openly. Saying, *He humbled himself, being made obedient even to death, death on the cross,* he then proclaims the meaning: *Because of this, God exalted him and gave him the name that is above every name, that at the name of Jesus every knee should bow, in heaven, on earth, and in the depths.** Because he was about to take possession of heaven and earth through the cross, he was placed on the cross as if he embraced heaven and earth. 6. Since in truth his death has already taken place not on the earth but above the earth, what can it mean except that, raised up as we are from the earth through his blessed passion, we taste *what is above,* not those *things on earth?** The fact that he died with arms outstretched is a sign of his great loving-kindness. Just as a hen gathers her chicks under her wing and defends them from a persistent raptor, so he, clasping us with maternal affection under the wings of his grace, makes us completely secure against the attack of heinous spirits.*

We have briefly discussed the divine mystery of the cross; now we will speak of the way it is an example of dying or living. 7. First we are taught by this example not *to fear those who kill the body, because they cannot kill the soul.** Then we are taught to be extremely courageous, brave enough to die for our own advantage as he did for the advantage of another. After that, let us contemplate in the cross a kind of example of good works. There are to be sure four dimensions in the cross, namely, length, width, height, and depth. There is width in the extension of the arms, length in the extension of the whole body; there is height in the title placed upon it, and depth in the positioning of the cross itself.

*Phil 2:8-10

*Col 3:2

*see Luke 13:34

*Matt 10:28

8. The width signifies charity; the psalmist describes it, saying, although *I have seen the limit of all fulfillment, your commandment is exceedingly wide.** For what is this width except the charity that embraces all, loves all, excludes not even enemies from the bosom of its affection? Charity is wide because every other precept is woven into it; it perfects all things. Therefore he says, *I have seen the limit of all fulfillment,* that is, I have understood the increase and summit of all perfection. Where? *Your commandment is exceedingly wide,* he says. In this wide commandment is the summit of all perfection. *Your commandment is exceedingly wide,* he says, that is, it exceeds measure, not because it might encompass more than it ought but because it ought not to be confined within limits. Thus the Scripture says, *Love the Lord your God with your whole heart, with your whole soul, with all your strength.**

*Ps 118:96

*Deut 6:5; Mark 12:30

9. Height signifies our hope, which we ought not to place in earthly and transitory things but in heavenly realities. For this reason the title was placed on the top of the cross; it is a mark of kingly status that signifies that we hope to reign with Christ in the future. As the Lord says, *Come, blessed of my Father, receive the kingdom that has been prepared for you from the beginning of the world.** Further, the bottom of the cross, not seen because it was fixed in the earth, signifies the fear we ought always to have of the hidden judgments of God. Perchance we know what we are now, but we are totally ignorant of how we shall be in the future. But because time produces nothing permanent in all these things, there is the length of the cross, signifying perseverance to us in these things.

*Matt 25:34

10. Here we are speaking about a way of living. What do we say about a way of dying? Listen powerfully to the apostle: *You know,* he says, *that our old*

*Rom 6:6

man was crucified with him, that the body of sin might be destroyed, that we might not serve sin.* This verse describes a happy kind of dying. There is something of the old man in us, something that belongs to the old life; let it be crucified and then let it die. All our vices and evil habits belong to the old life. Let us now see how all of them ought to be crucified.

11. Anger rises up; it persuades us to say what we ought not to say: that belongs to the old man. Therefore let it be crucified. How? Receive the nails of the precepts of God and thus nail down this old man so that he cannot move. Consider firmly what the Lord says: *Everyone who is angry with his brother, it will be a matter for judgment. And who said, You fool, etc. And who said, Raca, it will be a matter for* *Matt 5:22 *the fire of Gehenna.** Do you see what kind of nails [these are]? Who is it who cannot crucify his tongue with these nails so that it cannot be moved?

12. Those who are angry in their heart deserve judgment thereby, perhaps both temporal and eternal judgment (the latter perhaps because of cause, intention, manner, or person concerned). Who, then, [motivated by] this fear, would not control their anger, as if by some key, as if they crucified it? If the one who is not only angry against his brother in his heart but also gives vent to his anger through some words, even insignificant words, of his mouth, that is a thing for which he ought to be judged in council. [The question is] not whether he must be damned for it, for surely he ought to be damned, but by which kind of punishment. Who then would not restrain if he could even the movement of his face because of this consideration? Finally, if someone openly speaks a violent reproach to his brother, calling him a fool, in truth he is already brought to eternal punishment. Who then would not, because of this threat, lock up his tongue as if by a certain key so that it not be moved?

13. Appetite rises up, urging a person to *offer his members to sin as weapons of iniquity.** Let that one return immediately to the divine commands; let him hear the apostle saying that *God will judge fornicators and adulterers** and that the unclean *cannot obtain the kingdom of God.** With these commands like so many keys, he will crucify and mortify his members *that are on the earth.**

14. To put it briefly, just as the crucified people cannot move their hands, feet, or other members, so a person who wishes to die in order to live confines and restrains all his members from evil acts through the fear and precepts of God. For all [bodily members of the old man] must be held fast on the cross until they die. The apostle also says this: *That the sinful body may be destroyed,** that is, that all the disorder like a mass of sin must be destroyed so that it cannot move in us. Let these things about the manner and example of the passion of the Lord be sufficient. Now we must say something about the place, as we have proposed.

15. The place in which he was crucified is *outside the city.** For thus the apostle says: *In order that Jesus might sanctify the people through his blood, he died outside the gate.** And immediately explaining why this might be, he adds, *Let us therefore go to him outside the camp bearing his reproach.** What does it mean to go outside the camp? It means at least to bear his reproach. Hear how [Scripture explains it]: *I am the reproach of men and the most abject of the people.** My brothers, *let none deceive himself.** We cannot have it both ways; we cannot love the glory of the world and also bear the reproach of Christ. We cannot embrace both the cross and [worldly] delights. For surely the cross and [worldly] delights are contrary each to the other.

16. Let us go therefore outside the city: for there is the place where we can be crucified with Christ. There is a certain evil city that belongs to this world

*Rom 6:13

*Heb 13:4
*Gal 5:21;
Eph 5:5

*Col 3:5

*Rom 6:6

*Acts 7:58;
Luke 4:29

*Heb 13:12

*Heb 13:13

*Ps 21:7

*1 Cor 3:18

and this present time: all its joy, all its delight, all its happiness are to be found in the present. There one loves honors, riches, [worldly] delights, softness, sensuality, vanity, and other like things. It is good, brothers, to go out from this city and enter the one in which bitterness, reproaches, and tribulations are to be and where one may hope for eternal riches, enduring delights, endless joys, and happiness without end.

17. For our example, brothers, our Lord, our leader, our emperor, was ejected from the synagogue outside the city; he was mocked and crucified so that *1 Pet 2:21   we might follow him who preceded us.* *The disciple is not greater than the master. If they call the father of* *Matt 10:24-25   *the family Beelzebub, how much more his servants?** *John 15:18-19   If *the world hated him,** why would you wish to be loved by the world? The world held him in contempt, and you wish to be honored by the world? The very name of the place in which he was crucified conveys this truth. For it is called the place of Calvary, that *John 19:12   is, of the skull.*

18. Therefore whoever wishes to die with Christ, to rise up with Christ, to ascend to heaven with Christ, let them become bald. Let them shave their heads, as the Nazarenes were accustomed to do; let them make of their hair a sacrifice to God, and thus they may be bald. What are these hairs? Some superfluous part of the body. You see therefore what you must do. Cut back everything superfluous and make a grateful offering of it to the Lord so that you have nothing in this world except what is absolutely necessary. Thus the mount of Calvary may be within you, a true mountain of great excellence and great perfection. It is a great perfection, brothers, to seek nothing in this world except what is absolutely necessary, to fulfill what Paul ordains: *Having food and* *1 Tim 6:8;   *clothing, we are content with these.**
Aelred, Oner
26.23 (CCCM
2D:241)

19. Those who act in this way are plainly the sons of Core,* the sons of the bald man. They are sons of the bald who in this season mount the cross while the Jews mock, saying, "Ascend the cross, O bald man; ascend, O bald man." Thus the children mocked Eliseius the prophet,* as a type of the Jews who were mocking Christ and glorying in the fact that he was a bald man.* For they had all shaved their hair because all who clung to their love for and intimacy with him had fled.† In this way let us make progress in this solemn feast so that we wish with all affection to imitate this skull and with him be crowned with glory and honor, the one who at this present moment lives and reigns forever and ever. Amen.

*1 Chr 6:22

*2 Kgs 2:23

*Augustine, En in Ps 46:2 (CCSL 38:529–30)
†Matt 26:56; Aelred, S 62.16 (CCCM 2B:150)

Sermon 37

For the Feast of Saint Benedict

1. **B**rothers, we often celebrate the feasts of the saints, and [this celebration] ought not to be without fruit. It ought to be useful to us in some way; that is the reason such feasts are instituted.* For what do we think? Is there some benefit for those whom we praise and remember? Certainly not, brothers. Let us see, then, for what useful purpose the celebration of these feasts was established. Everyone lives either well or badly, and these celebrations ought to profit both of these categories of people.

*Aelred, SS 1.5, 9.2 (CCCM 2A:4, 70)

2. When we celebrate these festivities, one who lives badly ought to feel both shame and fear. Those who act badly do so because they are weak and unable to resist their desires, or they are malicious, loving evil and hating good. What does the one who sins through infirmity say by way of excuse? "I am weak, the desires of the flesh drive me, I am not able to overcome those appetites that arise in my flesh."

3. Behold, today we celebrate the feast of our holy Father Benedict. What was Saint Benedict? Without a doubt a man like you, like him, like me. His flesh is the same as your flesh. You and he are both of the same material. Why therefore was he able to do what you are not? When but a boy, young and tender, he left the world and fled from his parents. You, however, grown-up, wise, and prudent, you dream of the world and sigh after your parents. If you plead your serious temptations, he, as you know, was tempted

78

even more seriously. Nevertheless he resisted in a manly fashion; you succumb easily.

4. Let those who are like this conceive a great shame because they see that a mere boy seizes the kingdom of heaven *with such violence** while they themselves now seek soft living and delights. Let those who are lukewarm blush when they contemplate the fervor of Saint Benedict. Let the impatient blush when they hear of the patience of Saint Benedict. Let the proud blush when they read of his humility. Let gluttons blush when they contemplate his abstinence.

*Matt 11:12

5. Someone may ask, "But how can I overcome this natural desire?" How did Saint Benedict overcome it? He did what the apostle ordered: *Walk in the Spirit and you will not satisfy the desires of the flesh.** Therefore, my brothers, let us walk in the Spirit; let us not satisfy the desires of the flesh, and they will not overcome us. But what does it mean to walk in the Spirit? It means to live according to the Spirit. We ought to know that the Spirit has her desires and her counsels, and the flesh has its desires and its counsels. As it seems to me, we ought to understand by this—the phrase *to walk in the Spirit*, I mean—not our own spirit but the Holy Spirit who creates good desires in us.

*Gal 5:16

6. About good desires the apostle says, *The fruit of the Spirit is charity, joy, peace,* and others that he adds here. About the desires of the flesh he says, *The works of the flesh are manifestly fornication, uncleanness,* and others that he adds.* It is by the Holy Spirit that we desire charity, chastity, peace, and so forth. It is by the flesh that our heart, constrained by certain pleasures, feels itself drawn to evil desires, to fornication, uncleanness, and other evils. Who has not felt these two kinds of desires within?

*Gal 5:19-21

7. Therefore we need to take counsel about how not to fulfill these bad desires. If the flesh can make us fulfill its desires, then flesh has the victory. If the Spirit causes us to fulfill her desires, then the Spirit has the victory. Therefore flesh gives its counsels in order to draw us to its desires, and the Spirit gives her counsels in order to draw us to her desires. If, however, we follow the counsels of the Spirit, then we walk in the Spirit and do not satisfy the desires of the flesh but rather the desires of the Spirit. If, however, we follow the counsels of the flesh, then we walk in the flesh and do not satisfy the desires of the Spirit but rather fulfill the desires of the flesh.

8. Let us see what is the way of the counsels of the flesh. The desire of the flesh is fornication. In order to turn us over to this desire, the flesh counsels laziness and talkativeness; it counsels us to familiarity and conversations with women. It counsels us to let our eyes wander here and there to take in other sights that we might covet them. Through these [strategies], the desire of the flesh itself has power against us. 9. Again, the desire of the flesh is uncleanness. In order to make us satisfy this desire, [the flesh] counsels us to seek delicate foods so that we may eat to satiation. It counsels us to seek sleep, indolence, soft blankets, and soft clothing. These also betray us to uncleanness. Against this desire of the flesh are the desires of the Spirit, namely, chastity and purity.

10. In order, however, that we not fulfill the desires of the flesh, the Spirit gives counsel that we never be lazy, never wander, never waver, never be profligate in words, but always move toward some good work.* She counsels us to be serious, mature, to love silence and quietness.† She gives counsel that we spurn familiarity and gossip, which customarily feed unclean desires. She gives counsel that we mortify

*Aelred, Oner 28.23 (CCCM 2D:262), Spec car 3.33.79 (CCCM 1:144)
†Aelred, Spec car 1.34.107

the members of our body in abstinence, vigils, and
manual labor, that we have our heart [fixed] in good
meditations, prayers, compunction, and devotion.

(continued)
(CCCM 1:60),
S 21.33 (CCCM
2A:171)

11. Whoever follows the counsel of the flesh
satisfies the desires of the flesh. Whoever follows
the counsels of the Spirit, however, conquers the
desires of the flesh. The desire of the flesh is envy
and laziness. In order that it may lead us to this desire, it counsels someone to follow his own will, to
love familiarity with the high and mighty, and to be
called to the council chamber, to the distribution of
offices, and to the dispositions of the house in which
he dwells. 12. Whoever follows this counsel surely
satisfies the desires of the flesh, because he begins to
envy the one who attains these or seems capable of
attaining them. Against this desire of the flesh is charity, the desire of the Spirit. The counsel of the Spirit,
through which we can overcome flesh and satisfy the
Spirit, is that we love nothing in this world, that we
always seek the good of another rather than our own,
that we beware all those entanglements [of councils
and office]. Therefore, brothers, let us walk in the
Spirit; let us follow the Spirit's counsel.

13. See how Saint Benedict faced a like temptation. From one side, flesh would bring up its desire,
fornication; from the other side, the Spirit would bring
up her desire, chastity. In order that it might lead him
to its desire, the flesh counseled Benedict to go out
into the world, toward I know not what woman. In
order to lead him to her own desire, the Spirit counseled him to cast himself down in thorns and thistles,
and thus to conquer the desire of the flesh through
the pain of the flesh. Between these two desires and
these two counsels he fluctuated for a while, but he
chose the counsel of the Spirit, and thus, walking in
the Spirit, he did not satisfy the desires of the flesh.*

*Gregory
the Great,
Di 2.2 (SCh
260:36–38)

14. Therefore, brothers, whoever has been conquered by the desires of the flesh up to now ought to be greatly ashamed when he considers Blessed Benedict and his strength. Whoever is so wicked a fellow that he has come to love evil itself, let him consider the works and temptations that Saint Benedict endured. He will see that the Lord beats with labors and tribulations the one who has loved and done the good, and he will know what the one who loves evil may expect. As Blessed Peter says, *It is time for judgment to begin in the house of God. And if it begins with us, what will the end be for those who have not obeyed the gospel?** *1 Pet 4:17

15. If those who are in the house of God, those in whom God dwells, do not enter into the Kingdom of heaven except through great tribulations,* where *Acts 14:22 will they be who knowingly offend God daily and nevertheless suffer no annoyances thereby? *If the just man will barely be saved, where will the sinner and impious man appear?** Undoubtedly sinners and the *1 Pet 4:18 impious will hear that terrible voice of the Lord saying, *Depart from me, accursed ones, into the eternal fire prepared by the devil and his angels.** Now you *Matt 25:41 see what profit there is for the unjust, if they wish, if on the feast days of the saints they meditate on their lives and habitual behavior.

16. If any are tepid, let them begin to feel shame and through shame recover genuine warmth of virtue. If any are evil and cold, let them begin to feel fear and through fear climb out of the coldness of evil to the warmth of charity. Likewise through the feasts of the saints, those who are good and live well can make progress in hope and love. For whoever visualizes himself practicing the exercises the saints performed (and through which they came to holiness) can greatly hope to make progress himself through those exercises and so arrive at holiness.*

*Aelred, S
26.4 (CCCM
2A:210–11)

17. Notice that we considered a little while ago how Saint Benedict walked in the Spirit and therefore did not satisfy the desires of the flesh. What he himself did, he taught to others, and the counsel of the Spirit that he followed, without doubt, he recommended to us. What indeed does the whole Rule of Saint Benedict cry out except what the apostle said: *Walk in the spirit and do not satisfy the desires of the flesh?** What are those fasts, those manual labors, those vigils in his Rule except some counsels of the Holy Spirit, through which we can suppress the desires of the flesh and satisfy the desires of the Spirit? There is a great security, brothers, in following the counsel of the Holy Spirit; a great hope appears.

*Gal 5:16

18. There is no doubt but that the Holy Spirit has instituted this Rule through Saint Benedict. Therefore whoever preserves this Rule of Blessed Benedict, who imitates his life, is certain that he follows the counsel of the Holy Spirit. Whoever follows the counsel of the Holy Spirit in truth is certain that he walks in the Spirit. Whoever walks in the Spirit, however, does not satisfy the desires of the flesh. Cannot the one who walks in the Spirit, who tramples on the desires of the flesh, begin to feel great hope that, because he walks in the Spirit, he may arrive where those who do these things are? Therefore, brothers, walk in the Spirit. For the cravings of the flesh are against the Spirit, those of the Spirit against the flesh,* but if you follow the counsel of the Spirit, you will not satisfy the cravings of the flesh.

*Gal 5:17

19. On this feast of our holy Father Benedict, we must consider from how many dangers, how many vices, we are snatched by his teaching and example. We ought to consider this because he lived in this world not only for himself but also for us, and by this consideration we are set afire with love for him who

gave us such a father, such a leader, such a teacher.
We ought to consider the glory that our Lord conferred on him, and, judging by the glory that he has
on earth, we ought to guess how much glory he has
in heaven. This will lead us to love the one who has
prepared such good things for those who serve him,
to love him with our whole heart, and to desire him
with our whole mind.*

*Aelred, S
26.34–37
(CCCM
2A:217–18)

20. Do you see how useful it is that we celebrate
these feast days? Whoever lives badly and considers one who lived well cannot have any excuse for a
bad life; therefore, fearing damnation, such a one is
aroused to penitence. Whichever people truly live
well begin to feel a great hope of salvation because
they consider what degree of glory the one whose
feast day they celebrate reached through such a life.
Because they understand that a human being can do
nothing alone, they begin to love more ardently the
one who has done these things in his servants. With
this intention, brothers, and for this useful purpose,
we celebrate today the feast of our glorious father,
Saint Benedict.

21. For what is Saint Benedict like except a certain
burning piece of wood on the high altar before God?*
What are we like, except pieces of wood cold until
this point, we who do not feel that wonderful fire of
divine love by which he burns? Therefore, brothers,
let us join ourselves to him: let us consider the fervor
of his life and the charity of his heart. From this moment on, let us press upward; from this moment, let
us burn. For we cannot conquer the concupiscence of
the flesh better and more perfectly than if we bring
the fire of charity to bear upon it. For what is that
concupiscence of the flesh against the spirit except
a kind of rust on the natural soul? Therefore let us
take the fire to it.

*Ezek 1:13

22. For no one can be saved except through fire.* But there is the fire of tribulation and the fire of love. Each one of these fires destroys the rust of the soul. David was cleansed through the fire of tribulation, Mary Magdalene through the fire of love. As the Lord says, *many sins have been forgiven her because she has loved much.** In truth, brothers, it seems to me that both were cleansed through the fire of tribulation, both through the fire of love. For in David there was a great power of love, in him who says, *I love you, Lord, my strength.** And there was a great fire of tribulation in the penance of Saint Mary.

23. Therefore, brothers, if we wish to be truly cleansed, we will patiently submit to this fire of tribulation from this point on, and we will burn as much as we can with the fire of love. The fire of tribulation is the beginning; the fire of love, perfection. Through one, we come to the other. For *tribulation works in us to patience, patience to testing, testing to hope. Hope however will not be confounded, because the charity of God is poured forth in our hearts through the Holy Spirit who is given to us.** To this perfection our Lord Jesus Christ deigns to move us, who with the Father and the Holy Spirit lives and reigns, God forever and ever. Amen.

*1 Cor 3:15

*Luke 7:47

*Ps 18:2

*Rom 5:3-5

Sermon 38

For the Annunciation of the Lord

1. It is a shame, brothers, and a total disgrace, if Christians do not love Christ. But because you recognize him better than others do, it is right that you accordingly love him better than others. You remember his benefits often, you are accustomed to hear often of the marvelous love *by which he has loved us;** you also often celebrate the works of his charity in various liturgical offices. Truly all of this ought to work something significant in you; this seed, frequently scattered among you, ought to bear fruit. *Let not the birds*, that is, the demons, *carry it away* from the field of your heart and introduce there instead useless and poisonous thoughts; *let not the summer sun*, that is, the heat of carnal desires, *burn them; let not the thorns*, that is, the sharp points of self-will, *suffocate them.**

*Eph 2:4

*Luke 8:5-7, 11-14

2. Behold, brothers, today we scatter seed in the soil of your hearts, and it is truly seed. For what is today's feast except the seed from which will spring up the entire fruit of your salvation? Today *the grain of wheat dies in the earth, which, after it dies, brings forth much fruit.** The law given by Moses prepared human hearts for the reception of this seed; as the apostle says, *Because of transgressions, the law was put in place, until the promised seed should come.**

*John 12:24-25

*Gal 3:19

3. What does it mean that *the law was put in place because of transgressions*? [It was done] so that human beings might not transgress the will of God. In what way would they transgress the will of God except by

sinning? And what are sins except the thorns and tribulations by which the earth of our heart is choked up
so that it cannot receive that seed? Therefore, brothers,
the law was given and the people were told, *You shall
not kill, you shall not commit adultery, you shall not
steal,* and other similar precepts.* We were told this so   *Exod 20:13-15
that we might uproot these vices from the earth of our
heart and enable it to receive this grain of wheat, which
today *dies in the earth and bears fruit in patience.**   *John 12:24;
                                                                15:2; Luke 8:8
4. Therefore, my brothers, may you receive this
seed and let it not fall *on the roadway.** But first be   *Luke 8:5
on guard lest there be a roadway in your heart where
spiritual birds can fly; rather let it be a desert land,
vacant and dry, because in such soil as this, seed may
be received and not only received but preserved in
the best way. How may we understand *desert, vacant,*
and *dry?* A place where evil spirits may find no refuge
in which to remain, no road to cross over, no water—
that is, no flood of desires—by which to satisfy their
ill-intentioned thirst. What do they thirst for, after
all, except our perdition?*   *Aelred, S
                                                                14.16 (CCCM
5. Such was the heart of that blessed Virgin who   2A:118)
received that seed today, as the gospel narrates: *The
angel Gabriel was sent by God.** You know, brothers,   *Luke 1:26
why the angel was sent by God, namely, so that he
could announce to the virgin that the Lord was about
to be born. But I am considering something marvelous
that I wish to unfold before your charity. After the
gospel says that the angel first saluted Mary, saying
Hail Mary, full of grace, the Lord is with thee, why
does he then say, *the Angel Gabriel was sent from
God?* What do we think, my brothers? Is this God by
whom the angel is sent other than that Lord of whom
the angel says, *The Lord is with thee?*
6. You know, brothers, you must certainly know,
that the works of the Trinity are inseparable.* Whatever   *Anima 2.1,
                                                                24 (CCCM
                                                                1:707, 715)

*Aelred, SS
66.3, 67.5
(CCCM 2B:177,
182)
†Luke 1:26
‡Deut 6:4

the Father does, the Son likewise does.* Truth said this. Therefore, *the angel Gabriel was sent by God.*† *Hear, O Israel: The Lord your God is one God.*‡ He is the very one we adore as Father, Son, and Holy Spirit. *The Angel Gabriel was sent by God.* Brothers, these words, *by God*, must be pronounced with great weight. Now, as often as we read that God delegates angels to be sent, it hardly ever occurs that the phrase *by God* is added. It signals something great to us because it is said here that *the angel Gabriel was sent by God.* By the Father alone? Surely whatever the Father does, the Son does likewise. Therefore the angel was sent also by the Son.

7. And what does the angel say? *The Lord is with you.* Certainly he was announcing the great incarnation of the Son, because the Son alone took flesh, but the whole Trinity made that very flesh. Therefore it is not inappropriate for us to understand here that he said of the Son, *the Lord is with you.* For in the Scriptures our Lord Jesus Christ is customarily called by the more familiar title *Lord.* You see therefore that he himself sent the angel to announce his coming; nevertheless the angel knew that he had come. Why, then, was the angel sent by God? Perhaps so that the Virgin would not be astonished to have conceived if she did not know by what means she had conceived.

8. But for his part the Lord could have manifested his presence to the Virgin Mother not by the sound of his voice but by an internal inspiration, as he speaks to the angels. They do not hear his secrets from outside of themselves but contemplate them *Matt 5:8 *with a clean heart** within the font of Wisdom itself. And without a doubt, this manifestation, this vision, this speech is more excellent than that which may come through angelic creatures, corporeal signs, or the sound of external words. Does it not seem fitting,

brothers, that he should speak to his most beloved mother in the way that is more excellent than others? Why therefore was the angel Gabriel sent by God so that the Virgin would know the counsel of God?

9. I will tell you, I will tell you: it is because of the wonderful mercy of God that encompasses us. Truly the wisdom of God, who created flesh for himself in the womb of the Virgin, could lay bare all the secrets of his plan to his mother by interior inspiration. But how then could it be understood by others, how could it be written about, how could it be preached about? Therefore, the angel Gabriel was sent by God visibly, and he spoke aloud so that the mystery could be written about, preached about, and believed. He who deigned to be incarnate for us sent an angel for us, so that we who were not capable of what was revealed through a hidden inspiration could understand what was to be said.

10. There is another cause for which *an angel was sent by God*. This was so that through the words of the angel to Mary and the words of Mary to the angel, it would be made manifest how great was her humility, how undiminished her virginity, how pure the faith in her heart, and how greatly circumspect she was in her exchange with others. For there is an order in meeting together. Just as a bad angel and a woman in private conversation had bitterly given birth to the perdition of the whole world, so a good angel and a pure woman speak together in a friendly conversation for everyone's salvation.* These are therefore the reasons that *the angel Gabriel was sent by God*.

*Aelred, S 57.1
(CCCM 2B:98)

11. The name Gabriel means *strength*. Do you think, brothers, that he was sent to this office because he was called by this name? I judge rather that this angel was called by such a name because from the moment of his creation, his destiny was clearly to

announce. For God did not need to conceive a new plan for his Son to take flesh; undoubtedly he had foreseen it, had ordained it, from the very creation of the world. And as he had ordained his incarnation, so also he ordained the manner in which it might appropriately take place. 12. However, since it was the proper order of things that an angel be sent to the Virgin to execute this office, one was chosen from among the other angels. The proper name was conferred on him not because of his heavenly citizenship but for our sake, that we might also discern from the very name of the announcing angel who it was that he announced. He is called *strength* because through his ministry the incarnation of the Strength of God was announced.* Therefore, *the angel Gabriel was sent by God.*

13. Where? *Into a town of Galilee.*† Do we think, brothers, that this sweet *fame* arose in Galilee by accident or to no purpose?‡ We do not think this. See *what* a great thing was being done, namely, the joining of God and a man in one person, the reparation of the fallen, the destruction of death, the renovation of life, the restoration of the ruined angels, and the reconciliation of the whole world. When such a great event is beginning, nothing is done without a reason. The place, the time, the order, and, as I have said, every syllable of the words, all are full of sacred meaning. Why, then, was the Lord conceived in the flesh in Galilee?

14. Galilee means *the migration.** Has the Lord, then, been conceived in a migration? Do not begin to think, brothers, that the Lord was conceived only once. To be sure he was conceived in the flesh only once, but he is conceived spiritually every day. He did not wish to be conceived in the flesh except in a migration, because spiritually he is conceived only

*Aelred, S
57.6 (CCCM
2B:100);
Jerome, Nom 64
(CCSL 72:140,
24)
†Luke 1:26
‡Mark 1:28

*Jerome, Nom
64 (CCSL
72:140)

in a migration. Through the conception and birth of
the Lord, the migration of the whole world from the
power of the devil and the entry into the kingdom of
Christ begins. Therefore whoever can migrate from
vice to virtue, from a carnal to a spiritual manner of
life—for that one, the earth can already be called
Galilee, that is, the migration. He begins to build a
town here already, the town of Nazareth. *The angel
Gabriel was sent by God into a town of Galilee the
name of which is Nazareth.*

15. Nazareth means *a flower.** What kind of city
ought to be in our heart that it may be called *a flower?*
Consider that there are three aspects to a flower:
beauty, fragrance, and the beginning of the fruit. Our
heart ought therefore to have these three if we wish
Christ to be conceived there. Your heart has already
been made into Galilee. For you have passed over
from secular to religious life, from riches to poverty,
from pleasures to labors, from possessing too much
to doing without. It only remains for you to build
there the city of Nazareth. Because Nazareth means
a flower, this city must be built of those three that we
have considered in a flower: namely, beauty, fragrance,
and the material of the fruit.

16. If these three are in us, Nazareth will be there
spiritually, and there Christ will be conceived. For
where these three are wanting, Christ is not conceived
in any way. Beauty pertains to chastity, fragrance to
fraternal love, and the hope of fruit to spiritual fervor.
Chastity is the great beauty of the soul. For through
it, dishonor, the stink of inordinate desire, and every
filthiness of the flesh are repelled and excluded. Each
one ought to have this beauty from the beginning of
conversion, because in our conversion, if it be sincere,
Christ is conceived. Each ought also to have fraternal
charity, that he might be tranquil and quiet in the

*Jerome, Nom
62 (CCSL
72:137)

community and all the brothers breathe in the good odor that emanates from him.

17. For the human heart is like a vessel filled with honey or poison. As long as the vessel is closed, no one knows what is contained within. If, however, someone takes off the lid, immediately what is hidden within is known by its odor. Therefore, brothers, as long as a monk is in silence, as long as no one says anything to him, or gives an order or opportunity for him to show something of his inner self, it is as if the vessel is closed. What is hidden inside is not known. Let him come to a colloquy,[1] or let him be ordered to do something that is possibly difficult, or let him be corrected for some exterior deed—then the vessel is opened. Then one smells the good or bad odor.

18. If he is then made angry or gives himself up to slander and murmuring, if also, when he has the opportunity, he gives himself over to buffoonery, laughter, and similar frivolities, he does not offer a good odor to his brothers. He does not have fraternal charity in his vessel but, rather, a weakened will. He has not built Nazareth, and therefore Christ cannot be conceived in him. In contrast, whoever speaks with gravity, responds with humility, obeys with patience— whoever reveals no bitterness in his voice and shows none in his face—it is as if he gives forth the good odor of good ointment from his full vase. He shows that he has fraternal charity and therefore deserves to be loved by all.

19. Because of this charity he ought to have the wherewithal to hope for a great and good fruit. *What is this?** Spiritual fervor, without a doubt. One who

*Exod 16:15

---

[1] I have used the more formal term *colloquy* rather than *conversation* to suggest a situation in which a monk might have the occasion to reveal himself.

is lukewarm, unwilling, and apathetic does not hope for this fruit. If such a person is fervent, then he fervently follows the way of life prescribed for his vocation,[2] he fervently embraces all things; it is in this and because of this that he hopes for great fruit. We ought to have these three from the beginning of our conversion, when Christ ought first to be conceived in us. For if the migration has been made in our soul and Nazareth—that is, the flower of chastity for its beauty, of fraternal charity for its good odor, and of fervor of spirit for its hope of the fruit—has been built . . . .*

*The sermon is incomplete

[2] Aelred uses the Latin phrase *sequitur ordinem suum*. Since the word *ordo* carries ecclesiastical overtones, indicating one's place in the various ranks of the structured church, and since Aelred uses the *suum* to indicate a personal position within these ranks, I have tried, in translation, to capture both an orderly way of life and the monk's special position in the church.

Sermon 39

For the Annunciation of the Lord

*Gen 2:8

*Aelred, SS
10.1, 24.1
(CCCM 2A:81,
190)

1. **I**n *the beginning the Lord God planted a garden of delight, in which he placed the man he had created.** Although you understand the excellence and joy of this feast day sufficiently, nevertheless it is right that we say something more about it.* I myself know that whatever we can or do say about it, it is too little to express this mystery. For who could say how great is the mercy God showed us on this day, that mercy by which he always willed to bring about the redemption of humankind? Who could say to what heights God led humanity on this day, that high point to which human nature is raised up[1] to make one person with God? Who could say what profound plan God revealed on this day, the plan in which the Virgin conceived a man without the knowledge of a man? These realities are great, so entirely great that we could in no way perceive them. Nevertheless, we ought certainly to embrace that mercy sweetly, to honor fully with great respect the height that humanity reached, and to contemplate that profound plan with great affection.

---

[1] In its original literal meaning, the word *suscipio* described the act by which a putative father raised a newborn infant from the ground, thereby acknowledging paternity. Here Aelred uses the word to describe that action by which God, in the mystery of the incarnation, elevates human nature by uniting it to the divine word to make one divine person. In such a context, the resonance of the literal meaning provides great emotional power. Since Cicero uses this word in its original meaning, Aelred could well have known it.

2. O how blessed is our Lady, who was chosen for such a work above all other creatures and provided for it. Consider how great is the excellence of the one who was made queen and lady above all creatures, how great is her cleanness and purity, her in whom the Holy Spirit made for himself such a special small dwelling. Without a doubt, she herself is that paradise of delights whom the Lord chose for himself from the beginning; she herself is the paradise that God the Father prepared for the new Adam. Into this paradise the serpent could not enter because the old Adam did not dwell in it. But if it pleases you, let us see just what that [first] Paradise was, the riches and delights that were there, and thus let us make a comparison between this Paradise and that one.

3. Paradise is a certain land very far from the one in which we now are and is called Eden, that is, "sensual pleasure."* It is a beautiful place, full of the most beautiful trees and every physical beauty. And a certain fountain rises up in Paradise that waters the trees, flowers, and the like that are in it.† Already in truth you can see how rightly the heart of the holy Virgin ought to be called Paradise, a land undoubtedly fertile. For if it must be said that good land bears *fruit thirty-fold*, that better land bears *fruit sixty-fold*, and that the best land bears fruit a *hundred-fold*,* how even better than best is that land that bore these three kinds of fruit?

4. Thirty-fold fruit pertains to conjugal chastity, which raises the children it bears and educates them in *the teachings of the Lord.** Sixty-fold fruit belongs to the chastity of widows, whose fruits are *prayers, offerings*, and good works.* Hundred-fold fruit signifies virginity, because this is the perfect number, and no state in life is as perfect as virginity. Those who are accustomed to count on their fingers number all

*Jerome, Nom 5 (CCSL 72:65); Ambrose, De para 1.4, 3.12 (CCSL 321:266, 272)
†Gen 2:6

*Matt 13:8

*Eph 6:4

*1 Tim 2:1; 5:5, 9

the numbers up to a hundred on their left hand and,
when they get to a hundred, change over to their
*Jerome, Adv
Jov 1:3 (PL
23:213B–214A)
right.* By the left hand is signified this present life; by
the right hand, that life that they will receive, those
who will be seated on the right hand on the Day of
Judgment. Virginity, however, belongs more to that
life in which *they will not marry nor take wives but*
*Luke 20:36;
Matt 22:30
*be like the angels of God.**

5. Now you perceive how fertile is this, our paradise, in which there are all kinds of fruit. It is a great
wonder that in other [holy people] none of these
kinds of fruit may be found together. Because if one is
married, she is not a widow or virgin; if widowed, she
will be neither married nor a virgin; if she is a virgin,
she will not be a mother or a widow, but in Blessed
Mary there were all these simultaneously. She is herself mother, virgin, and widow. Whose mother is she?
*Luke 1:42
What kind of *fruit is from her womb?** Who can say
it worthily? The mother of her God, the mother of
her Lord, the mother of her Creator. If, however, you
would consider the fruit of her widowhood, think on
those tears next to the cross of her son, those prayers
and sighs after his ascension. Concerning the fruit of
her virginity, it is better to keep silent than to speak,
because we can say nothing worthily on that point.
For who could say how many virgins remained virgin
through her example or through what manner of pains
and torments they preserved their virginity?

6. It is sufficiently clear how fertile this, our
paradise, is. For what were those virtues in her soul
except, so to speak, spiritual trees? Such a tree is
patience: how firmly it stands, how sweet the fruit
it bears. So too are piety, humility, and the other virtues. Now let us see of what character is the fountain
that irrigates that paradise. The Lord says in a certain
place, *Whoever drinks the water that I give, it will be*

*in him as a fountain of water bubbling up for eternal
life.** Who doubts but that he gave this water to his   *John 4:13-14
most beloved mother?

7. But what sort of water is this? Let us hear what
he says in another place: *If you are thirsty, come and
drink, and from your womb the living waters will
flow.** And if we are perhaps uncertain as to what   *John 7:37-38
this water may be, the evangelist adds, *This he said
concerning the Spirit whom those believing in him were
about to receive.** You see now that the water that   *John 7:39
the Lord gives is the Holy Spirit. And who drinks
the water that I give, he says, it will be in him like a
fountain of water bubbling up into eternal life. That
is the fountain that irrigates this paradise. Today this
water is clearly given to her, a fountain remaining
in her perpetually, as the angel said: *The Holy Spirit
will come upon you, and the power of the most High
will overshadow you.** This fountain fills the spiritual   *Luke 1:35
paradise with such abundance that it suffices not just
for her but for the whole world.*   *Aelred, Inst
                                                          incl 29 (CCCM
8. But what does Scripture say concerning that   1:663), S 57.4
fountain that was in Paradise? *It was divided into*   (CCCM 2B:99)
*four springs.** To be sure, four rivers flow out from   *Gen 2:10
this fountain of which we speak; they are the source
and beginning of all spiritual streams. *The name of one
is Phison, which encircles the whole earth of Havilah,
where gold is found as well as precious stones and
lapis lazuli, and the gold of that land is the best.**   *Gen 2:11-12
9. Therefore, brothers, whoever makes of his soul a   Vulg
paradise for God, whoever has received in himself this
life-giving fountain, let him know that from this fountain four rivers immediately rise up. These are the
four virtues, which are the source and beginning of all
other virtues but which no one can have at all unless
the fountain of the Holy Spirit dwells within him.
These are the four virtues: prudence, temperance,

*Ambrose, De
para 3.14 (CSEL
32:1); Aelred, S
55.20 (CCCM
2B:86)

*Prov 21:20

fortitude, and justice. They are the four sources from
which all virtues arise.*

10. The first river, called Phison, signifies prudence. Gold is found in this river, and gold signifies
wisdom. That is why it is written that *a desirable
treasure rests in the mouth of wisdom.** No one can
arrive at wisdom except through prudence. For the
one who does not possess prudence cannot discern
between the wisdom of this world, which is folly, and
the wisdom of Christ, which is true. And thus the one
who does not have prudence is deceived by error and
thinks folly to be wisdom and wisdom, folly.

11. And you, brothers, who are seeking the true
wisdom that is Christ, you must have prudence so
that you can know when *Satan transforms himself
into an angel of light.** Those who do not have this
prudence are often led astray and, thinking to do well,
do badly, because they fall into vice that appears to
them as virtue. This is why Blessed Mary, when she
heard the salutation of the angel, *was troubled and
wondered what kind of salutation this was.** Prudent
virgin that she was, she knew that Satan, as we have
said before, transforms himself into an angel of light,
and therefore she did not wish to acquiesce in those
sweet words until she knew for certain that the angel
was from God.

*2 Cor 11:14

*Luke 1:29

12. In that river is found a precious stone that has
the appearance of fire and signifies charity. For without prudence, no one can arrive at charity. Through
prudence one knows what one ought to love and what
not. There is also a green *lapis lazuli,** which signifies
the freshness that we ought to have in our life. We
ought not to languish or wither away but be always as
if in the fresh springtime of our holy manner of life.

13. *And the name of the second river is Gheon,
which encircles the land of Ethiopia.** Right next to

*Gen 1:12

*Gen 2:13

this river, the law was given to the children of Israel when they were in Egypt, bidding them observe the Passover and eat the lamb with girt loins. This river signifies temperance, by which people curb their vices and appetites so that they might worthily *eat the Passover* of the Lord.* Because of this, it is well said to circle the land of Ethiopia. Why Ethiopia, if it does not wash the blackness of Ethiopia away? The land of Ethiopia is our flesh, which from a kind of natural concupiscence in our members is as if it were black and discolored. It is necessary that this river of temperance circle our land, wash it clean, and carry this natural blackness away, making it shine with the splendor of chastity.

*Luke 22:15; Ambrose, De para 3.15–16 (CSEL 32 1:274–76)

14. It is not necessary to show how perfect this virtue was in Blessed Mary. For through this virtue, she had conquered all the allurements of the body, controlled the concupiscence of the eyes, and restrained the movement of all the members of her body under the rule of holiness. We have just heard read the gospel that says, *Having come into her the angel said: Hail, Mary, full of grace, the Lord is with thee.** That gospel sufficiently reveals her virtue, for by saying that the angel had come *into her*, it shows that she had hidden herself away in a certain secret place from all exterior occupation and from all allurements.*

*Luke 1:28

*Aelred, SS 9.18, 58.21 (CCCM 2A:74, 2B:112)

15. *The third river is called the Tigris; it rushes against the Assyrians.*† This river is intensely swift and fierce and signifies fortitude, the virtue that is strong and fierce and that nothing can resist. It is through this virtue that martyrs overcame fire, iron instruments of torture, wild beasts, and all sorts of torments. Rightly is it said to rush against the Assyrians, that is, *against evil spirits.** For this virtue resists all the clever machinations of the devil. Solomon

†Gen 2:14; Ambrose, De para 3.17 (CSEL 32 1:276)

*Eph 6:12

foresaw this virtue in Blessed Mary when he asked,
*Who can find a valiant woman?** The Lord* was speaking about her fortitude when he *said to the serpent: I
will put enmity between you and the woman.**

16. *The fourth river is the Euphrates,** which in
Latin means *fertility* or *abundance of fruits.** This
river signifies justice, in which undoubtedly there is a
great abundance of fruit. For justice is that by which
one returns to all people what is their due.* Through
this virtue people return fear to their lords, obedience to their superiors, and charity to their brothers.
Through this virtue one is unyielding to vices, honest
toward other people, humble with companions, and
beneficent to those in need.* And see how perfectly
this virtue was in Blessed Mary. It was justice that
caused the humility of her response: *Behold the handmaid of the Lord.*† It was justice that caused the sweet
visitation she deigned to make to one who was her
inferior, that is, Saint Elizabeth.*

17. As well as we could, though not as well as we
ought, we have described the kind of paradise into
which the new Adam entered today. Today, brothers, our Adam,* the Lord Jesus Christ, entered into
this spiritual paradise in order to fight against the
*ancient serpent** that overcame the old Adam. From
this comes this festivity, brothers; from this comes
the joy. Let us not be afraid. For our *joy ought to be
full.** We need not fear that the serpent will seduce
this Adam to evil or entice this woman into sinning.

18. Brothers, if we wish this Adam to dwell in our
heart, let us prepare for him a paradise there. May
the soil of our heart be fertile and fecund, virtues
abounding there as if they were spiritual trees. May
the Spirit be there, a certain unfailing fountain that
waters us with spiritual grace, compunction, devotion,
and every spiritual sweetness. May these four virtues

*Prov 31:10

*Gen 3:14-15

*Gen 2:14

*Ambrose, De
para 3.18 (CSEL
32 1:276)

*Cicero, De
fini bon et mal
5.23; Aelred, S
31.27 (CCCM
2A:257)

*Aelred, S
31.27 (CCCM
2A:257); Spec
car 1.33.96
(CCCM 1:56)
†Luke 1:38

*Aelred, S
58.26 (CCCM
2B:114)

*1 Cor 15:45

*Rev 12:7-9;
20:2

*John 16:24

be there, like four rivers, which wash us from the filth
of vices and make us pure and unspotted so that we
may be ready for the embrace of our Lord.

19. Here let us beware lest we touch *the tree of the
knowledge of good and evil.** The tree of the knowl-   *Gen 2:9, 17
edge of good and evil in our soul is self-will. The Lord
prohibits us from touching that tree. For those who
love to touch that tree must fear being expelled from
this paradise;* that is, they must fear lest they lose   *Gen 3:23-24
the spiritual sweetness and virtues that they have. For
our Lord wishes us to submit and follow his will, not
our own, like the one who comes not to do his own
will but *the will of him who sent* him.*   *John 6:38

20. Therefore, brothers, let us beg our Lord Jesus
Christ himself that through the intercession of his
most sweet mother he might build this paradise in us,
that we might cross over from this paradise to the one
in which he himself lives with the Father and the Holy
Spirit and where God reigns forever and ever. Amen.

Sermon 40

For the Day of Easter

1. **A**s our Lord Jesus Christ deigned to be born for us, to be tempted for us, to be beaten for us, and to die for us, so also did he deign to rise for us. Yet his temptation, scourging, death, and entombment belong to our redemption; his resurrection strengthens our hope. For by the former he paid for us what we owed, by the latter he showed us what to hope for. Just as by the death of his flesh he freed our soul from death, so by the scourging he took he freed us from the scourging of our soul. For without a doubt, we were in the scourging and we were in the tomb, and whatever he himself suffered in the body is what we have suffered in the soul.

2. Let us now consider the order of the passion and thereby arrive at the glory of the resurrection. First Judas betrayed him with a kiss, and afterward he was tied and led toward Caiphas; then his face was veiled and he was beaten with fists. After this he was led to Pilate. From Pilate he was sent to Herod and from Herod again to Pilate. At last, whipped, spat upon, crowned with thorns, and having drunk bitter gall, he was crucified and buried. He suffered all these things in his body because we had suffered all these things in our soul, and thus by the passion of his body, he liberated us from the spiritual passion of our soul.

3. For we were betrayed by a kind of deceitful kiss. Listen to the kiss: *Taste and you will be like gods.** This kiss had sweetness and delight on the out-

*Gen 3:5;
Aelred, SS
35.20, 49.6,

side, but poison lay concealed within. After this kiss, we were bound. How? Without a doubt by our own inordinate desires. For as Scripture says, *the woman, seeing that the tree was beautiful to see and sweet to eat, took and ate from it.** At first, therefore, she was as if seduced by a kind of sweet kiss—certainly it tasted sweet in the soul to be *like gods.** But afterward she was so bound by her *inordinate desires** that she could not restrain herself, even if she hoped for no other advantage from it.

4. Thus bound, humanity was handed over to Caiphas, that is, to cupidity, whose servants and attendants *veiled his face.** For who are the servants of cupidity except the vices themselves, which veiled humans' face so that they could not perceive the true sun, true justice? They were veiled as if by two bonds, that of ignorance and that of inordinate desire. For these two make a human being totally blind. At length they were beaten with fists—and what causes these blows if not sadness and error? 5. Clearly human pride took a beating: the first blow was the error that the human person perversely coveted in place of divine knowledge, and the second, sadness, because that error did not satisfy him. For if he had been punished by error alone, he would not be much cured, because he would secretly enjoy his error. Rightly was he told, *prophesy.** What is there to say to one who was thrown out of Paradise and worn out by error and tribulations except *Prophesy*? Otherwise you mock and reproach him and say, "Show now the divinity that you so perversely coveted."

6. After this he was handed over to Pilate, that is, to the devil, prince of this world. In a marvelous way the demons themselves ridiculed the human species in their midst when a man being mocked by one devil was handed over to another for mockery. We find

(continued)
59.29 (CCCM
2A:292, 2B:23,
127)

*Gen 3:6; 2:9

*Gen 3:5
*Jas 1:14

*Luke 22:64;
Mark 14:65

*Luke 23:64

*Dan 10:20

in Daniel that another devil was the prince of the kingdom of the Greeks, and still another that of the Persians.* Truly, who can say in how many ways the human species has already been scourged? 7. What more? Mocked by unclean spirits, people have been led to such perversity that they enjoy it when they do evil and exult *in the worst things.** This is not to be wondered at. He was thus crowned with thorns, because his glory and honor were in his own iniquities. For the more prone he was to perverse and crude things, and the more he leaned toward all vices, the more he appeared to glory in himself. But he was not able to escape from the bitter draft; gall was mixed in either his food or his drink. All the sweet things of his life were mixed with the bitter and the painful.*

*Prov 2:14

*Aelred, SS
11.1–14, 44.3,
62. 2 (CCCM
2A:89–92, 345;
2B:144)

8. At last he died and was buried. He died because he was separated from God. He was buried because he had reached a point of contempt for God. Even if people are vicious and sinful, inasmuch as they confess and recognize their sin, they are not punished by death. When, however, they advance so far in their evil life that they neither recognize nor confess their sin, then they are dead from deep within. As it is written, *confession is as far from death as if it were not.** Moreover, if they go so far as to be oblivious of God and hold him in contempt, even despairing of his mercy, they are buried. About this point Scripture says, *the impious man when he came into the depths of evil was contemptuous.**

*Sir 17:26 Vulg

*Prov 18:3 Vulg

9. Because we had suffered all of these things in the soul, our Lord Jesus Christ wished to suffer all of them in his body and, through the sufferings of his body, to cure the sufferings of our soul. And because Christ suffered all these things for us, so that he then rose from the dead, without a doubt where he rose we too have risen. *If therefore you have risen with Christ,*

*seek the things that are above.** But we must see to
whom the apostle spoke: undoubtedly to those who
have risen with Christ. And who are those who rise
with Christ except those who share in all that Christ
has suffered?

*Col 3:1

10. I am silent about other people, but I wonder
whether the apostle speaks especially to you—to you
who have certainly suffered many temptations, as if
you were being beaten with Christ; to you who die
with Christ through daily labors and tribulations; to
you who are, as it were, buried in this cloister and in
this silence for Christ. You who suffer all these things,
not in your soul against Christ, but in your body for
Christ, you have certainly risen with Christ. For now,
you have risen in the soul; afterward you will arise in
your body. Therefore *seek the things that are above.**
But since not all those who share in this resurrection
are the same in perfection, let us briefly see how all
ought to seek the things that are above, all according
to their own way.

*Col 3:1

11. For there are the beginners, the advanced,
and the perfect. The beginners are those newly come
from the world, who are a great deal plagued by carnal desires. The advanced, those who have already
gained a certain calm in regard to their carnal vices,
are vehemently attacked by spiritual vices. We call
fornication, extravagance, gluttony, drunkenness, and
others of this kind carnal vices. These are customarily
the first to assail people when they leave the world.
Afterward, spiritual vices like pride and vainglory immediately begin to assail the one who starts advancing
in virtue.

12. It is necessary therefore that beginners, who
have already risen with Christ through confession,
seek the things that are above. The virtues are above,
the vices below. Above is chastity, which belongs to

heaven; below, lust, which belongs to hell. Above is moderation, which raises the mind to heavenly things; below is gluttony, which drives the mind toward the belly. Below is the love of temporal things, beautiful garments, and the like, for example; above is contempt for the world, because the one who condemns the world is superior to the world, while the one who *loves the world** surrenders to the world.

*1 John 2:15

13. Therefore those who are beginning ought always to despise those things that are below, namely, vice and sin, and always keep before their eyes the virtues, which are above. Those, however, who have already made progress in virtues and are tempted by pride, let them see why they take pride in themselves. If it is because of the virtues that they have, let them know that these are already no longer virtues. For proud virtues are not virtues.* Let them understand that those who are proud are from below, not from above. 14. For if they grow proud, whether because they seek some praise from another or because they glory in themselves, each attitude is from below, not above, because both are of human origin. Therefore, if they have already risen with Christ, let them seek the things that are above, not by faith alone but also by good works, so that they may fulfill what the apostle said: *He who glories, let him glory in the Lord.**

*Aelred, Spir amic 1.63 (CCCM 1:300)

*1 Cor 1:31

15. Those who have already made such progress in perfection that after the mortification of all their vices they also think humbly of themselves in good and perfect works, let them truly ascend higher and seek the things that are above. Let nothing suffice for them except always to aim higher. Let them begin to raise their hearts from every earthly thought, close their eyes to all visible reality, and be zealous to surmount every creature so that they may see *the king in his beauty.**

*Isa 33:17; Aelred, Anima 3.9 (CCCM 1:735)

16. Therefore let beginners strive toward virtue; those making progress, toward true humility; the perfect, toward contemplation. Thus what the apostle said will be fulfilled: *If you have risen with Christ, seek the things that are above.* And he adds, *Savor the things that are above, not the things on earth.** What is the difference between seeking something and savoring it? A very great difference, brothers. Would that those who seek the truth would all savor the truth itself! As we have read, all the children of Israel collected the manna, but not all of them savored the manna in the same way.* How many people today seek the truth and find it! Nevertheless they do not savor the truth itself when they have found it.

17. Many read the gospels and the prophets; indeed they also diligently seek the truth of opinions, but they do not savor them when they find them. For if they savored that internal sweetness of truth to be had in Scripture, they would not live in such a perverse and morally abandoned way as they do. Many also say, "O, if only I knew where I could serve Christ in an honest life, no one would deter me from it." Yet after they have found the pure, evangelical life, many have no taste for it but have, rather, a greater taste for the sweetness of the world.

18. Thus the children of Israel greatly desired to leave Egypt, to throw off the service of the Pharaoh, and to sacrifice in solitude to God.* But afterward, when they had come into solitude, when they had seen the miracles and signs that the Lord did in their sight, when they had tasted the heavenly manna, they began to have a greater taste for the food of Egypt. They desired *the flesh pots** and felt distaste for the manna. Therefore, brothers, it is not enough if you have sought the truth, it is not enough if you have sought and found the things that are above; also savor the things that are above.

*Col 3:2

*Wis 16:20-21

*Exod 8:23

*Exod 16:3;
Num 11:4-6

19. Savor, that is, frequently meditate upon and thoroughly consider how great is the excellence of truth, what security there is in purity, what happiness in the service of God. Contemplate this and reject whatever your flesh might say to you. Follow reason and weigh carefully how great are the things of heaven and eternity measured against those sweet temporal and earthly things. By frequent meditation, acquire not only the knowledge of the truth, as many evil people have done, but also the taste for the truth. 20. If thus we have arisen and raised ourselves above the earth in mind, intention, zeal, and love, then we will truly share in the resurrection of the Lord. But since our effort is too little unless his grace also assists us, let us pray for his most gentle mercy. May he give us both *the intention* and [the power to] *bring it to completion by his own good will*,* Jesus Christ our Lord, who lives and rules as God, forever and ever. Amen.

*Phil 2:13

Sermon 41

For the Day of Easter

1. Today we can say, "Abundance has made us poor, not an abundance of understanding but of subject matter."* For who is adequate to speak of the glory, sweetness, and joy of this day? Who knows what to talk about? *This is the day that the Lord has made: let us rejoice and be glad in it.** This day feeds the hungry and heals the sick; it is life and resurrection for the dead. The one who is tired can rest on this day. The one who is sick can be cured on this day. The one who is dead can arise on this day. *This is the day that the Lord has made: let us rejoice and be glad in it.*

2. This is the day of eternity, in which the Creator lives eternally. It is the day of creation, in which God has created all things. It is the day of perdition, in which humanity fell into damnation. It is the day of restoration,[1] in which God has redeemed humanity. It is the day of resurrection, in which God has glorified humanity. *And it is the day that the Lord has made.* The day of eternity has no morning; it has no evening.

*Aelred, Spir
amic 1.30
(CCCM 1:294);
Ovid, Meta
3:466

*Ps 117:24

---

[1] Aelred generally follows that Augustinian anthropology according to which God created the first human beings in his three-fold image with the faculties of memory, reason, and will. Sin blurs and damages this image but does not destroy it. Augustine and Aelred speak of redemption as the restoration of the image, according to the person of Jesus, who is himself the image of the Father. The word that Aelred uses here is *reparo*, which also carries the meaning "to acquire or procure again." This connects to the Pauline vocabulary of redemption, a buying back. I have chosen to translate it as *restore*, in various forms, to make the Augustinian heritage more clear.

*Aelred, Spec
car 1.19.54
(CCCM
1:34–35)

It has no beginning or end.* The day of eternity is
God himself, who has no beginning or end, who does
not vary or change but is always in the same condition,
to which point the prophet says, *You are always the*

*Ps 101:28

*same and the years do not decrease you.**

3. It is a day of mutability in which God created
all things, because he made all things out of nothing,
and all things are mutable. That day has a morning

*Aelred, Spec
car 1.19.54
(CCCM 1:35)

and an evening, that is, a beginning and an end.* For
there is no doubt that time began, and it has been
written about the end of the world, *Because time*

*Rev 10:6

*will be no more.** But that day does not have a night,
because had all things remained in the same state in
which they were created, there would be no terrible
night of eternal damnation nor any exterior darkness
into which are sent those who, of their own accord,

*Matt 22:13

rush into interior darkness.*

4. It is the day of perdition that humanity created
for itself when it sinned, to which Saint Job says, *Let*

*Job 3:3

*the day on which you were born perish.** For on that
day we all were born, because we all come forth from
the mass of perdition. On that day we also will die,
because *through one man sin entered into this world,
and through sin, death; and thus death entered into*

*Rom 5:12

*all men.** That day has a morning and an evening. The
morning is the day of a person's birth; the evening,
his death. From the beginning of his birth up to the
end of his life, he experiences the pain of perdition
that he first incurred. As Scripture says, *There is a
heavy yoke upon all the sons of Adam, from the day
they went forth from their mother's womb until the*

*Sir 40:1

*day they returned into the womb of the mother of all.**

5. Whoever does not follow that sun, which on
this day was born for us, will after that day undoubtedly rush into that unhappy night in which there is
the darkness of evil, the exterior darkness. Therefore

the saint, who knew how to recognize the evil and misery of that day and how to fear the unhappiness of that night, justly desired that the day of perdition perish, because he longed for the day of human restoration to arise. That is the day on which the Lord was made, *when the word was made flesh and dwelt among us.** This day had a morning in the Lord's nativity, a noontime in the display of his miracles, an evening in his passion.

*John 1:14

6. It had a morning, when *the light rises on the righteous in the darkness, the Lord merciful and compassionate.** It had a noontime when that sun was thus exalted and power went out from him and healed all,† when his fame went through the whole region,‡ when the light of his holy preaching illuminated the darkness of human consciences, when he sent fire upon the earth* so that cold human hearts might be set aflame and say, *Was not our heart burning within us?** That day had an evening when the Lord himself hung on the cross, when the sun was darkened,* when the disciples fled, leaving him,* when the words of the psalmist were fulfilled: *In the evening, weeping enters in.**

*Pss 111:4; 110:4
†Luke 6:19
‡Luke 4:14

*Luke 12:49
*Luke 24:32

*Luke 23:45
*Matt 26:53
*Ps 29:6

7. But this weeping does not remain for long, because immediately *joy breaks out in the morning,** when the day of glorification begins because of the sublime resurrection of the Lord. *This is the day that the Lord has made: let us rejoice and be glad in it.** Just as God redeemed humanity on the day of restoration, so he glorified humanity on the day of resurrection. For we await the fullness of glory on the day of our own resurrection, when this mortal [flesh] shall put on immortality and corruption, incorruption,* when the word that was written shall come to pass: *death will be swallowed up in victory.**

*Ps 29:6

*Ps 117:24

*1 Cor 15:53, 50

*1 Cor 15:54

8. And what will this glory be like? When our body has perfect health, perfect beauty, perfect

strength, and perfect alacrity, when there will be no labor, no fatigue, no temptation, no persecution, no fear that something must be suffered or lost, no greed for something that must be possessed. And what [more] will I say? Nothing will be against our will, nothing against our joy, nothing against our desire, but everything whatsoever there is *in heaven, on earth, in the sea** and in the depths of the earth, whatever we will see, whatever we will experience, whatever we will hear—every single thing that exists will be totally for the increase of our glory.

*Pss 112:6;
134:6

9. But why do we exert ourselves to express in words what is ineffable? For *eye has not seen, nor has ear heard, nor does it enter into the human heart.** See already, brothers, that the whole of our glory will be in God and from God, in our neighbor and from our neighbor, in us and from us. And both love and vision make up this glory. In a wonderful way, love increases vision and vision love, because as much as we love, that much shall we see, and as much as we see, that much will we love.

*1 Cor 2:9;
Aelred, SS
17.22, 71.13
(CCCM
2A:139, 2B:224)

10. You know already, brothers, and by all means you ought to know, what the apostle said: *They will be two in one flesh; this is a great mystery, it applies to Christ and the church.** And what does this mystery mean? It means at least that Christ and the church are one. If we do not corrupt faith by a bad life, brothers, *we who believe in Christ** are surely the church. As the apostle says, *insofar as we have believed in Christ, we have put on Christ.** But Christ is our Head, and we are his Body. Consider now what kind of joy you ought to have on this day. Today Christ has risen. This is the beginning of our glory. *This is the day that the Lord has made: let us rejoice and be glad in it.*

*Eph 5:31-32;
Gen 2:24

*Gal 2:16

*Gal 3:27

11. This day had a morning when our Lord rose; it will have a noontime when his glory, splendor, and

brightness, which begin today in the Head, are transferred to all the members,* when *our lowly body is
configured to the body of his brightness.*† Then will
he make our *justice shine forth like a light and our
vindication like the noonday.** Then our noontime
will be transferred into the noon of that first day,
the day of eternity, so that it cannot fail or fade into
evening but remains always in its fervor, in its light,
in its brightness, in its sublimity. Then we will sing
in reality what we just now sang in hope: *This is the
day that the Lord has made.*

12. The Lord made this day not alone as an exception to all others, but alone as the most excellent
and luminous of all. For this day is not one of those
seven in which God created the heaven and the earth
but is the eighth day, in which he united heaven and
earth. Those days were changeable, variable, rising in
the east, setting in the west. This day begins today
at some point but never fades; it will increase to the
noontime and then shine out always in its brightness.
And see, brothers, why in Scripture this day is called
the eighth.

13. As you know, brothers, God created all things
in six days; on the seventh, *he rested from all the works
that he had performed.** We do not experience in this
earthly life any more than seven days. These days
always repeat; they hasten through seasons, months,
and years. There are not more days. But how long
will these days last? How long this mutability, this
temporality, this variability? All of this will continue
up to the day of resurrection. Then these seven days
will end, and that one day will succeed these seven.
Therefore that which follows the seven, what ought
it to be called except the eighth? Certainly that day
will not be one of the seven, because in them there
are mutability and variation, rising and setting; in it

*Aelred, Spir
amic 3.134
(CCCM 1:350)
†Phil 3:21
*Ps 36:6

*Gen 2:2

*Aelred, Spec
car 1.33.96; Iesu
2.11 (CCCM
1:56, 258)

there are eternity and stability.* Justly then *this is the day that the Lord has made: let us rejoice and be glad in it.*

14. This day began today, because the resurrection itself began. Therefore, brothers, it is after the seventh day that the Lord himself rose from the dead. For on the sixth day, as you know, the Lord was crucified; on the seventh day, that is, the Saturday, he rested in the sepulcher. After the seventh day, and therefore as on an eighth day, our Lord rose from the dead,* because the one who knows all things before they came to be, even before he created the world, saw how the world had to perish. And he saw how it ought to be restored. Therefore he willed to create the world in a way that would signify the manner in which he wished to restore it.

*Aelred, S 5.7
(CCCM 2A:47)

15. For without a doubt, the Lord did not need the passage of time to create all things, not he *who spoke and they were created;** nevertheless he willed to distinguish the work in a certain way and divide it among the seven days. And although he could in no way be fatigued, he willed nevertheless to rest on the seventh day. Why? Undoubtedly because the manner of creation signified the manner of restoration. Therefore when the Jews calumniated him in the gospel because he violated the Sabbath by healing a sick man on that day, the Lord answered, *My father works up to this moment and now I work.** Does it not seem to you that he openly said, "you have calumniated me because I do not rest on the Sabbath, but as yet the seven days [continue] in which it was right for my father to work, and the eighth day has not yet come in which he ought to rest"?

*Ps 32:9

*John 5:17

16. Now let us consider when God the Father with his Son began not to create but to restore the world. And let us note the six days of its re-creation,

as we read of them in its creation. Let us consider
that the first day is the nativity of the Lord, the second, the institution of the sacraments, the third, his
preaching, the fourth, the choosing of the disciples,
the fifth, the demonstration of miracles, the sixth,
his passion. Thus far, our salvation has been worked
out *in the midst of earth.** Now may it please you to   *Ps 73:12
pay attention to how this second operation fits those
works that he did in the first six days.

17. For on the first day he created the light. What
light? That by which the world, which then was darkened, is illuminated, as it was written: *For the earth
was empty and void, and darkness was upon the face
of abyss.* Therefore *God said: Let there be light. And
there was light.** Do you not see how clearly this work   *Gen 1:2-3
signifies the birth of Christ? For what was this whole
world except empty and void and darkened? But in
the birth of Christ *the people who walked in darkness
saw a great light, a light rose upon those dwelling in the
region of shadows of death.** Thus light was created on   *Isa 9:2; Aelred,
the first day. Clearly it was created. For just as Our   S 9.3, 6 (CCCM
Lord, the Son of God himself, was made wisdom and   2A:70–72)
justice for us, so he was made the light. It also says
that God divided the light from the darkness. This is
a great division, brothers, between light and darkness,
between the old Adam and the new. The former is
darkness; the latter, light.

18. On the second day, God *made the firmament
and divided the waters that were above the firma-
ment and those that were below the firmament.** The   *Gen 1:7
firmament that the Lord made on the second day of
restoration is the excellence of the sacraments, which
the Lord instituted in baptism, in anointing, and in the
reception of his body and blood. *The waters are the
people.** But we who are the waters below, dwelling in   *Rev 17:15
this exile and on this pilgrimage, we are absolutely in

need of submitting to this firmament, that is to say, to the sacraments of Christ. For those holy angels who are the waters above, they are above this firmament. For they are healthy and have no need of medicine.

19. On the third day, *the earth produced green plants bearing seed and trees bearing fruit that contained seeds.** This creation spiritually signifies the preaching of the Lord. For at first the people were like a land empty and without fruit, but when the Lord preached, they immediately brought forth the fruit of penitence, the fruit of good works. *Zacheus was a sterile land, a sinful man, the prince of publicans.** But when the Lord said, "let the earth produce green plants bearing seed," immediately *he gave half of his goods to the poor and, if he defrauded anyone, he repaid them four-fold.** What will I say of that sinful woman? She was a land in darkness up to that point, an empty land, a sterile land. But what fruit of penitence did she produce on the third day! What fragrance came forth from that fruit! Further, *the house was filled with the fragrance of the ointment.**

20. On the fourth day God made the sun, moon, and stars.* God did this spiritually by the choosing of the disciples. There the order of apostles is like the sun, the society of lesser clergy like the moon; there the numerous followers are like stars. They are the lights of the world, as the Lord said: *You are the light of the world.**

21. On the fifth day he created the birds and fish.* The miracles of our Savior can be called the birds because [they suggest] contemplation, the fish because [they suggest] profundity. For whoever wishes to consider well the miracles of the Lord ought to fly with the wings of contemplation so as to know how exalted they are, and to walk down into the depths, as it were, to know how profound they are.*

*Gen 1:12

*2 Kgs 2:19;
Luke 5:8; 9:2

*Luke 19:8

*John 12:3

*Gen 1:16

*Matt 5:14

*Gen 1:21

*Job 38:16

22. On the sixth day, the human person was *created according to the image of God** and, in the passion of the Lord, was reformed in that same image. He has recovered his ancient dignity, because he returned to Paradise, from which he had been expelled.* The Lord [indicates this return], saying to the thief, *This day you will be with me in Paradise.** By this time, the Sabbath followed, and *the Lord rested from all of his labors,** lying down in the tomb until the eighth day, on which he rose from the dead. And *this is the day that the Lord has made: let us rejoice and be glad in it.* Mark this well: there is work for six days, rest on the seventh, and glory on the eighth. Therefore this is more excellent than all other days, more glorious, happier. Justly, *this is the day that the Lord has made.*

23. Understand, brothers, where our exultation and joy ought to be: on the eighth day. Happy are those who exult on this day, happy those who have such a good conscience that not only do they not fear for the eighth day, that is, for the resurrection of the dead, but rather exult in it. But in the meantime, brothers, because we have seen the very resurrection of the Head, let us live as *soberly, justly, and devoutly** as we are able, through humble obedience and sincere love, so that we may truly be as members of his Body. And so let us exult in his resurrection today, so that on that day we deserve also to exult in our own, through the sweet benevolence of the one who with the Father and the Holy Spirit lives and reigns, God, forever and ever. Amen.

*Gen 1:27

*Aelred, S 57.4
(CCCM 2B:99)

*Luke 23:43

*Gen 2:2

*Titus 2:12

Sermon 42

For the Day of Pentecost

1. **B**ehold, I will consummate a new covenant with Jacob, not like the covenant that I gave to his fathers in the day on which I took possession of his hand and led him from the land of Egypt: I will give my laws into their minds and write them on their hearts.* I am compelled to offer something from my limited [resources] concerning the construction of this spiritual tabernacle.* But considering that, for some, this heavenly edifice gleams with wisdom, that it shines with knowledge for others, that it flames with a double ray of charity upon others and glows with angelic chastity upon all, and that a diverse variety of virtues like some collection of different precious stones glows so that a red hue reflects on the face of the one gazing at it—considering all this, I say that I blush with embarrassment lest I obscure the beautiful variety and varied unity of our Joseph's tunic by my words.*

2. But it is not hidden from your charity that often something darker is spread out under the many and precious colors so that the latter may appear brighter by comparison to the other.* Perhaps therefore my sermon will produce at least this much, that, when you happen to draw out sweetness from the spiritual drink provided by a more learned person—for who is not more learned than I?—it may grow sweeter still to the taste in contrast with this confused water that I give you to drink. I have said this in advance so that you do not expect to hear anything great or

*Heb 8:8-9; Jer 31:31-32, 33

*Aelred, S 8.3, 8.8 (CCCM 2A:65, 66)

*Gen 37:3

*Aelred, S 59.19 (CCCM 2B:124), Inst incl 25 (CCCM 1:657)

profound from me or throw in my face the words of
the poet, *The mountains have given birth, a silly little
mouse is born.**

3. Yes, and since the Holy Spirit is called love,
charity, goodness, kindness, and any other name that
can indicate something even sweeter, someone who is
more familiar with his sweetness, accustomed to taste it
more frequently, may speak more worthily of him.* For
who am I that I go on about his excellence on this day,
about what sweetness, consolation, hope, and security
he guarantees us? 4. For what could our Lord Jesus
Christ better offer to us as evidence of his love than
the Holy Spirit, who is the love and unity of the Father
and the Son? Thus he would press upon our minds that
through the unity and charity by which they are one in
essence, we might bring about a certain unity in him and
with him, not by identity of substance but by clinging
to the Spirit. This is according to the apostle: *The one
who clings to the Lord is made one spirit with him.**

5. How could he offer his children a greater benefit from his fatherly compassion than to lighten the
weight of the law, which both we and our fathers
found insupportable? He reduced that law to one
precept and brought it to perfection by pouring his
Holy Spirit into us. In respect to this, he proclaimed
this promise through the prophet: *Behold, I will fulfill
a new covenant with the house of Jacob, not according
to the covenant that I gave to their fathers.* Here obviously two things are to be noted and remembered,
namely, the Old Testament and the New. Although
the Old Testament was still in place, nevertheless the
New was prophesied. He spoke with careful attention. He did not say, "I will send"; he did not say, "I
will give," but *I will fulfill.*

6. For the *Law was given through Moses,** but it
was not fulfilled—*for the law led nothing to perfection.**

**Horace,
Ars Poet 139

**Aelred, S
66.2 (CCCM
2B:177)

**1 Cor 6:17

**John 1:17
**Heb 7:19

*John 1:17

Grace, however *and truth,* contained in the new covenant, are not just given but brought about and fulfilled *through Jesus Christ.** For the perfection of the law is charity. However, *the charity of God has been poured out into our hearts by the Holy Spirit who is given to us.** Charity is preserved through the pouring forth of the Holy Spirit. The practice of charity fulfills the new covenant. *Behold,* he says, *I will fulfill a new covenant with the house of Jacob,* that is, I will show you life brought to fulfillment in the new covenant; this life was not in the old covenant, and I will bring you to fulfillment in the new covenant.

*Rom 5:5

7. Because he gave the new covenant today, we will attend to it a little later by comparing it with the old covenant. Now, however, let us consider very carefully what he said: *I will bring it to fulfillment.* In the birth, passion, and resurrection of Christ, our redemption has been accomplished; in this sending of the Holy Spirit, it has been brought to fulfillment. In that which he bore for us in his humanity, he remade us; in the sending of the Holy Spirit, he perfected us. His way of life on earth is instruction for our life; this sending of the Holy Spirit is the fulfillment of human life.

8. In his infancy he taught humility, and in his childhood, piety; in adolescence, knowledge; in young manhood, strength. In that strength, he fought to the finish, unto death, and by his death he overpowered death. His resurrection followed, in which he revealed the secret of his plan. He ascended into heaven, drawing our understanding toward heavenly things, and today, through the infusion of the Holy Spirit, he gave an understanding of wisdom, the perfection of charity, the fulfillment of the law.

9. In infancy he taught humility, which is born in us through fear of the Lord and confession of sins.

If we listen diligently to him crying out, *Do penance, the kingdom of heaven is approaching,** [it is] as if we were hearing him say, *Let there be light** at the beginning of our re-creation. First he says, *Let there be light,* so that the morning star may arise in our hearts and there may be a division between the light of our new conversion and the darkness of the iniquity we have committed. *And let there be evening,* out of consideration for our weakness, *and morning,** for the beginning of our enlightenment. Thus, out of the spirit of fear of the Lord,* let there come for us *a first day,** like our first blessedness. All this was shown to us by the Lord, first by example in his infancy and afterward by word in his preaching when he said, *Blessed are the poor in spirit*—that is, the humble and God-fearing—*because yours is the kingdom of heaven.**

10. In childhood, he taught piety. What we call *piety* the Greeks call *theosebeian,* that is, the cult of God;† that's why the impious are properly called infidels and strangers to the cult of God.‡ We are instructed in this piety by an investigation of Sacred Scripture, to which the twelve-year-old boy Jesus led us by his example, when he sat in the midst of the elders in the temple, hearing them and asking questions.#1 Therefore *let there be a firmament* for us, according to the command of the divine voice, and let that firmament be called *heaven,** as the prophet describes it, saying, *heaven is spread out like a skin,*† which signifies Sacred Scripture.2 *Let it be in the midst of the waters, dividing the waters above from*

*Matt 3:2
*Gen 1:1

*Gen 1:5

*Isa 11:3
*Gen 1:5

*Matt 5:3; Luke
6:20; Aelred,
S 27.11–12
(CCCM
2A:224–25)
†Augustine, Civ
Dei 10.1; Enchir
1.2 (CCSL
47:273, 46:49)
‡Gregory
the Great,
Mo 25:20,
25 (CCSL
143B:1250)
#Aelred, Iesu
1.8 (CCCM
1:255)
*Gen 1:6, 8
†Ps 103:2

---

1 From here to the end of the sermon, Aelred recasts material found in S 27.

2 The word *skin* undoubtedly evokes the parchment on which the sacred words of Scripture were inscribed.

*Gen 1:6
*the waters below,** namely, human and angelic knowledge, that it may be below the angelic intellect, but above our own.

11. Nevertheless, let us not grow proud because of this intellect, but, according to the example of the Lord, let us be made gentle by divine eloquence so that we are meek, listening and asking questions rather than engaging in disputation. And *let there be evening* for us by the consideration of our ignorance *and a morning* by the illumination of divine grace.

*Isa 11:3

*Gen 1:8;
Isa 11:2

*Matt 5:4
Thus, through the gift of piety from the Spirit,* let us keep watch for *the second day** as the Lord describes it in the second beatitude: *Blessed are the meek, for they shall possess the earth.**

12. In his adolescence, he encouraged knowledge. In adolescence indeed he was baptized; the one who had no trace of sin took up the remedy for sin. Neither indeed did he need this, but he showed to us the kind of knowledge that was necessary for us. For it was not necessary for us to know the nature of herbs or the movement of the stars, but rather to know what and where he is, his daily failings, how much he advances, how much he regresses. And since this knowledge is his appointed task, sorrow is also appointed, the sorrow of his pilgrimage, which comes as he considers his own neediness and his desire for his own country, and he washes himself sweetly by his own tears as if by a kind of baptism.

13. By the word of the Lord *let the waters that are below heaven be gathered in one place*—these waters signify human thoughts, earthly and in flux—and

*Gen 1:9; Pss
142:6; 62:3
let *a dry land appear** in our heart, where we thirst for God and experience a shower of compunction coming from above. Then *let the earth bring forth*

*Gen 1:11-12
*green vegetation and seed-bearing trees making fruit,** which means "from the seed of thoughts, let the fruit

of good works come forth." *Let there be an evening in us* from the fear of our weakness and *a morning* from the hope of divine consolation, and thus, from the Spirit of knowledge,* let *the third day* dawn for us, the day of the third beatitude, about which the Lord says, *Blessed are they who mourn, for they shall be consoled.**   *Isa 11:2

    *Matt 5:5

14. In his young manhood, he showed strength, teaching us so *to hunger and thirst for justice* that we would not fear to suffer either *persecution** or death for justice's sake. But lest we be exalted because we practice justice, or discouraged because the persecution is great, let *two great lights appear in the firmament* of Sacred Scripture. The greater light, which presides over the day, is the example of the Savior himself, which prevents us from being exalted in the day of human achievement; the lesser light, which presides over the night, the stars, is the example of the patience of the church, which prevents us from being overthrown by the cruel night of persecution. And although it might be evening, given the consideration of human persecution, let there be morning if we remember divine justice. Thus from the gift of the Spirit of strength let there appear to us the fourth day, namely, the fourth beatitude. The Lord says of this beatitude, *Blessed are those who hunger and thirst for justice, for they shall be satisfied.**   *Matt 5:6, 10

    *Matt 5:6

Sermon 43

For the Nativity of
Saint John the Baptist

*John 14:2

1. **T**he Lord says in the gospel, *In my Father's house there are many mansions.** What are these mansions? Without a doubt they are the many mansions of rewards and crowns. See, brothers, if all people were one in life, one in merit, one in holiness, there would certainly not be many mansions, but one mansion, and all would arrive at that mansion. But because there are differences in life, different ways of living, different degrees of perfection—if I may say this—such differences in heaven are called mansions.

2. Each mansion has a certain title,[1] and a sure way of measuring is established, of course, [to determine] what kind of person ought properly to be in one man-

*Aelred, Anima 3.47 (CCCM 1:752)

sion and what kind in another.* Accordingly, a certain mansion is prepared in heaven for the married; there is a certain way of measuring established as well as a manner of living appropriate for the married if they wish to arrive at that mansion. Another mansion is prepared for widows, and there is a title written on this mansion indicating what kind of widows ought to enter it. We understand that it is the same for all the states in life[2] in the church. 3. And therefore in every

---

[1] One of the meanings of *titulus*, the Latin word Aelred uses here, is a sign indicating that the house to which it is affixed is for rent.

[2] Aelred uses the term *ordes, ordines* here and throughout the sermon. It reminds us of the early use of the term to indicate all the

state in life in the church, people can be saved if they are able to live according to the designation and rule of their state in life. Accordingly, a most excellent mansion has been prepared for monks, and a standard has been prescribed that it behooves a monk to hold to if he wishes to ascend to that mansion. Solitaries have their own mansion provided they hold to the law that has been founded for those who tend toward this mansion.*

*Aelred, S 69.3 (CCCM 2B:201)

4. The Lord shows us these laws or standards of measurement or titles in the reading of Sacred Scripture and in the example of the saints. In Saint Zachary and Elizabeth, the perfect life of married people is described, and in Saint Anna, the perfect life of widows; in the primitive church that began in Jerusalem the heavenly life of monks is depicted. In Saint John the Baptist, whose feast we celebrate today, the Lord shows us how the life of solitaries ought to be.* 5. We also find all of these states in life in the Scriptures. For the blessed apostle describes quite clearly the law that married people ought to hold to. Likewise, in showing the perfect life of widows, he says, *Truly the one who is widowed and made desolate will hope in God, be instant in prayers and sacrifices by night and day.* The total perfection of the monk is in giving up his own will. The prophet describes this perfection when he says, *If you prevent your foot from doing your own will on my holy day and you have glorified me when you did not do your own will, I will raise you up above the height of the snows.*

*Aelred, S 69.4 (CCCM 2B:201)

*1 Tim 5:7

*Isa 58:13-14; 14:14

6. As to solitaries, some are solitary only in body, others only in spirit, and still others both in body

various ways of living and serving in the early church. From the twelfth century onward, it was restricted to the clerical ranks. In this sermon, Aelred is clearly speaking of what we now call states in life.

and spirit. Those who are solitaries only in body sit alone, remote from the faces of others, but they care little for purity of heart; they are outwardly quiet, but inwardly they choose to entertain a tumult of bad thoughts and desires. The prophet spoke of such a spirit when he said, in derision, *The enemies see him and mock his sabbath.** Others are bodily among people, but inwardly they have great quiet and great peace; they are zealous for purity of heart and the contemplation of God. These are the solitaries in spirit. There are others who are both quiet in body and inwardly enjoy peace and the contemplation of God. These two are solitaries to be praised.

*Lam 1:7;
Aelred, S
17.11 (CCCM
2A:136)

7. Saint Jeremias describes their perfection and the very way of perfection itself when he says, *It is good for a person to carry the yoke from his adolescence; let him sit alone and be silent because he has been raised above himself.** The perfection of those who are truly solitaries is to be raised above themselves. And the way is to carry the yoke from adolescence, to sit alone and be silent. *It is good for a person,* he says, *to carry the yoke from his adolescence.** These stages may be noted in human life: first infancy, then childhood, afterward adolescence. From that point on a person begins to be an adult.[3]

*Lam 3:27-28

*Aelred, Spec
car 1.34.108
(CCCM 1:61),
S 69.3 (CCCM
2B:201)

8. You ought to know that your soul also has these stages. For example, a stage of the soul is described in the book of Wisdom: *For old age is venerable not through the passing of time or by counting the number of years. Understanding is the gray hairs of a man and a blameless life, the attainment of old age.** Look

*Wis 3:8-9

---

[3] Aelred uses the very specific *vir* here, but throughout he uses *homo*, which is the more generic term for person or persons. I have chosen to translate it here as *adult*; I believe that captures the sense Aelred intends, consistent with his use of *infant*, *child*, and *adolescent*.

at the differences among those stages that we have just called to memory. In infancy, ignorance rules; in childhood, evil desires rule; in adolescence, reason and sense arise against vices.

9. Therefore, however long someone lives without any caution or foresight, like a blind person without sense and without reason, such a one is surely an infant in spirit. Again, so long as someone follows evil desires and does not resist, that person is undoubtedly a child in spirit, even if a hundred years old. Of such a child it is written, *Because a child of a hundred years old will die and a sinner of a hundred years will be cursed.** But when someone begins to understand himself, to hate vices and to love virtues, when he begins to rise up against the world, the flesh, and the devil, then to be sure he is an adolescent. After that, if he wishes to arrive at the perfection of one who is solitary in spirit, he ought to bear his yoke so that he may be an adult, perfect in knowledge and virtue. *For it is good for a person to carry the yoke from his adolescence.*

10. Now we must inquire about this yoke of which we speak and trace out how we may understand it. For a yoke is mentioned in many places in Sacred Scripture, sometimes understood in a bad sense, at other times in a good. It occurs to me that there are five ways to understand *yoke* in Sacred Scripture: there is a yoke of iniquity and a yoke of misfortune; there are also a yoke of weakness, a yoke of fear, and a yoke of charity.

11. The yoke of iniquity is what the devil put on the neck of Adam; it remained on him and on all his sons up to the coming of Christ. The prophet complained loudly of this yoke, saying, *For behold I was conceived in iniquity and in sins did my mother conceive me.** And in another place, *For my iniquities overwhelmed my head and as a heavy weight they weigh upon me.** Through Isaiah, the Lord promised

*Isa 65:20

*Ps 50:7

*Ps 37:5

that this yoke was about to be lifted from the neck of his people: *In that day,* he said, *the weight will be lifted from your shoulder and the yoke from your neck; it will putrefy in the presence of oil.**

12. Of which weight, which yoke, does he speak? That of the king of the Assyrians. For he was speaking figuratively about the people of God, who were then oppressed by the king of the Assyrians. *For all things were contained for them in figures.** For if you pay attention to the letter, what would it mean that the yoke will putrefy in the presence of oil? But the people signified the people who belong to the Lord God, those, namely, who were predestined for eternal life. There are those who, whether among the Jews or among the Gentiles, sighed under the yoke of the devil and its weight. Under this yoke they groaned and cried and begged the Lord to help them. Therefore for their consolation the Lord said through the prophet, *The weight will be lifted from their shoulder and the yoke from their neck.*

13. About the yoke of misfortune it is written, *A heavy yoke is upon all the sons of Adam, from the day they go out from their mother's womb until the day they return to the womb of the mother of all.** The miseries of this life are the yoke of misfortune: labors, sorrows, weariness, poverty, the death of family members, every sort of illness, of tribulation. O my brothers, who can count all these things? But already we have come to the yoke of weakness. This weakness is not of the body, but of the soul. It is the impossibility or the difficulty of doing good. We suffer this yoke in two ways: through the corruption of nature and through unrelenting habit.*

14. This corruption of nature is a certain drive for pleasure[4] in the members of our body that leads us to

---

[4] Aelred uses the word *delectatio* here, meaning "pleasure" or "delight," but it is clear from the context that he means the drive or thirst

evil; we endure it whether we will or no. The apostle describes it, saying, *I see another law in my members, etc.** This drive for pleasure is said to be natural, not because our nature was created in this corruption but because after the sin of Adam, in whom this corruption first arose, this drive passed over into all of his descendants. Before baptism and faith in Christ this drive is not just a weakness, but sin, and justly deserves damnation. We are redeemed from this sin through faith in Christ and baptism. From that point on, it is only weakness and, if we do not consent to it, is not reckoned to us as sin.*

*Rom 7:23

*Aelred, S
64.20 (CCCM
2B:168)

15. Another yoke weighs very wretchedly upon the neck of the wretched, namely, the yoke of bad habit. People place this yoke upon themselves. At first, when people fall into a particular sin, they so regret it and sorrow over it that they easily avoid falling into the same sin. If, on the contrary, they repeat that sin, they then stand up against it with more difficulty. If, however, it turns into habit, they cannot control themselves without difficulty, even if they will to do so; often they mourn and lament in the very act of sinning, but they do not have the strength to abstain. They sigh under the heavy yoke of evil habit that so weighs on their neck that even should they will it, they cannot rise up.

16. Jeremias the prophet says to such people, *If the Ethiopian can change his skin and the leopard his varicolored [coat], you will be able to do good when you have learned evil.** For it is impossible that an Ethiopian become white or a leopard solid-colored. So is it impossible for those who, when they have learned evil through habit, to rise up by their own power to pursue the good. That yoke is signified by the stone placed over Lazarus, who was already [dead] for four

*Jer 13:23

---

for pleasure that is part of the dynamic of human nature. He speaks favorably of delight elsewhere. Here he views it more negatively.

days and smelled bad; this signifies the one weighed
down by evil habit, from whom a bad odor comes
forth, that is, the fetid odor of a bad reputation.*
Jesus alone can raise him up. Therefore it behooves
the one who bears this yoke to cry to him and say,
*From my urgent needs, take me away.**

17. These are the bad yokes, wretched; all of them
come from the sin of the first man. If we wish to escape this oppression, it behooves us to submit to the
yoke of our Lord of which the prophet speaks: *It is
good for a person to carry his yoke*, etc. See that however long someone remains in wretchedness and this
state of oppression, he remains in a condition of old
age and belongs to the old man; he remains an infant
and a child, and yet in a condition of old age. He is an
infant and a child because he does not follow reason
but rather the desires of the flesh; nevertheless he is
in a condition of old age because he belongs to the old
Adam and not to the new. But if he would become an
adolescent and a youth, let him first accept the yoke
of the fear of the Lord. Understand what I say. There
are many among us who can remember their old life
and can recognize in themselves what I say.

18. Sometimes people are so foolish, so given to
vices and sins, that they neither care for nor think
about God—or indeed about anything that might
draw them away from their evils—but freely do everything that they want to do, without an argument
from heart or conscience. Such people are infants,
children without discretion. On the other hand,
sometimes they begin to consider themselves carefully, to reflect upon their evils and sins, and their own
conscience immediately begins to argue against them,
to reprove them. Then they begin to think about the
end of their life, to consider what might happen to
them if perchance they should die, and thus they

begin to fear. When this fear takes possession of their heart, they begin to draw back from evil deeds and already begin to submit to the yoke of fear.

19. This fear compels such people to accept the yoke of law and discipline, that is, to be under the power of another and to live under one or another written rule, as we do under the Rule of Saint Benedict or as canons do under the Rule of Saint Augustine. At this point their adolescence begins, because then they begin to resist vices and sins and to be strong against the devil and his persuasions.[5] At this stage, that is, under this yoke, there are labor and tribulation, and one begins to experience what the Lord said in the gospel: *Narrow is the way that leads to life.** For what a person does in fear is not done with delight but with great exertion.

        *Matt 7:14

20. However, one must persevere under this yoke so that it may not be said of him what the Lord said through the prophet: *You have thrown off my yoke; you have broken my chains.** If people truly persevere under this yoke, they will certainly grow from adolescence into perfect adulthood; thus they will receive the yoke that is sweet and the burden that is light. This is the yoke of charity about which the Lord says, *My yoke is sweet and my burden, light.** Then such people will find rest for their soul. For the yoke *putrefies in the presence of oil,** the yoke of fear in the presence of charity; *there is no fear in charity, but perfect charity casts out fear.**

      *Jer 2:20 Vulg

    *Matt 11:29-30

        *Isa 10:37

       *1 John 4:18

21. Blessed John the Baptist, this man of whom we speak today, bore that yoke without a doubt, not

---

[5] The word Aelred uses, *suggestiones*, is the name of rhetorical figure in which an orator answers his own questions. He here creates a lively appreciation for the devil as a master orator, who raises the questions a wavering soul might ask and then answers them brilliantly.

just from his adolescence but even from his infancy, because even in the womb of his mother he was full of the Holy Spirit, who is love, charity, and sweetness. For then was *the charity of God poured forth* in his heart *through the Holy Spirit who was given* to him.*

*Rom 5:5

Therefore when Blessed Mary came to salute Elizabeth, bearing her son in her womb, John was filled with the charity of God and therefore leapt for joy in the divine sweetness. Because he had carried the yoke of charity even from the womb of his mother, he found it sweet to sit alone and keep silent.

22. Since he had experienced the sweetness of Christ, every pleasure and joy of this world was a burden to him; therefore he immediately left the world and dwelled in the desert, where he could freely taste and see *how sweet the Lord is*.*

*Pss 33:9; 30:20

Therefore if we keep to the letter of everything the prophet says—that *it is good for a person to carry the yoke from his adolescence*—it is exactly what Saint Benedict says in the beginning of his Rule. For there he speaks of solitaries who do not seek the desert *in their first fervor** but who first bear the yoke of discipline in submission until they vanquish in themselves all their vices and evil passions.

*RB 1.3-5

23. Such as these can usefully be solitaries, even physically. But to be sure, it is better that we understand this as a rule for the spiritual solitary, such as we all ought to be. For if we first bear the yoke of fear in submission and then the yoke of charity in delight, we are surely able to sit alone spiritually, be silent, and thus be raised above ourselves. [The text] says, *He will sit solitary and will be silent because he has been raised above himself*.* Consider this. Three things

*Lam 3:28

impede this solitude: wandering about, suspicion, and curiosity. Whoever can ward off these three can sit, be silent, and be raised above themselves whether in the cloister, in the field, or even in the public arena.

24. Here *sitting* signifies stability, *silence* signifies quiet, and *being raised up* signifies the heights of contemplation. He who can avoid the three [impediments] we have spoken about above can have these three. For the one who wanders certainly cannot sit; the one who is suspicious cannot be silent; the one who is curious cannot gather his heart to that which is one. These are the dying flies of which the prophet speaks: *The dying flies diminish the sweetness of oil.** Oil is the anointing of the spirit in the love of God and contemplation. But the one who wanders is not able to experience this sweetness. There is a certain wandering of the body, and there is a certain wandering of the spirit.

*Eccl 10:1

25. Bodily wandering is a certain restlessness that does not permit a monk to be in one place but compels him now to go out and now to come in, so that he can scarcely do one work or stay in one place for an hour. For example, if he begins to sing, he can hardly endure it until he has completed one or two verses. If he begins to read, he gets up before he has finished reading one page, and, if he is not able to leave the cloister, at least he goes to another part of the cloister. 26. Then he begins to think that he may have some reason to speak with the prior. So he runs from office to office; he seeks through a sign from this one and that one where the prior may be, as if he were in great necessity. If he finds him, he makes a sign, enters the office, prostrates himself, asks forgiveness, and represents[6] what he has done or what he has thought, not so much because of sorrow for sin as for the desire to talk. Such a one surely cannot sit alone, be silent, and rise above himself.

---

[6] The verb *fingo* that Aelred uses here suggests fabrication or exaggeration in the representation that the wandering monk makes to the abbot.

27. Spiritual wandering is when a monk holds himself bodily in one place and wanders here and there in his spirit. For whoever is suspicious always has his eyes on something outside of himself; he never pays attention to himself but rather to the life of one and the behavior of another. He suspects everybody of evil. If he sees others talking or signing in turn, he always thinks that it is either about himself or that it is something evil. That monk cannot be silent in any way but is always in judgments and detractions. Similarly, one who is curious always has his ears perked up for rumors and leisurely conversations,[7] his eyes open for investigating what another monk does and says. That person is unable to experience the spiritual sweetness of the oil.

28. Therefore, brothers, let us sit, so that we may persevere in quietness of body and spirit; let us be silent, so that we may remove both from our mouth and our heart all that is meaningless, suspicious, and disparaging; thus we may be able to be raised above ourselves. Brothers, it is a great human perfection to be raised above oneself. Toward what is he raised, this one who is raised above himself? Consider. Sometimes people lower themselves beneath themselves, sometimes they preserve themselves in themselves, sometimes they raise themselves above themselves.

29. What is below a person? Undoubtedly the earth, the sea, the air, the sun, the moon, the stars, all corporeal things, gold, silver, and one's own body. All these are beneath a person, because they are of a nature inferior to that of a human being. What therefore is above a person? Nothing except God alone, to be sure. Therefore, if a person raises himself above him-

---

[7] The phrase Aelred uses, *habet aures erectas*, is a phrase commonly used to describe dogs on the alert.

self he is not raised up to anything other than God. But how and by what wings can someone raise himself above himself or lower himself beneath himself?

30. Brothers, whatever transition a soul makes, whether to good or to evil, she[8] does not do so except through love. If she loves transitory and perishable things, which are inferior to her nature, she certainly lowers herself below herself. If, however, she turns her whole love toward herself, it is as if she preserves herself in herself, but because she herself is wretched, however long she loves only herself, she cannot be anything else but wretched. If, in contrast, she raises her whole heart and all of her love toward God, then she raises herself above herself, and because that is true beatitude, she cannot be otherwise than blessed.

31. The blessed man whose feast day we celebrate today knew and understood this. He held all earthly things in contempt—all earth's delights, all earth's vanities, all earthly pleasures and honors—and he raised his whole heart above himself to the one who is truly blessed and eternal. Therefore he is eternally blessed with him. Through his merits, may our Lord Jesus Christ lead us to that same blessedness, he who with the Father and the Holy Spirit lives and reigns, God, forever and ever. Amen.

---

[8] Here the subject to which all the following pronouns refer is the feminine *anima*, the soul. See S 33n2. The feminine pronouns that Aelred uses for grammatical reasons indicate that his teaching applies to all.

Sermon 44

For the Nativity of
Saint John the Baptist

*Aelred, SS
6.1, 15.3, 45.1
(CCCM 2A:53,
121, 353)

1. **I**t is certain, brothers, that we ought to celebrate all the feast days of the saints set up in the church with joy and devotion,* but especially those feast days that have authority not only because they were instituted by the holy fathers but above all because of the gospel. Among the feast days that have such authority is that of Saint John the Baptist. For, as you heard in the gospel yesterday, when the Lord announced to his father Zachary that a son would be born to him, among other things that he said was also this: *And many will rejoice in his birth.** These are the many about whom the Lord said, *Many will come from the east and the west and will recline with Abraham, Isaac and Jacob in the kingdom of God.**

*Luke 1:14

*Matt 8:11;
Luke 13:29

2. Accordingly, brothers, because we are among the many, let us rejoice in the birth of Blessed John. However, let not our joy be in such things as those in which the worldly customarily find joy, that is, in precious vestments, delicate foods, and many meaningless things. They have their joy in such things, all of which are outside of themselves, and therefore they go out of themselves; they care for the body that is outside, and they neglect the soul that is within. For our glory and joy ought to be within because our greater care is for the soul rather than the body. This is why the apostle says, *This is our glory, the witness of our conscience.**

*2 Cor 1:12;
Aelred, Inst
incl 25 (CCCM
1:657), S

3. Our joy must also necessarily be mixed in some way, because the same apostle says, *As if sad, always however rejoicing.** Note what he says: *As if sad, always however rejoicing.* Who could have perfect joy in this life? This body weighs us down, the devil troubles us, temptations attack us; from all this comes sadness.* We ought nevertheless to have great joy in the hope we have in the Lord, through whom we will be freed from these evils and come to perfect joy. The Lord gives us an analogy about that sadness and that joy: *A woman,* he says, *when she is in childbirth, has sadness.**

4. That woman signifies the soul that is bearing spiritual children, of whom the prophet says, *Your children shall be like olive branches around your table.** Those children are good works. Therefore, as a woman giving birth has sadness about the pain she experiences and yet has joy because of the hope she has for what she bears, so it is for us. In spiritual childbirth we have sadness because of the labors and temptations without which we cannot do good works. But we ought also to have joy because of the hope for the blessedness we will have because of the good works that we are practicing with a certain measure of sadness.

5. Therefore we ought to rejoice not only because of the reward given for these tribulations but also because we are worthy to suffer some trouble for our Lord and to pay back something to him for the trouble he himself suffered for us. Therefore it is written about the apostles, *The Apostles went in to face the council rejoicing because they had been made worthy to suffer indignity for the name of Jesus.** And truly, brothers, I do not know if anyone can have in his conscience this joy of which we speak if he does not know that he suffered something for the Lord.

(continued)
26.15 (CCCM
2A:213)
*2 Cor 5:6, 10

*Aelred, S
40.7 (CCCM
2A:319)

*John 16:21

*Ps 127:3

*Acts 5:41

6. We can rejoice in these festivals of the saints insofar as we take care to imitate their faith, their manner of life, and the suffering they endured for the Lord. Accordingly, let us now observe the life and conduct of that man whose feast day we celebrate today, and, insofar as our life is in accord with his, let us rejoice. As you know, he fled into the desert because he did not wish to live among the worldly; he wore *camel skins* because he did not care for precious and comfortable garments; he ate *locusts and wild honey* because he did not seek rich and refined foods.* 7. Pay attention to his way of life, his withdrawal from the world, the roughness of his clothing, the meanness of his food and drink. I believe that you know that your life is greatly in harmony with the life of this man, and you rejoice. For you are similarly far removed from the world, you are dressed in cheap clothing, you make use of rough foods. Is it not just, my brothers, that you who imitate his life share in his joy?

8. But where did his joy come from? You well understand that his joy could not be from external things, because in external things he had nothing but labors and severity. It might be that he rejoiced because everyone wondered at his way of life and praised him for it. Many behave likewise. They do not rejoice because they do well but because they are much praised. Such was not Blessed John. Had he been such a man, would he not have accepted the kind of praise that would lead people to believe that he himself was the Christ, as many were doing? But he himself dissuaded them from believing this; he said, *I am not the one whom you believe me to be.**

9. Do you see how clear it is that he had no joy in human praise? Therefore where did his joy come from? Let him tell us himself, and let him show us what we ought to desire: *The one who has the bride is*

*Matt 3:4; Mark 1:6

*Acts 13:5 Vulg

*the bridegroom; however the friend of the bridegroom
stands and hears him and rejoices with joy because
of the voice of the bridegroom.** That man called our
Lord, that is, Christ, *bridegroom.* But of whom is he
the bridegroom? Of this flesh? Absolutely not! Christ
is the bridegroom of the soul. Who else would it be?
The one who has the bride is the bridegroom. Who
can make the human soul his bride, except our Lord?
Who can unite a human soul to himself and make
himself one with her and make her a sharer in his joy
and his sweetness except the Christ?

*John 3:29

10. That is why he says that *the one who has the
bride is the bridegroom.* And what was Saint John?
Listen to what he was: *the friend of the bridegroom
stands and hears him.* Truly, brothers, this John who is
the friend of Jesus Christ is great. Who can be greater
than the friend of Christ? He has servants; he has
friends. What more could he have? Without a doubt
he could not have lord or father. No one at all can be
greater than his friend. Therefore *among those born of
women there arose none greater than John the Baptist.**

*Matt 11:11

11. *The friend of the bridegroom stands. The friend
stands*; he is not moved, he does not waver, he does
not fall but stands. Therefore one of the friends of
the bridegroom says, *the Lord lives, in whose sight I
stand.** Blessed the one who stands in the sight of the
Lord. There are many who stand in the sight of other
people but fall down in the sight of the Lord. But the
friend stands. He sinks down who passes over from
a good life to an evil one; he falls who hangs onto his
vices, sins, and carnal desires. But the friend of the
bridegroom stands; he holds straight his way, he *who
does not turn toward the right or the left,** he who does
not bend toward the earth.

*1 Kgs 17:1

*Isa 30:31;
31:21

12. Such was this *blessed man.** He did not fly
upward; he did not bend himself down; therefore he

*Ps 1:1

stood. The one who wished to fly upward said, *I will put my seat to the north, and I will be like to the Most High.** Blessed John did not wish to fly. Men were inciting him to fly when they said, *Are you the Christ?** But he did not wish to fly, but to stand in the position in which the Lord had placed him. *I am not the Christ,* he said.* Oh, how unhappy was Adam, who did not wish to remain in the position in which the Lord had placed him but wished to fly and be like God. He did not wish to be a friend but an equal; therefore from being a friend he was made a wretched slave.

13. The friend, however, stands and listens to him. Happy the one who can listen to the bridegroom. Only the soul who is the bride can do so. Some hear him as a king, others as a judge, still others as a teacher. But the friend of the bridegroom, whose soul is the friend of the bridegroom and the bride of the bridegroom, hears him as a bridegroom. Adam heard him when he was walking in Paradise, but he heard him as his judge; therefore he feared and hid himself. David heard him as his king when he said, *You yourself are my king.** Moses heard him as a teacher when he said to him, *Go, do all things according to the example that I showed you on the mountain.**

14. But which is the soul that can say, *I will listen to what you speak within me, Lord God? Within me,* he says. There the friend of the bridegroom stands, there he listens to him and rejoices with great joy at the voice of the bridegroom. Oh, how interior is that joy!* *All his glory is from within.*† There, within, there he rejoices with great joy at the voice of the bridegroom. Brothers, just as you have heard that you share the rigors that Saint John endured, understand how you thus share his interior joys, not those outside. There within, you are accustomed to listen to the voice of the bridegroom and to rejoice at his voice.

*Isa 14:14

*John 1:19;
Luke 3:15

*John 1:20; 3:28

*Ps 43:5

*Exod 25:40;
Heb 8:5;
Num 8:4

*Aelred, S
64.14 (CCCM
2B:166)
†Ps 44:14

15. Where do your frequent tears and sighs come from, except from what you hear within—I know not how sweet it may be, how delightful? As you read in Ezekiel, sometimes a hidden voice came to his soul; sometimes it came from below the firmament, sometimes from the firmament itself, sometimes from above the firmament.[1]* Sometimes the Lord makes the soul feel something of his sweetness; he thereby makes him consider the beauty of creation and thus how beautiful is the one who created such beautiful things. But this is the voice from under the firmament.

*Ezek 1:22-25

16. The spiritual creature that the Lord made is the firmament and is sometimes called *heaven* because of its unity and sometimes *the heavens* because of its multiplicity. Concerning these heavens it is written, *The heavens proclaim the glory of God.**   *Ps 18:2
And immediately afterward, [the psalmist] called the heavens the firmament and said, *And the firmament announces the works of his hands.** *Ps 18:2
My brothers, consider what great joy arises in the soul when she[2] can see how marvelously, how mercifully, how sweetly our Lord works in these heavens, in this firmament.

17. [Consider] how the soul finds joy within herself when she considers that fishermen become rulers of the whole world, publicans become evangelists, thieves are changed into preachers! What [joy] when the Lord places before her eyes the great mercy at work in herself; she sees herself, once given to luxury, become chaste; once drunk, become sober; once wrathful, become patient; once proud, become humble!

---

[1] From this point until the middle of Section 18, Aelred borrows freely from Gregory the Great's Hiez, Homily 8.12–16 (CCSL 142:108–19).

[2] Again, feminine pronouns refer to the soul.

If the Lord says this in her heart and shows his great mercy, who does not rejoice at the voice of the bridegroom? But these things are the voice from the firmament itself.

18. But when the Lord illuminates the soul with his presence and in some marvelous way reveals his secrets—now of Scripture, now of heavenly joy, of his sweetness, of the mysteries, of his divine plan—then the soul hears the voice from above the firmament. It is not through a creature of the world, nor through a human being or angel, but through his own proper presence that the Lord makes that soul hear what he is pleased to say. In that way, Paul heard the mystery of the gospel. Therefore he said, *Paul, an apostle not from men nor through a man,* and so on.* And again: *I received the Gospel that I have announced not from myself nor from any human being but through the revelation of Jesus Christ.*

*Gal 1:1

*Gal 1:11-12

19. The friend of the bridegroom certainly heard this voice. And he heard it very early. For in the womb of his mother he heard the voice of the bridegroom, and therefore he rejoiced as his mother said to Blessed Mary, *As soon as the voice of your salutation sounded in my ears, the infant in my womb exulted.* If he had such joy in him when in the narrow confines of his mother's womb, just imagine what kind of joy he had in his heart when he saw him, when he touched him with his hands, when he saw the Holy Spirit descending like a dove upon him, when he heard the voice of the Father from heaven. [Imagine] what kind of joy he had when he saw and experienced all those things outside of himself and heard the causes of all those things within himself!

*Luke 1:44

20. Do you see now, brothers, how much you are in harmony with him, both in the life that you lead and in the joy that you have within? Without a

doubt you worthily and rightly rejoice in the birth of John, because his birth has been manifest in you who imitate his way of life. Therefore praise him. How? It certainly seems to me, brothers, that your life must be his praise. For you who have chosen to live as he lived reveal how much he must be praised.* And deservedly so. Without a doubt and with great security, you are able to imitate him whom our Lord calls his angel. Who can have doubts about the life that an angel teaches?

*Aelred, SS 18.4, 27.22, 45.39 (CCCM 2A:140, 228, 364)

21. *Behold,* he says, *I will send my angel, who will prepare the way before your face.** The Lord said this about him through the prophet a long time before he was born. For the Lord himself says in the gospel that this was *written* about [John].* He himself was sent before our Lord as the dawn before the sun, that dawn before which Jacob could not receive the blessing of our Lord. You know how Jacob wrestled the whole night with an angel, and when the *dawn* arose, the angel wished to depart from him. And he said to him, *I will not let you go until you have blessed me.** And immediately he blessed him.†

*Mal 3:1; Matt 11:10; Luke 7:27

*Matt 11:10; Luke 7:27

*Gen 32:26 †Mal 3:1; Gen 32:29

22. You know how the whole human race was under a curse. Jacob stands for the holy fathers who came before the incarnation of the Lord; by tears, prayers, and a good life, they wished to constrain our Lord to take flesh, him who would remove this curse and give a blessing. Because of their great desire, they were almost impatient, but he was waiting for the time he had himself foreseen together with the Father. Perhaps the wrestling match signified that [conflict]. And what did the Lord say? *Behold I send my angel who will prepare a way before your face; and immediately he will come to the temple,* and so forth.*

*Mal 3:1; Matt 11:10; Luke 2:27

23. It is as if the angel had said to Jacob, "Why do you constrain me to bless you? First the dawn must

arise, and then I will bless you." Brothers, that wrestling match took place during the night. It was night as long as that curse lasted, as long as the devil, who truly is the night, ruled in this world. At length, the dawn came before the sun rose, that prophet before our Lord. He prepared the way for the sun, as the gospel says: *He was not the light,** that is to say, he was not the full shining of the sun. But just as the dawn is not the sun but somehow a witness that the rising of the sun is coming, so Blessed John was *not the light but came forth as a witness concerning the light.**

24. In truth, immediately after the angel was sent, after that dawn appeared, the sun rose and completely drove away the darkness. Jacob received the blessing he had so long desired. It seems to me that that [same] angel *prepares the way of the Lord,** not only then but even now, because, following his example, you mortify the members of your body and are eager for the renunciations and austerities of this life.* Without doubt the way is prepared by which our Lord wills to come to your hearts so that, like true friends of our Lord *the bridegroom,* you may be able to hear his voice within you and rejoice *at his voice.**

25. Therefore, my beloved brothers, let us hold with all fervor to this way that this friend of Jesus has prepared by his example, so that when we have shared in the austerities he himself endured, we may share the interior joy that he experienced. Thus may we come to that perfect and eternal happiness to which he arrived through the mercy of our Lord Jesus Christ, to whom be the honor and glory forever and ever. Amen.

*John 1:8

*John 1:8

*Matt 3:1;
Isa 40:3;
Mal 3:1

*Origen, Super
Lc 4.6 (SCh
87:134)

*John 3:29

Sermon 45

For the Assumption of Saint Mary

1. However much we ought to love, honor, and praise all the saints, we owe our allegiance to our Lady, Saint Mary, above all. For we ought to conform our will to the will of our Lord as much as we are able; since she was the one whom he loved more, we ought similarly to love her the more. We ought not to doubt at all, but believe firmly and without wavering that no creature was so loved by God, none so honored, none so glorified, as she herself. From her, the creator himself deigned in a certain way to be created; by her, he who governed all things himself deigned to be governed. At her most holy breasts, he who nourished all things deigned to be nourished; from her, he through whom we all were born deigned to be born.

2. How could he love any creature so much that he deigned to be born and created by her? For he who created her according to the power of his divinity was created from her according to the humanity he assumed from her. What will I say of the tender love that he showed to her when he deigned to sit in her lap, to suck her breasts, and, as a boy, to obey her precepts? What when he exalted her today above all other creatures, above the angels and archangels and above all of the assembly that is in heaven?* Thanks to all this, we can satisfy ourselves that he loved her and loves, honors, and glorifies her above all creatures. And therefore we ought to do likewise, beloved brothers.

*Eph 1:21

3. Granted that we ought always to love and always to honor her and to arouse our minds to praise her. Nevertheless, on this day when we recall the memory of her assumption, we ought especially to enter into her praises with all devotion and tender love, because today her excellence and glory were most fully revealed. Many and great are the delights of this solemnity; they ought to taste the sweeter to us because they represent her glory and joy, and from her, all our sweetness receives its beginning. For after God, she herself is our advocate; after her son, she alone is our hope; and as her son our Lord is the *mediator** between the Father and us, so she herself is the present mediator between him and us.* With a certain right, she demands the salvation of sinners, for which reason she herself deserves to become their mother. For if no sinner existed, neither the God-Man nor the mother of God herself would exist.

*1 Tim 2:5

*Aelred, S 58.26 (CCCM 2B:114)

4. And therefore, beloved brothers, even if I were made entirely into a tongue,[1] I could not satisfy my desire to speak of the excellence of this feast day and of the glory and praise of the most blessed mother of God,[2]* because just as she is more excellent, more blessed, and more gentle among all the saints of God, so too she who is to him not only a creature, a handmaid, a friend, and a daughter but also a mother tastes his sweetness more intimately. Therefore, as we have said, it is right that we undertake this feast

*Jerome, Ep 108.1 (CCSL 55:306, 305)

---

[1] The Latin *lingua* can be translated either *tongue* or *language*. I have chosen the more literal meaning because it seems to suit the context, in which Aelred imagines becoming the instrument of praise. He is also speaking about Mary's giving birth to Jesus, the God-Man and Savior, as the foundation of her many privileges and glories, grace that begins with human physicality.

[2] From here to the end of section, Aelred uses material found also in S 20:11–30. The parallelism between the two sermons continues, in fact, to the end.

with greater sweetness and joy and nourish ourselves more abundantly on this feast day with a spiritual banquet. As we said a little while ago, brothers, we ought always to praise and honor her and remember her tender love with all devotion. But today we ought to rejoice with her even more, because today her joy was filled up to the brim.

5. She had great joy when the angel saluted her, great joy when she felt the coming of the Holy Spirit, when the marvelous union between the Son of God and her flesh took place in her womb, so that the one who was the Son of God became also her son. She had great joy when she held such a son in her arms, when she kissed him, when she took care of him, when she heard his words, when she saw his miracles. And because she was greatly saddened in his passion, it was marvelous that she again had great joy in his resurrection and even more up to his ascension. But the joy she receives today overwhelms all that joy.

6. Granted that she had great joy in all these things, nevertheless she was in great woe after the glory of his ascension, when his corporeal presence, in which she had greatly delighted, was taken from her. This is not to be wondered at. For *where her treasure was*—and that treasure was her beloved son and Lord—*there also was her heart.** And granted that her every desire and love was there where he was, nevertheless, as long as she was living in corruptible flesh, she could not erase from her memory what she had seen of him according to the flesh. For his deeds and his words were always taking place in her soul and, above all, an image of his beautiful face revolved in her heart.

*Matt 6:21

7. Therefore, beloved brothers, do not wonder that I said that she was wretched in this life, because, to my mind, no one experienced the miseries of this

*Ps 44:3

life more, no one cried more, no one suffered more the heavy burden of tarrying here in the flesh. For no one loved *the most beautiful of the sons of men** as much as she, no one desired him as much; therefore no one sighed for his presence or wept at his absence as much as she did. For who can understand, brothers, how much our Lady loved her son, how much she desired him? If Peter loved his Lord, how much more did she love her Lord, who was also her son. Brothers, it is unnecessary for me even to wish to begin to show her love, that love that is so great that no human mind is adequate to reflect on it.*

*Aelred, S 19.14 (CCCM 2A:150)

8. For as long as she lived, our Lady was in misery because of her very great desire; with tears and groans, with prayers and sighs, she always desired quickly to join the one whom she desired. But today our Lord Jesus Christ rescued her out of this life of misery, bore her up to heaven, and, congratulating her, placed her on a throne in his Kingdom. Therefore he provides us with a great cause to jump up with joy. Our queen, our Lady, our mother, our own *flesh and our blood*[3]* is raised up above the choir of angels as one ready to pray for us. She is conveyed to the right hand of her son as one ready to protect us. If therefore she *is for us, who can be against us?**

*Gen 29:14; 37:27

*Rom 8:31

9. Today she crossed over out of this world and ascended to the heavenly Kingdom, where she began to contemplate the brightness, power, and divinity. Her joy and desire are complete, so that she can rightly say, *I have found him whom my soul loves, I held him and will not let him go.** For in this day her good desires have been satisfied with good things, her *youth renewed like that of an eagle.** For the *eagle who*

*Song 3:4

*Ps 102:5

---

[3] The Latin is *os nostrum et caro nostra*, literally "our mouth" or "our face and our flesh."

*climbed above all the heavens in order to fill up all things** is Jesus Christ our Lord, who ascended into heaven before her that he might prepare a place for her.* Today he receives her in that place and conforms the body of his most blessed mother to his own body, with its proper glory.

10. Granted that I may not dare to affirm this—because if someone would wish to deny and vigorously to refute this we do not have the sure testimony of the Scriptures to prove it—nevertheless it is sweet to us to hold this opinion. [We hold therefore] that because of a very great love for his mother, he who can do all things not only took her soul to heaven but also raised up her body so that she might be in his presence with both body and soul and would already receive the bodily immortality that we all hope for on the Day of Judgment. It seems altogether credible that the one who can do all things, he who bore his own holy body above all the heavens, would also [raise up] the body of his most sweet mother. Since he received his own body from her, he did not allow her to be separated from her body for a long time.

11. Again, consider that human flesh suffers this corruption, this death, for the condemnation due to original sin: someone is corrupted in the flesh in this life because of his own concupiscence and illicit desires,* and the corruption of the flesh is the penalty for sin. Surely, then, the flesh that in this life was corrupted by sin would putrefy after this life and in some way perish completely. But her flesh ought not in any way to be subject to this penalty, because she was cleansed from every vice and every corruption of sin so that the Son of God himself might worthily be born of her and rest in her.

12. We know also, brothers, that some who have conquered perfectly the desires of the flesh and

*Eph 4:10;
Obad 1:4;
Jer 49:22
*John 14:2

*Gal 5:16

preserved their virginity have so much merit from our Lord that even now their bodies are whole and healthy and preserved from all corruption.* If our Lord conveys such a gift to his sinful servants, what kind of gift do we think he will have conveyed to his most blessed mother? For if their bodily members are incorrupt after so many years, it is not incredible that the members of her body may also have been resurrected. If the flesh of some or other sinful servant merited this, we ought not to judge that her flesh, from which came forth the flesh of the source, will have merited less glory. And therefore no Christian ought to doubt the incorruption of her holy body.

13. Brothers, because it seems to me that the flesh of the mother may in some way be one flesh with the son, therefore I believe that where the flesh of the son is, there also the flesh of the mother may be assumed. After the death that he suffered *for us, rising from the dead, he dies no more and death shall have no dominion over him.* I believe that, in like manner, he also raised his mother from the dead so that she might live in eternal blessedness with him, that she might remain with him, reign with him, rejoice with him, delight in him. Brothers, this is how I understand what we sang a little while before in her praise: *What is that one who goes forth like the sun,* and so on.* For just as *he who is the sun of justice, who shines upon all those coming into this world,* ascended into heaven in that body that he assumed from our Lady, in a similar way, unless I am mistaken, she ascended into heaven body and soul, through his grace.

14. *What is that one who goes forth* and so forth?* I think that this is the voice of the angels, citizens from on high, who were reigning in heaven with the Lord and saw how on that day the Lord proceeded and she followed. Because of the joy and great admi-

*Aelred,
Vita E 2 (PL
195:782A–C), S
14.21 (CCCM
2A:119)

*Rom 6:9

*Song 6:9

*Mal 4:2;
John 1:9

*Song 6:9; Resp
for the Feast of
the Assump-
tion (Hesbert
4:7455)

ration they felt for her marvelous dignity and glory, they seem to say, *What is that one who proceeds*, and so forth. We ought not to doubt that today our Lord Jesus himself, her son, with all his court that is above in heaven, came to meet his most beloved mother, our Lady, with great festivity, great joy, and a great procession.

15. Just think how great was the exultation in that heavenly court when she entered with a company dressed in purple and white. What exultation, what joy! I think that Jesus himself on that day increased the joy of his whole court—if, indeed, such increase is possible—conferring more sweetness upon them and conceding to them a greater abundance of his gifts. This is not to be wondered at. Because today she rose into heaven, she from whom was born the one who is the font of all sweetness. Today *King Solomon rose up to meet his mother and sat upon his throne; he placed a throne for the mother of the king who sat at his right hand.**

*1 Kgs 2:19

16. When, therefore, she had come in, all wanted to embrace her and hold her, each on the step[4] where he was. But though she was allowed to see the brightness of the angels, their glory and blessedness, this was not enough for her; she desired to see him alone whom she loved above all things. Therefore she rose above all, until she came to the very throne of God, to the embrace of her son, where he sits at the right hand of the Father,* so that all were saying, as if in admiration, *What is that one who proceeds*, and so forth?

*Heb 10:12

---

[4] The Latin word Aelred uses, *gradus*, may be translated literally as *a step* and in an extended sense as *a degree* or *station* or *position*. The vision Aelred evokes here is the multitudes of heaven ranked hierarchically according to their state of life as well as their degree of holiness. I think that a series of steps, up which the Virgin Mother ascends, reflects the vision that Aelred imagines.

17. At first, when she came to that step on which stood the holy women who in this life were married, chaste, and fruitful, like Sarah and Rebecca as well as Rachel and many others, what must have been their exultation? How much must they have desired her company? They knew our Lady and well understood that she was both married and fruitful, and therefore they sought her presence. She certainly was married, as they were; she had a son, as they had given birth to children; but she was a virgin before, during, and after birth, as they had not been. Rightly therefore she passed them by, because she experienced no contagion of the flesh. And those women were not envious of her glory but rather congratulated her and said, *What is this one*, and so forth.

18. You ought not to be amazed that our Lord provided that *his mother be betrothed*.* For it was not appropriate that this sweet, holy, and undoubtedly modest girl should be accused of adultery; even before he was born, her son, who can do all things, did not wish to endure that his mother be so shamed. If she had not been betrothed, brothers, when the Jews saw her pregnant they would certainly have asked about it. What would our Lady have responded? If she said, "I am a virgin who has conceived, God is the one I am carrying"—would not those enemies of God immediately have *covered their ears** as if for blasphemy? Without any trial, would they not have stoned her, both for adultery and for lying?

19. But someone may say, "Could not he, who can do all things, save his mother, either so that no one would know that she was pregnant or so that they would not stone her even if they knew?" Most certainly he could, brothers. But if he had done this, it would have been a miracle, and it was not yet time for him to show his miracles in that way. Certainly

*Matt 1:18

*Acts 7:57-58

she was *betrothed to a man*,* but her betrothal did   *Matt 1:18
not revoke her virginity; nor did it lead to fruitfulness,
but preserved her integrity, brought about modesty,
and prevented infamy. Therefore, he honorably provided that she be betrothed because, at that time, it
was more honorable that people think she was the
wife of Joseph rather than believe his mother to be
an adulteress. Today it is abundantly clear that she
was not betrothed in the manner of other women,
and therefore she bypassed the company of all the
other women, because, as we have said, she knew no
contagion of the flesh.

20. After that step on which the married women
stand, the step of the widows follows. And when they
saw our Lady ascending, they certainly came to meet
her. There was Naomi, whose story is told in the book
of Judges, the woman who gave Ruth in marriage to
Boaz,[5] from whose seed Blessed Mary descended.
There too was that marvelous widow Judith, who as a
figure of the church destroyed the devil when *she cut
off the head of Holophernes*.* There was Saint Anna,   *Jdt 13:10
who knew Blessed Mary and her son in this life. When
all these with their companions saw Blessed Mary
coming, they received her with great joy and greatly
desired her company, because they said that she was
a widow too, and not without reason.

21. Undoubtedly we can call her a widow. After
the ascension of her son and spouse, she despised all
the glories of the world, all its delights, all its pleasures, and all its honors. She took delight in nothing else but tears and her desire to return to him.
For from the moment that our Lord ascended to his
homeland and retreated bodily from his disciples,
surely *the voice of the turtledove was heard in our*

---

[5] It is rather in the Book of Ruth that this story is told.

*Song 2:12

*land,** that is to say, in the holy church. The nature of the turtledove is such that when its mate dies, it does not seek another but remains always in lamentation and sorrow. As long as our Lord was bodily on earth with his disciples, they were in joy and happiness, but as soon as he departed from them, they sorrowed and cried and imitated the turtledove, which does not wish to receive temporal consolation.

22. This is what the Lord himself said: *The friends of the bridegroom are not able to mourn while the bridegroom is with them. The days are coming when the bridegroom will be taken from them, and then they* *Matt 9:15 Vulg *will mourn.** That day had already come, and the bridegroom in his bodily presence had been taken away from them; therefore they began to mourn. And if the friends of the bridegroom were greatly mourning, we can know with certainty that she herself, who was both the mother and the bride of the bridegroom, was mourning even more. Further, the apostle Paul says, *Let the true widow who is all alone* *1 Tim 5:5 *hope in God.** How rightly did the most Blessed Mary lament to be all alone, when she saw him in whom alone she delighted, by whom she was fed, by whom she was made joyful, taken away from her!

23. What does it mean, brothers, that we read hardly anything of the words and deeds of Saint Mary after the resurrection and ascension of the Lord, though of the apostles and the disciples of the Lord [we read much]? Perhaps it is because she was a woman. But we read much about Blessed Mary Magdalen, about the mother of Jacob and other women: how they cried at the sepulcher of the Lord, how *Matt 28:1-10;
Luke 14:1-10;
John 20:11-18 they spoke with angels and with the Lord himself.* Aside from that, and woman though she may be, no prophet or apostle or any other person can be compared to her. Nevertheless we read that Peter healed

the crippled, cured paralytics, healed many through
his shadow, and, more than this, raised Tabitha from
the dead.* Nothing like this do we read of our Lady,
Saint Mary. Why? Each can think what he wishes; I
think that the reason is that she so loved her son, our
Lord, and so desired him that she could not let herself
attend to any outside activity.

*Acts 3:1-10;
9:33-34;
5:15; 9:40

24. For after the ascension of the Lord, Holy
Scripture says nothing of her except that she was
with the disciples in prayer. *And the Apostles and
Mary the mother of Jesus went up to the upper room
and they remained praying with one mind.** Such
a mention is made of her where it is a question of
prayer, so that we might know that she very much
gave herself to that exercise with others where she
could, by prayers and sighs, desire the presence of
her son. Rightly, therefore, we say that Blessed Mary
was a widow. But she was not only a widow, but also
a virgin; she therefore mounted above all widows,
and just as she transcends the merits of all widows,
she is not unworthy to be numbered in the ranks of
all those who have mounted above [the widows]. But
the latter were not envious. Rather they admired her
great excellence when they saw it and rejoiced as if
they were saying, *What is that one,* and so forth?

*Acts 1:13-14

25. Who can worthily think or describe how much
the holy virgins rejoiced at her coming and with what
speed and devotion they received her? Certainly they
who were closer to her in purity and chastity rejoiced
more in her coming and hoped more confidently for
her companionship. This is not to be wondered at.
For the more pure their life, the more dazzling their
flesh with the flower of virginity, the more chaste
their affection, the sweeter their words, that much
more certain is their hope, that much more bold their
voice, and that much more do they desire to enjoy her

companionship. How would they not have presumed that they might have her on their step, when such is their dignity that they follow the Lamb *wherever he goes?**

*Rev 14:4

26. But however much they follow wherever he goes, will they remain where he will remain? Plainly there, and not there. He says, *Where I am my servant will also be.** Therefore they will be there in his Kingdom, but not in the same lofty [condition]. Again, *There are many mansions in the house of my Father.** Granted that one Kingdom is promised to all, nevertheless those who are closer to the Lamb are undoubtedly in a more lofty [condition]. I think that although they follow the Lamb wherever he goes, nevertheless, as we have said, they do not come to the same lofty condition as the Lamb himself.* For what does it mean to follow the Lamb wherever he goes? How does the Lamb walk?

*John 12:26

*John 14:2

*Bernard, Miss
1.8 (SBOp 4:20)

27. Certainly the Lamb of God is also the Son of God. Nevertheless he has this name not because of his divinity, by which he is equal to the Father, but because of his humanity, in which *he was led like the lamb to the slaughter* in order that he might bear *the sins of the world.** He is called Lamb according to his humanity, because according to humanity he was led like a lamb to the slaughter, *like a lamb he was sacrificed** and was offered for the sin of the whole world. According to divinity he does not walk or cross over from place to place. According as he is the Lamb, he walked, preached, taught, and crossed over from death to life, from earth to heaven. Nevertheless his walking describes his way of life when he was with sinners in this world. To follow this Lamb is to imitate his way of life. Not everyone follows the Lamb wherever he goes. For only virgins can do this. In what way? Let us see what was their way of life on earth.

*Isa 53:7;
John 1:29

*Isa 53:7;
1 Pet 1:19

28. Without a doubt, the Lamb went before on
the road of obedience and humility, on the road of
patience and sobriety, on the road of justice and charity—above all, in virginity of heart and body. Therefore let us also follow. For what true Christian does
not follow on this road of virtues? Others can follow
him in humility, in patience, in charity, in virginity of
heart, but they cannot follow him wherever he goes;
they do not imitate his entire way of life unless they
are also virgins in the flesh. For only virgins imitate
his entire way of life and thus follow the Lamb wherever he goes. However, not all virgins, but only those
who, beyond the virginity of the flesh, also have other
virtues in which they follow him.

29. For if they do not imitate his patience, humility, and charity, however much they have virginity of
the flesh, they do not follow the Lamb wherever he
goes. But without a doubt, among all the other virgins
who follow the Lamb wherever he goes, the one who
gave birth to that Lamb from her own flesh is the
best, the most excellent, and the most precious. She
not only followed him but, more than that, in some
marvelous way preceded him by giving birth to him,
nourishing him, carrying him in her arms, enfolding
him in her lap.* Therefore she rightly ascended above   *Bernard, Miss
all the virgins in order that she might arrive at that   1:7 (SBOp 4:19)
Virgin of Virgins, who is Christ. The other virgins
were not envious but rejoiced at her exultation as
if they were saying, *What is that one who goes forth*,
and so on.

30. She arrived at the highest orders of angels,
but the glory of the angels was not sufficient for her.
For who among the angels could be compared to her
who had given birth to the Lord of the angels himself?
Afterward, if we were to consider all the virtues that
the angels possess, I believe that we would find all of

them in Holy Mary more abundantly than in all the angels together. But because it would be very long to treat [each order] singly and to compare their virtues with those of Blessed Mary, let us consider those two orders that are above the others, namely, those of the cherubim and of the seraphim.*

31. *Cherubim* means "fullness of knowledge." But whence has this order that fullness of knowledge? Without a doubt from him *in whom are hidden all the treasures of wisdom and knowledge,*† that is, from our Lord Jesus Christ. But who cannot easily see that she who gave birth to the font of wisdom shares in wisdom and knowledge above all other creatures? The *seraphim* are called the fire, because that order burns with love for their Creator above all others.* But if they burn so much with the love of their Creator and their Lord, how much more does Blessed Mary burn with love, not only for her Lord and Creator, but also for her most beloved son?

32. Therefore, because she loves more than all the angels, archangels, thrones, dominations, cherubim, and seraphim, without doubt she ascended above them all. They all admired her excellence and, with great exultation, said, *What is that one who goes forth,* and so on. It is as if they said, "What is that one who has such authority and power that she is like the sun of justice, Christ himself, the very son of God? She transcended all others according to the flesh and thus walks after him past us all, advancing toward his throne." 33. As he ascended above all, so his most sweet mother ascended over all so that she might be nearer to him than all. O, how blessed are you, most holy Virgin! The heavenly court receives you with great eagerness; the whole church joyfully honors you with many sure signs of great joy. The sinner turns to you with confident eyes in order not to despair; the

*Aelred, SS 24.46, 26.41 (CCCM 2A:202, 219); Augustine, En in Ps 79.2, 98.4 (CCSL 39:1112, 1381)
†Col 2:3

*Jerome, Nom 50 (CCSL 72:121–22)

just one frequently prays to you in order to persevere; the fallen one leans on you in order to rise up; the one rising up seeks your hand in order not to fall short.

34. *Who is this that comes forth like the sun and beautiful as Jerusalem?* Great praise, brothers, for the Blessed Mary: *beautiful as Jerusalem.** What is this Jerusalem? Do not think of that earthly Jerusalem that the king of Babylon could destroy and the Romans overthrow. Far be it from me that I compare Blessed Mary to such a city! There is another city to which she ought rightly to be compared. It is that one of which we spoke a little while ago. The one *which is on high, which is free, which is our mother.** It is the holy company of the holy angels that is rightly called the vision of peace.* For that company sees *King Solomon,* not the one *seduced by foreign women,*† but the one whom the *kings adored* on the lap of the Virgin.‡ He is truly called Solomon, the true peacemaker, or rather peace itself, as the apostle says: *He himself is our peace who makes both sides one.** That [company of angels] sees him *face to face,*† and in the vision of him, they remain blessed for eternity.

35. One part of this Jerusalem is on earth, constructed of living stones; that part is holy church, and all the saints within are as her stones. These stones are diverse in worth. One has the appearance of gold like a topaz because of charity. Another is green like the emerald because of good works. Another has luster like a pearl because of chastity. Another is like a diamond that is not easily broken, because of patience. See how great is the worth of the Blessed Mary: she is beautiful like Jerusalem. She is not compared to any one of the stones in that city but to the city as a whole. How can this be unless she alone has in herself all the virtues that are separate in each separate being? And therefore what is said of the whole society of the

*Song 6:9; Resp for the Feast of the Assumption (Hesbert 4:7455)

*Gal 4:26

*Jerome, Nom 50 (CCSL 72:138)
†Neh 13:26; 1 Kgs 11:1
‡Matt 2:1

*Eph 2:14; Aelred, S 4.10 (CCCM 2A:39)
†Gen 32:30

*Song 4:7

church can be said of her alone: *You are all beautiful, my beloved.**

36. Among all the members of holy church, at least those that make pilgrimage in this life, none can be found who is not less beautiful in one or another part of himself. For all say, *We all offend in many things.** And one of the best members of Christ says, *I see another law in my members fighting against the law of my mind.** Without a doubt, where that law appears, in that part there is less beauty. And therefore Blessed Mary alone has complete beauty, since from the moment the Holy Spirit came upon her and the power of the Most High overshadowed her, she experienced in herself no disgraceful concupiscence. She received a marvelous beauty not only in her soul but also in her body; thus she was *wholly beautiful.* Therefore is she rightly said to be as beautiful as Jerusalem, she who alone has all the virtues that no one finds except in the full company of holy church. And therefore it follows that *the daughters of Sion saw her and called her beautiful.**

*Jas 3:2

*Rom 7:23

*Song 6:8; Resp for the Feast of the Assumption (Hesbert 4:7455)

37. The church herself is Sion or Jerusalem. But she is the Jerusalem of those who are already in that heavenly homeland, in that vision of true peace, where they do not endure the war against the vices, as we do in this life. For we do not have the peace that they have. She is called *Sion,* that is, "the act of watching" or "the watchtower."* The watchtower is a place set up so that one can see from a long distance what one wants to see; it is customary for men at war to place someone in a watchtower so that they may be able to catch sight from afar of those who are coming and guard against them. Such is holy church in this life. It is a watchtower for us to stand in as if at war, fearing always lest our enemies seize us. We must fear, brothers, lest we sleep in this watchtower. *Blessed is*

*Jerome, Nom 50 (CCSL 72:121); Augustine, En in Ps 64.3 (CCSL 39:825)

*that servant whom the Lord will find watchful when
he comes.* *

38. Therefore the daughters of Sion are the holy
souls, daughters of holy church, who all see Blessed
Mary and call her blessed. She is undoubtedly blessed,
she who was chosen from among all women that she
might be the mother of the Lord. Blessed is she whom
the angel humbly saluted. Blessed, the one who bore
the Son of God and nevertheless did not lose her
virginity. Blessed, whom the whole heavenly court
received today. Without a doubt, those holy souls to
whom the holy church gave birth in this life saw her
in this court. They saw her, and with great exultation
they called her blessed.

39. But let us also see her, beloved brothers—let
us see her excellence, her humility, her charity, her
purity. Let us see her, and let us praise her not by
the voice alone but also by imitating her. For if we
truly wish to praise her, let us imitate as closely as
possible her most holy way of life and, what is more
to our benefit, her humility.* May our souls be not
handmaids but queens that they may praise her. For
the queens praised her.† And they praise her rightly
because she is the lady of ladies and the queen of
queens. Let us be wary therefore that our souls may
not be handmaids.*

40. The handmaid is that soul that serves her
flesh, that does not will to control her flesh properly
but obeys its desires. Such a soul can not worthily
praise the queen, because *praise is not beautiful in
the mouth of sinners.** Therefore *let not sin reign in
our mortal bodies,** and then we will be truly queens
and will be able truly to praise that queen.* Because
if perchance our soul experiences some slavery to sin
and endures some opposition from its handmaid, that
is to say, from the flesh, if perchance we do not dare

*Ant for the
Common of
Confessors
(Hesbert
4:7455)

*Aelred, SS
23.15, 27.22
(CCCM
2A:187, 228)
†Resp for Feast
of the Assump-
tion; Song 6:8
*Aelred, S
24.38 (CCCM
2A:200)

*Sir 15:9
*Rom 6:12
*Aelred, S
20.36 (CCCM
2A:164)

to praise the queen, let us not be slow to pray to her and implore her aid.

41. Let us raise our eyes to heaven, where she herself ascended today. Let us contemplate her glory there and not forget her kindness. For without a doubt, just as she is more excellent and more blessed than all creatures, so she herself is more generous and more merciful than all creatures. Therefore let us beg her confidently and confidently place our trust in her. For we have many indications of her kindness. We know that many have been taken from the snares of the devil through her kindness, and many who were at the point of desperation were reconciled through her grace. There are many who were in the most grave torments after death but were snatched from those penalties because they loved her in their lifetime and zealously put themselves under her protection.*

*Aelred, S 19.14 (CCCM 2A:150)

42. May she be our common joy, our common glory, our common hope, our common consolation, our common reconciliation, and our common refuge. If we are sad, let us flee to her, that she herself may gladden us. If we are cast down, let us flee to her, that she may glorify us. If we are in despair, let us flee to her that she may draw us up. If we are troubled, let us flee to her that she may console us. If we suffer persecutions, let us flee to her that she may protect us. If we are out of harmony with her son, let us flee to her that she may reconcile us. May she be our guardian in this life and our protector in death. May she guard us now from sin, and may she then recommend us to her beloved son.

43. Therefore, beloved brothers, let us raise our hearts and the eyes of our heart to this our Lady, our advocate, and our helper. Let us consider what great hope we can have in her. She is herself illuminated by the sun of justice* in a most marvelous way; by the

*Mal 3:20

abundance of her light, she dispels the darkness that Eve, the first mother, led into the world. Confidently let us pray to her; she is the one who can support us because of her excellence and wills to do so because of her mercy. Let us pray that she intercede with her son for us* so that he who deigned to be born of her for us might deign, through her, to be merciful to us.

*Rom 8:34

44. Therefore, beloved brothers, let us honor and love her as much as we can and pray that in her most gentle mercy she may deign to entreat her most gentle son on her behalf. What we do not deserve by our own merits may we thus obtain by her patronage guaranteed by our Lord Jesus Christ, who with the Father and the Holy Spirit lives and reigns forever and ever. Amen.

Sermon 46

For the Feast of All Saints[1]

1. The skins of which the tent was composed signify the heavens into which our Lord entered. This is why the prophet said, *Covering the heavens like a skin.** In *the likeness of sinful flesh,** [our Lord] appeared black in the sight of the Jews; according to this flesh he himself felt the nails and the lance; according to this flesh he died and was mocked, and this flesh of his was his tent. Therefore this holy assembly says, *I am black like the tent of Cedar; I am dark like the skins of Solomon.**

2. Therefore, my brothers, if we wish to have this beauty within us, it is necessary for us to cleanse our hearts and be peacemakers. And if we do this, we will undoubtedly come to that beatitude shared without end by the blessed in whose honor we are gathered here today, that is, to the vision of God. For thus says the Lord, *Blessed are the pure of heart for they will see God. Blessed are the peacemakers for they will be called the children of God.** Purity of heart is twofold. For first the heart ought to be cleansed from greed, afterward from weakness.

3. Greed is when you love something more than God and more than the neighbor, loved because of God. We ought to love God, because without him we cannot be happy, the neighbor, because with him we can be happy. If we love something else in this world,

*Ps 103:2
*Rom 8:3

*Heb 10:20;
Aelred, S
26.28 (CCCM
2A:216)

*Matt 5:8-9

---

[1] The beginning of this sermon is lost.

that comes from greed and is like a beam in the eye
of the heart that prevents us from seeing God. But if
we voluntarily throw away all these things, then the
beam is cast out, but there remain temptations and
thoughts, like *dust in the eye*,* and we cannot bear to
open the eye of the heart. 4. We ought to hasten to
subdue this greed, because however fully we conquer
it, that much more fully our heart is cleansed, and
however fully it conquers us, that much more is our
heart soiled. Without a doubt, the one who has been
healed of greed here will be healed from all weakness after this life and will be capable of seeing God;
that is perfect happiness. Then such a person will
have perfect peace, peace between the self and the
neighbor, between the flesh and the spirit, between
the spirit and God.

*Matt 7:3-4

5. Even though you cannot have this peace as
perfectly as you would like in this life, nevertheless
we ought to make peace in this life so that we might
be peacemakers, making peace between ourselves
and the neighbor, between the body and the soul,
between ourselves and God. For *blessed are the peace-*
makers, because they shall be called the children of
*God.** The one who is zealous for making this peace
in the self, for winning the war against vice and against
the temptations of enemies, has already received a
certain likeness to the Son of God, who is truly the
peacemaker, who destroyed the devil, who reconciled
human nature to God. But we cannot make this peace
or overcome in the battle against vices and against the
temptations of our enemies unless the one who gave
the law gives a *blessing*,* unless the one who teaches
what we ought to do helps us to be strong to do it.

*Matt 5:9

*Ps 83:8

6. By means of this peace, all the saints whose
feast day we celebrate today arrived at very lofty
heights. They preserved this peace not only among

the successes of this world, but more fervently still in the midst of its persecutions. They kept always in their heart what the Lord promised, for, immediately after he taught about this peace, he added, *Blessed are those who suffer persecution for justice's sake,* and so on.* Therefore some of those who refused to forsake this justice were stoned, some scourged, others burned on the fire, others devoured by beasts, others hung from trees, others skinned alive. Certainly, my brothers, no tongue can say how many torments and mean attacks, how much disgrace these saints bore because they refused to forsake this justice. And the Lord predicted this, and therefore he affirmed those saints, saying, *Blessed will you be when men hate you,* and so on.*

*Matt 5:10

*Luke 6:22

7. At first there was no greater disgrace among the people than to be a Christian. In comparison with these, what are we who cannot suffer one stern sermon for Christ? In no way is there any greater honor on earth than to serve Christ. For when kings themselves, as well as aristocrats and rich people, see something that they think is religious, they honor it, almost with adoration. Similarly no one is considered so vile in this world, even by the worldly and those who live badly, as the one who abandons the state of life in which he first began to serve Christ. Nevertheless, there are many who, when they cannot have all their own will, when they happen to hear one harsh word, immediately threaten to depart,* as if their leaving hurt someone else more than it hurt themselves.

*Aelred, S 8.7
(CCCM 2A:66)

8. What would we do if all the worldly people wished to praise and honor us, if they promised us money and riches to abandon our way of life, if they warned us with pain and torment and disgrace unless we walked away from it? What would we do then, we

who grow angry over nothing, who threaten to leave immediately, when it is an honor to serve Christ and a disgrace not to serve him? Therefore, beloved brothers, let us follow the example of the saints whose feast day we celebrate today, and we who do not have anyone attacking us from outside or driving us to abandon our warfare, let us conquer and overcome that in ourselves that is against ourselves.

9. Let us have our eyes on that blessedness at which the saints arrived by means of the temporal pains of this life. *God has* already *wiped away the tears from their eyes;* already *there will no longer be mourning or cries of sorrow,* and indeed *no more sadness.** Already they see their *king in his comeliness,*† the one for whom they suffered, and in that vision they have perfect happiness. Now we are not asked to conquer beasts and torments for Christ, but to conquer our own soul for him, to overcome our own flesh and its desires for Christ.

*Rev 21:4
†Isa 33:17

10. Let us contemplate that it is more felicitous to rejoice with Christ in the company of the saints than to be tormented in hell with the devil. With what countenance could we hope for the glory that the saints have, those who suffered such pains in this life, if we desired to live softly and, as much as possible, to attain rest and the pleasure of the flesh? Let each one judge as he will; it does not seem to me that a person can simultaneously have delight of the mind and care for the belly, nor have eternal rest there if he does not experience hardship here.

11. Therefore, brothers, let us follow the examples of the saints whose feast day we celebrate today; let us entirely flee the repose and delight of the flesh and bear willingly with the adversities and temporal pains of this life for Christ. Let us cleanse our hearts in this way and become peacemakers so that we love

nothing in this life more than God and our neighbor; thus we may deserve to mount to the summit of perfect blessedness that consists in the vision of God.

12. For perfect blessedness is the vision of God; nor can people be happy in any way until at length they arrive at this vision. However, this vision is promised only to the pure of heart, and therefore our every effort, all our exercises, ought to tend toward this one end. Whatever we do, let us never judge ourselves perfect until we arrive at this purity. Therefore we always have cause for humbling ourselves, because we can always find in our heart something that separates us from God.

13. See the great dignity of the rational soul. Nothing is closer to God than a pure heart, and nothing at all lies between God and the pure heart, for as immediately as the heart is pure, it will see God. However, the vision itself is knowledge, and knowledge itself is the greatest happiness. Whoever will see God will love God, without any doubt. For the vision of God is beautiful to see, is pleasurable to listen to, is sweet to taste; the vision of God is so lovable to embrace that, if one could experience it, one could not fail to love it.

14. In this vision, in this hearing, in this embrace, in this tasting there is such love that we bear what we dislike. There is such satisfaction that we endure crucifixion; there is such fullness that we hunger for nothing from outside; there is such jubilation, such praise, and such glory that there is nothing better to desire. In that vision true peace is to be found; there true happiness, there tranquility, there perpetual steadiness, there true rest, a dwelling place, true delectation, the end and consummation of all good things. If such a homeland pleases us, brothers, then the road to it—be it as hard as we have said above— also pleases us, and we do not turn away from it.

15.[2] For this is the road, brothers, by which it is fitting to return to that homeland and to be ranked with the society of those whose feast day we celebrate today. They climbed this laborious road that rises before us and attained that dwelling place above. No persecutions, no adversities, could tear them away from this road. They heard the consolation that the Lord preached in these words: *Blessed are those who suffer persecution for the sake of justice, for theirs is the kingdom of heaven.* And this one: *Blessed will you be when men hate you,* and so on.*

*Matt 5:10; Luke 6:22

16. May true praise for all the saints be on our lips, brothers, but let us not praise with the lips and censure by our action. For we truly praise them if we trouble ourselves to imitate them. When we do something freely, we prove that we love the thing we do, and however much we silence our tongue, we praise by our action. Let us hasten, beloved, to enjoy their sweet company to the full, to contemplate with them that *one more beautiful than the sons of men,** *whose beauty makes the sun and the moon wonder.** Let nothing impede our swift advance, neither the successes nor the adversities of this life.

*Ps 44:3
*Ant for the Feast of Saint Agnes (Hesbert 3:1968, 3407)

17. Since *without Christ, we can do nothing,** let us ask our Lord that through all the merits of his saints he will hold us to this road and by his compassion lead us to that dwelling place on high, and that he will crown us with eternal joy with them—Jesus Christ our Lord, who with the Father and the Holy Spirit lives and reigns, God, forever and ever. Amen.

*John 15:15

---

[2] From here to the end of the sermon, Aelred depends on or reworks the material in S 27.21–23 (CCCM 2A:227–28).

Scriptural Index

Scriptural references are identified by sermon and paragraph number, but only one reference per paragraph.

Topical Index

This index is intended to give a sense of topics emphasized or explored in these sermons but is necessarily incomplete. It includes neither *Christ* nor *God*. Topics are cited by sermon and paragraph number.